DELEUZE
AND CINEMA

For Xhrise.

DELEUZE AND CINEMA

THE FILM CONCEPTS

Felicity Colman

Oxford • New York

English edition
First published in 2011 by
Berg
Editorial offices:
First Floor, Angel Court, 81 St Clements Street, Oxford OX4 1AW, UK
175 Fifth Avenue, New York, NY 10010, USA

Berg is the imprint of Bloomsbury Publishing Plc.

Library of Congress Cataloging-in-Publication Data

A catalogue record for this book is available from the Library of Congress.

British Library Cataloguing-in-Publication Data

A catalogue record for this book is available from the British Library.

ISBN   978 1 84788 037 6 (Cloth)
        978 1 84788 053 6 (Paper)
e-ISBN 978 1 84788 771 9 (Institutional)
        978 1 84788 770 2 (Individual)

Typeset by JS Typesetting Ltd, Porthcawl, Mid Glamorgan.
Printed in the UK by the MPG Books Group

www.bergpublishers.com

Contents

Abbreviations

C1 Deleuze, G. [1983] 1986. *Cinema 1: The Movement-Image*, H. Tomlinson and B. Habberjam (trans.). London: Athlone.

C2 Deleuze, G. [1985] 1989. *Cinema 2: The Time-Image*, H. Tomlinson and R. Galeta (trans.). London: Athlone.

politics as played out in French film journal *Cahiers du Cinéma* and French post-Hollywood films of the 1960s and 1970s.[1] Underwriting Deleuze's philosophical methods in the cinema books are the attitudes and opinions of the *Cahiers'* writers, alongside those of philosophers, directors, mathematicians and literary authors. While Deleuze is not always in accord with *Cahiers'* writers, their ideas provide impetus and orientation for many of his arguments on the nature of the cinema. The influence of cahiers upon Deleuze is extensive, to the point where Deleuze frequently utilizes exactly the same scene analysis as those film theorists he references. In this sense, Deleuze's approach to the cinema can be considered, as film theorist D.N. Rodowick commented, to be in the 'mainstream' of these debates (1997: xii).[2] In particular the editorial opinions of the *Cahiers'* writers who comprised the November 1972 editorial team are reflected in Deleuze's topic choices in his cinema books. They were Jacques Aumont, Pierre Baudry, Pascal Bonitzer, Jean-Louis Comolli, Serge Daney, Pascal Kané, Jean Narboni, Jean-Pierre Oudart, Phillipe Pakradouni, Sylvie Pierre and Serge Toubiana (cf. Reynaud 2000). This generation saw *la politique des auteurs* as taking a radical approach to film, although now both the term and the form of this radicalism has passed into the stylistic historical avant-garde. Deleuze's cinema books arrive at what is arguably the end of the era of the dominance of the *Cahiers* critical line of thinking and the advent of *le cinéma du look* – that is, an era in the early 1980s of filmmaking that attended to a certain stylistic production, characterized in the work of Jean-Jacques Beineix, Luc Besson and Leos Carax. Second, Deleuze's contemporary philosophical milieu was one where French philosophy was culturally important enough to be accorded recognition through media forms, including regular television programmes about philosophy (cf. Reynaud 2000: 17; Chaplin 2007: 5ff). Third, is the shift in pedagogic focus by Deleuze, when his university lectures began to engage cinema from 1981 (Dosse 2010: 397–405). The two-volume works are the result of Deleuze's lecture series on cinema, as a very specific media that engages in a political commentary and determination of culture as a political aesthetic (see Deleuze's interview in *Cahiers du Cinéma* from 1976 in Deleuze 1995: 37–45).

Form and Content: How to Read this Book – Biases and Expectation

In this book, I describe the key concepts and themes of the two cinema books (C1 and C2) in approximately the order that Deleuze presents them. For economy I have selected the core topics for understanding the Deleuzian ciné-methodology and provide thematic chapters on key aspects of Delueze's system, including his transsemiotic method, vectors, topology and politics. Each chapter begins with a brief summary of what the reader will encounter in that chapter and the terms of the Deleuzian ciné-concept. These issues provide resources for screen analysis, or philosophy, but the terms of this practice must be first understood through praxis. 'A theory has to be used,' Deleuze (2004: 208) notes; 'it has to work.' After presenting a case study or focussed discussion on the significance of the relevant chapter concept or theme, each chapter then takes the reader through three ways of approaching the concept:

1. what x concept is (in broader as well as Deleuzian terms);
2. how Deleuze uses x concept;
3. the function of x concept.

For each chapter, I suggest a way of accessing the more difficult aspects of Deleuze's ciné-philosophy is for the reader to watch the key film/s discussed and then consider the Deleuzian concepts presented. Like Deleuze, I discuss a wide range of films, and while the big screen and sound of the cinema theatre is the best place for viewing, most are available online.

Through this method of exegesis, I also present my own taxonomy of Gilles Deleuze's cinema books as a system for engaging with screen-based forms. I do this from the position of being a student, teacher and producer of screen media forms – films, games, mobile media screens, television and theory. My focus engages with the filmic medium as I follow Deleuze closely in the following chapters. However, the reader will note that my terminological preference is for 'screen media', rather than 'film' or 'cinema', where I give an example that would be successfully engaged by any number of screen media (films of all levels of production – commercial, amateur, artistic, experimental – made on all types of media recording formats, analogue and digital – mobile, dv, 35 mm, video, etc; computer games of all levels of production – mobile, flash, platform-based, commercial experimental, similarly for television, and internet news media products, etc.). While Deleuze writes specifically about cinema, and the rise of a cinematographic consciousness through the types of cinema made in the twentieth century, his discussion focus is on the philosophical concepts generated by the time-based form of the moving screen image. The Deleuzian ciné-system is thus applicable to any screen media that has the capacity for image, sound and movement.

In this book I engage with Deleuze's work in terms of a feminist position that I have previously described his work as enabling. This takes the approach of never thinking that you have found, or even can find, an end-point or limit to some type of knowledge form (Colman 2005b: 100–102). Deleuze's method provides a positioning theoretical springboard for all types of enquiry, and reader's biases toward certain styles or genres of screen materials are easily accommodated by Deleuze's generative approach to film theory and film history.

Deleuze's cinema books are complex and skilful, yet in parts they seem obvious, and in others elliptical, and the promise of the new logic required for the 'becoming' time-image that is argued for at the end of *Cinema 2* not entirely evident (C2: 275). This call for a new logic continues Deleuze's thinking in *Difference and Repetition* where he states, 'The search for a new means of philosophical expression was begun by Nietzsche and must be pursued today in relation to the renewal of certain other arts, such as the theatre or the cinema' (Deleuze 1994: xxi). Deleuze's philosophical oeuvre has become part of the philosophical canon, but within that discipline, his cinema books remain only scantly accounted for, and are absent from many philosophy and film theoretical works. The main (English language) exponents of Deleuze's system for film work include the respective works of Steven Shaviro (1993), D.N. Rodowick (1997), Barbara Kennedy (2000), Patricia Pisters (2003), Ronald

Bogue (2003), Anna Powell (2005; 2007) and David Martin-Jones (2006). For the purposes of this book, a discussion of the Deleuzian components of the ciné-system is the focus, providing a pathway into the various nuances of the above authors. Bogue's work in particular provides the point of reference for the technicalities and neologisms that Deleuze employs, while Pisters's work provides examples of applied Deleuzian ciné-theory.

Deleuze concludes his two volumes on cinema with the reminder that 'philosophical theory is itself a practice, just as much as its object' (C2: 280). It is with this coda in mind that this book, *Deleuze and Cinema: The Film Concepts*, combines a detailed account of Deleuze's ciné-system, and engages in the practice of the philosophically based film theory advocated by the cinema volumes.

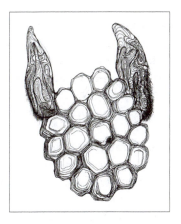

1

Ciné-system

Deleuze's two volumes on cinema provide a model of ciné-philosophy. Deleuze sets himself the task of compiling a taxonomy of the cinema and ends up with a processual ciné-system. This is a model of ciné-philosophy that can be used as a methodology for analysis of all types of screen-based media. This chapter examines that model as a ciné-system, open, infinite, and critically questioning how screen media can possibly prefigure, produce or presuppose the subject of its discourse.

By which system can a little egg be cooked in a huge pot?

C1: 176; see *The Navigator* (1924)

Screen-based work and film is a dynamic medium. Through the duration of the delivery of its content, no matter how limited or formulaic, the media form changes by accommodating incoming information and reconfiguring the forms already in play. It is through specific activities on screen that cinematic forms can be productive of ideas that in turn give rise to new forms or consolidate pre-existent ones. As Deleuze argues, film is a creative practice that uses a processual system.

No matter what the content, the type of interface and/or gesture required to access and operate it, screen forms are moving sound-images on time-based platforms. Educational models would describe the screen thus: by engaging visual, audio and sensory methods, cognitive data and ideas are communicated, affective domains are enabled (political and cultural attitudes and value systems), and psychomotor skills are tested (through interactive media forms and ideas about these forms) (cf. Anderson and Krathwohl 2001; Bloom and Krathwohl 1956; Krathwohl *et al.* 1964). Deleuze engages a similar group of elements, but does not limit discussion of the screen form to only reading the psychological, affective or cognitive capacity of the medium. In addition to addressing these significant issues are the philosophically and cinematographically framed questions of the forms that contribute to and determine such elements.

When producing or analysing screen-based work, the significance of film form and the relationship between form and style is foremost, even in theories coming from quite different traditions (cf. Andrew 1976; Beller 2006; Bellow 2000; Bresson 1977; Bordwell and Thompson 2003; Eisenstein 1949; Eisner 1973; Gledhill and Williams 2000; Godard and Ishaghpour 2005). The relationships produced by such different approaches in turn create fundamental questions for film philosophy and film theory concerning the political implications of aesthetic forms such as cinema and screen-based images (for discussion of the relationship between film, theory and philosophy compare essays in Colman 2009c and Wartenberg and Curran 2005). The work of film theorists such as David Bordwell (1985), Raúl Ruiz (1995) and Kaja Silverman (1988) are exemplary in explicating the significance of film form, and for discussions engaging the relationship between form and style, see the respective works of Jean-Luc Nancy (2001), Linda Williams (2008) and Jacques Rancière (2004; 2006). Deleuze will cautiously frame an answer to this question through his examination of the constitution of the world through screen forms; at various points in the cinema books using the term 'englobing'; describing the sense of the nature of the cinematographic to encompass perception, thinking, and politics.

The discussion of form provides a platform for many of the ideas Deleuze sets forth in his system. In this, Deleuze's project is furthering the implications of Henri Bergson's comments where he refers to the cinema as a model for human perceptual processes: 'The mechanism of our ordinary knowledge is of a cinematographical kind' (Bergson 1983: 323). Although we can see the influences of other philosopher's logics on the development of the method Deleuze employs in his cinema books, including the work of Foucault, Guattari and Gottfried Leibniz, Deleuze attributes his primary cinematographic thinking on movement and duration to Bergson (see Mullarkey 2009a; 2009b: 88). Deleuze draws this discussion through the work of philosophers including Plato, Kant and Spinoza, but also from diverse authors including Arnold J. Toynbee, and theories by a range of film directors including Godard, Glauba Rocha, Hitchcock, Yasujirô Ozu and Pier Paolo Pasolini. Deleuze concludes his study by pronouncing: 'Cinema itself is a new practice of images and signs, whose theory philosophy must produce as conceptual practice' (C2: 280).

What is the Deleuzian Ciné-system?

Deleuze uses the term 'system' to describe cinema in terms of his approach: 'The image itself is the system of the relationships between its elements, that is, a set of relationships of time from which the variable present only flows' (C2: xii). Deleuze creates a classification system that describes what these 'elements' of cinema are in order to discuss how they systemically work to produce a film, and how those elements are then capable of becoming autonomous producers of other systems (cf. the various body-becomings charted in MacCormack 2008: 113; or in *The Wizard of Oz* (dir. Fleming, 1939)).

Deleuze carefully looks at language systems, such as semiotics, for the means with which to express what is happening on screen and in the perceptive body of the addressee. It is a dynamic system that is anti-structural. Deleuze will however privilege his vitalist, pedagogic vision for addressing the forms and concepts created in the practice of film.

Within the system are sets of images. Deleuze divides them into two parts – movement and time, but these two are part of the same set. Of his approach to these types of cinematic images, there are three main questions that Deleuze circles in his system:

1. How does a screen form produce content?
2. How do screen-based forms become autonomous?
3. How does cinema produce philosophical concepts?

These three points are questions that Deleuze has in mind in every chapter of his cinema volumes. No matter what the content focus, the composition of the screen form is concerned with the organization of information, including abstract informational forms such as time and space. In reference to the first point, Deleuze describes the screen form as the set – the *ensemble* of things (including the *mise-en-scène* or *milieu*). In Deleuze's terminology the term image 'set' is not to be confused with 'set-theory', although elements of that approach are definitely present. Rather, the type of 'set' that Deleuze invokes, as Arkady Plotnitsky argues, is a conceptual set that does not always involve spatial figures. Rather, the set provides a more extensive meaning, closer to a 'topos theory' that looks at points in space: 'A *set* is composed of *elements* capable of having certain *properties* and certain *relations* among themselves or with elements of other sets' (Cartier, cited by Plotnitsky 2006: 188 original emphasis; see chapter 12 Topology). The key words are italicized: *elements, properties, relations* – these are the components that Deleuze describes.

Thus, Deleuze's approach here is neither ethnological nor linguistic in terms of its classification of material. Rather, to answer the second question, Deleuze draws up a philosophical semiology for screen analysis, combining the systemic meaning. As he states at the beginning of the preface to the

French edition of *Cinema 1*, his study is 'a taxonomy, an attempt at the classification of images and signs' (C1: xiv). While Deleuze gives credit to the American theorist C.S. Peirce's study of images and signs as being one of 'the most complete and the most varied', Deleuze uses Peirce's descriptions of signs just for taxonomic purposes, not for semiotic analysis (C1: xiv; C1: 69). Throughout the cinema books, Deleuze situates Peirce within a certain sphere of classification, combined with insights from linguist Louis Hjelmslev, film maker Pasolini, philosopher Bergson, and consolidated over work with Guattari in *A Thousand Plateaus* wherein any systematic analysis of signs must be understood as having political consequences by virtue of the ways in which the image can produce mental images – this is the third question that Deleuze's system encircles (C1: 198–200, C2: 30–34; Hjelmslev 1961; Pasolini 2005; Deleuze and Guattari 1987: 43–45). Drawing on Bergson and Guattari's work, Deleuze distinguishes between the terms of mechanistic and machinic, which might be invoked when thinking of a system that describes concepts and forms based on a technological platform. Deleuze makes it clear that when he engages the sense of a 'system', and the use of terms such as 'components', it is in a machinic sense and not in a mechanistic sense, and this is why his theory is applicable to all kinds of screen media – analogue, digital, mobile, fixed, text, image or sound based.[1] The definition of the elements that might comprise a film or screen form – what is cinematography, what is acting, what comprises a shot, sound, lighting, dialogic style etc. – is the subject of numerous side discussions Deleuze undertakes throughout his volumes. An example of this technique: in looking at how cinema presents a world of images that contain multiple layers of time within them, Deleuze questions how French director Jean Renoir is able to present a multi- dimensional image, one that is not flat or just 'double-faced' (C2: 84). He writes: 'It is a depth of field, for example in *La Règle du jeu*, which ensures a nesting of frames, a waterfall of mirrors, a system of rhymes between masters and valets, living beings and automata, theatre and reality, actual and virtual. It is depth of field which substitutes the scene for the shot' (C2: 84–85; Renoir 1939).

In addition to describing the elements of the image, Deleuze offers two basic propositions for critical screen analysis: the movement-image and the time-image. Both movement and time are technical and abstract concepts that screen-based works dramatize. Movement images and time images engage processes that activate further models and forms on screen and in thought. Deleuze notes the points at which cinema invents a new logic for addressing movement and time.

First, in Deleuze's terms, the movement image produces its own world, its own universe in fact, a process of what philosopher Henri Bergson termed a 'metacinema' (C1: 59). Matter is 'a set of movement-images' (C1: 61). Deleuze will prove that this 'set' is in fact an 'infinite set' wherein each set is extensive and forms what Deleuze terms a 'Whole' or 'Open' as it 'relates back to time or even to spirit rather than to content and to space' (C1: 59; C1: 16–17; see chapter 2 Movement). The movement-image, as Deleuze names it, thus has its own generative process of 'cinematographic consciousness'; it is a living thing.

Second, Deleuze expands his ciné-semiotic language to describe the time-image. Deleuze's discussion of the time-image is oriented by philosophical focus on the perception of forms, the description of reality, and the undertaking to account for the methodology of filmmaking techniques and practices. Influential for his entire philosophical oeuvre, Deleuze wrote monographs on philosophers especially concerned with issues of difference and time: Kant (Deleuze [1963] 1984), Spinoza (Deleuze [1968] 1990a; [1970] 1988a), Nietzsche (Deleuze [1962] 1983a), Bergson (Deleuze [1966] 1991), and books on Foucault (Deleuze [1986] 1988b) and Leibniz (Deleuze [1988] 1993), the latter two published in France directly after the two cinema books. To take analysis of Deleuze's construction of the time-image taxonomy, in addition to further consideration of Bergson's work in *Matter and Memory* (1896) and *Creative Evolution* (1907), some background on Leibniz, Foucault and Nietzsche's philosophy is useful for reading the frequently dense passages in *Cinema 2*. The work that Deleuze engages from each thinker's oeuvre provides distinctive paradigms for the taxonomy that Deleuze constructs of the time-image.

Deleuze engages Bergson's focus on duration for the task, taking into account and building upon the different forms of habitual time such as 'recognition', 'representation' and 'perception', also discussed in *Difference and Repetition* (1994: 133–142). Considering these issues up in relation to the screen medium, Deleuze's discussion is wide-ranging in scope, for example, accounting for the creation of recognizable forms of movement and time, such as the perception-image; the dramatization of time by the cinematographic image; addressing classical temporal difference created between forces of the world characterized by figures of the Apollonian and the Dionysian; Nietzsche's concept of the eternal return, and Bergson's vitalist concept of duration. Deleuze develops Peirce's semiology to provide new words for an account of the range of time-signs. Deleuze applies and develops some of Bergson's temporal schemas from *Matter and Memory* (Bergson [1896] 1994). Bergson's theories on issues of duration, recognition and memory are engaged by Deleuze as temporal laws that account for the different ontologies of time that the cinema produces. Deleuze's discussion of time addresses the body, the brain, politics, the event, the philosophical question of the true and the false, variations of temporal concepts such as dreams, memory, amnesia, déjà-vu, death and their operation in film. In parts of *Cinema 2*, Deleuze's discussion of time within his open-system seems impossibly dense. However, the determining logic to this system is the discussion of the components' creation of 'cinematographic autonomy' that cinema creates (C2: 243) through the nature of its open-system.

Foucault's work highlights concepts of temporal processes upon subjectivity, and the different registers of affective exchanges that power can hold over people – as Deleuze develops in his book on Foucault (1988b). Foucault pointed out that the corporeal control of activity through the monastic inheritance of the timetable that continues to govern the epistemic direction of everyday human life: 'for centuries, the religious orders had been masters of discipline; they were specialists of time, the great technicians of rhythm and regular activities' (Foucault [1975] 1977: 149–150). Foucault's work on how such historical control over human events has helped determine the chronological regimes of thinking and action that tacitly control human impulses, and applications of knowledge. Extending the Foucauldian critique of such passive and unquestioning behaviour that Deleuze undertakes with Guattari

in *A Thousand Plateaus* (where they develop the concept of rhizomatic thinking), the cinema books offer an absolute critique of modern philosophy's positions on structuralism, the representational theory of mind and the notion of
'Truth'. Rather than focus on how a certain type of narrative 'reality' is 'cap-
tured' on screen, Deleuze directs us to see how the nature of the 'becomings' of
each character (C2: 145; 150) determines the type of time-images produced.
The points of potentiality for thinking of the new logic of the time-image
include references to new dimensions, and the crystalline state as a seeding
of these dimensions. At the beginning of the *Movement-Image*, Cinema 1,
Deleuze refers to time as the 'fourth dimension' revealed through those images able to 'open' themselves, as in Carl Dreyer's 'ascetic method' (C1: 17).
As we discuss in the chapters in this book, Deleuze introduces many terms to
discuss the range of the variations in modes of time on screen and the type of
philosophy that is generated by time-images.

Deleuze argues that the cinematic image is not singular, but is comprised of
an 'infinite set' (C1: 58). Cinephiles know this already: a screen-based or filmic
idea is never complete; there may be another version, there may be alternative scenes or endings in circulation; there may be alternative formats; there
may be an extended discussion and revision of a screen form. The image is
always in the process of determining its ensemble; a set of images which form
signaletic material (as explained in the movement-image, and the perception-
image) (Deleuze 1995: 65). This set is not the same as 'set-theory', rather
(as we discuss in the chapter on topology), this is a conceptual field or phase
of elements that enable Deleuze to build the complex dimensions of screen
space. Through his work Deleuze draws on various branches of conceptual
mathematics, such as in *Difference and Repetition*. The work done in the
cinema books enables a specific type of philosophical direction to be taken
in Deleuze's subsequent books, *The Fold: Leibniz and the Baroque* (1993),
Foucault (1988b) and *Pure Immanence: Essays on a Life* (2001b) which, with
Guattari in *A Thousand Plateaus* (1987) and *What is Philosophy?* (1994),
becomes a model of topological political philosophy. Deleuze and Guattari's
development of the concepts of smooth and striated political spaces draw
on Bernhard Riemann's conceptual mathematics in order to describe the

movements and conceptual sites of territory and the processes of de- and re-territorialization (1987: 142–145). In the cinema books, this mathematically informed conceptual approach is evident throughout, in particular the political consequences of the forms that such divisive territorial movements take on screen are made clear through Deleuze's method in addressing genre films and political cinemas. The set of images that Deleuze uses to define what comprises the screen set is the subject of this book: Deleuze's ciné-system.

How Deleuze Uses the Ciné-system

Deleuze 'does philosophy' on cinema to the extent that he demonstrates that film is a medium that shows us the immanent constitution of things (images, content, ideas), as opposed to being transcendent (mysterious, opaque, sublime). There are different kinds of concepts that Deleuze engages throughout, and other philosophical problems that he has worked on previously – in *Difference and Repetition* and in *The Logic of Sense* (Deleuze [1969] 1990b) – where the issues of 'the 4th dimension' and Plato's concepts of Forms of 'the Real' are addressed. In philosophy, Forms are framed and identified by the question, '*what is x*' (McMahon 2005: 43; Salanskis 2006: 50). Identified throughout the cinema books with a capital F to indicate that Deleuze's sense is in reference to Plato's theory of ideas, Forms are the named properties or essences of things. In conjunction with neo-Platonic screen Forms (and the philosophical debate over the immanent or transcendent nature of things), Deleuze also engages Bergson's two forms of perceptual recognition: 'automatic or habitual recognition' (C2: 44), the range of narrative forms that cinema engages and the forms that the creation of different types of 'whole' image set that the screen produces (cf. C2: 161).

Deleuze's method for discussing the time-image is predominantly influenced by Bergson, whose work on the internalization of time appears to be similar to Kant. However, as Deleuze points out, the process of the actualization of this Idea, and the realization that 'we are internal to time' and are thus a component part of that interiority – that is, 'we inhabit time' – this is Bergsonian, not Kantian (C2: 82). As Deleuze discusses the time-image, he also engages in philosophical debates with thinkers including St Augustine, Peirce, Kant, Leibniz, Bergson, Nietzsche and film makers including Hitchcock, Pasolini, Resnais, Welles. Each aspect of the various time-images has a specific function within the Deleuzian ciné-system, and to invoke one calls upon a depth of possible configurations and nuances for the particular time-image under discussion.

In the first cinema book, Deleuze takes the time to detail a crucial aspect of his cinema system. This, as I argue in chapter two of this book, is Deleuze's thesis on *the notion of the cinematic body as a social, living system* (C1: 59; my emphasis). The system is an open-ended system – as more things enter it, or as it comes into contact with other systems, then there are an infinite number of possible outcomes. Even the actualization of something within a screen system – another film on war, or another film on family life, or another film on human or animal comedy, drama, tragedy, science-fiction, fantasy, and so on – does not mean that the possibilities are exhausted with that making. On the contrary, Deleuze's cinema methodology shows how an open system does work, or could work, but he also describes how there are many films that succumb to being closed-systems, making clichéd and static images. Deleuze also tries to demonstrate how open-systems can be co-opted for all kinds of political purposes, and how we can be attentive to the aesthetic dimensions of the system.

Deleuze's investigation into the concepts that cinema is able to produce continues his work in his 1969 book, *The Logic of Sense*, on ancient Stoic ontology. This is a process-oriented philosophical exploration of creation of 'becoming' (cf. Braidotti 1994; Bonta and Protevi 2004; Roffe 2007: 43–47; Burchill 2010; Colman 2010). This ontological process is a perpetual process – as clearly demonstrated by the cinematographic consciousness that must be distinguished from other art forms. Screen-based audio-images are time-based in different ways to literature or painting, or even performance works. Screen-based images are subject to technical restrictions and advancements, just as other arts are (writing developments in technologies of printing and design, for example), but cinema uses a different kind of method. While its closest medium allies may be found in music and photography, the cinema is a moving surface of intersecting components – things and ideas – that create images that dominate all other modes of communication. These images produce forces (which Deleuze describes as 'affects'), complex notions about time and space, the organization of things in the world, the politics of thought as it is produced by the cinema. In short, Deleuze questions how the cinema can affect the organization of the world, by altering perception of that operation. Thus Deleuze introduces terms such as 'worldization' (*mondialization*) and the 'world-image' in order to describe moments where films produce constructed sound/images (C2: 59).

Deleuze is in pursuit of a methodology that will enable him to adequately describe the breadth of types of images that cinema produces. So he comes up with his own type of screen-sign method, but it is useful to think of it in the terms as set up by Deleuze in *Proust and Signs* (Deleuze [1964] 2000), *The Logic of Sense* (Deleuze, [1969] 1990b) and by Deleuze and Guattari in *Anti-Oedipus: Capitalism and Schizophrenia* ([1977] 1983) and in A *Thousand Plateaus* ([1980] 1987).

First, the pragmatics of signs holds a key function in Deleuze's philosophy. Through consideration of the Proustian method for engaging with previously unknown objects and coming to recognize that meaning can be discerned through attention to the taxonomic relations of objects, things, and people and their repetition under different conditions and over time, through to the diagrammatic flow of differentiating 'belief or desire' (Deleuze and Guattari 1987: 141; 219), a significant philosophy of the sign emerges in the cinema books. This philosophy forms a *transsemiotic* of the screen image, which indicates the rhizomic, or multiple ways that signs (including those produced by sound images) produce a 'mixed semiotics', comprised of four components: generative, transformational, diagrammatic, and machinic (*ibid.*: 145–146). Each of these elements combined create different types of screen analysis, and we see this rich method applied in academic and practical work (whether consciously Deleuzian or otherwise). For example, the development of the generative (and transformational) terms of a 'minor cinema' (see Genosko 2009a) or the possibilities of 'schizoanalytic' screen analysis (see Buchanan and MacCormack 2008), a diagrammatic method being engaged in many filmmakers works, such as Lars von Trier's film *Dogville* (2003) or Terence Davies' *Distant Voices, Still Lives* (1988) and the work of Bruno (2002) and Conley (2006).

Another significant part of the system is provided by an exploration of movement and contrast. Deleuze engages a dialectic method in order to describe the composition of screen Forms. According to the screen situation, elements of a set engage in differentiating forms of dialectical movements. This is a dialectic that is certainly comparable to other thinkers, and Deleuze draws from Burch's dialectic as much as a Nietzschian comparative ethics. Deleuze's dialectic of difference is entirely critical of a Hegelian dialectic. Hegel uses a comparative and oppositional dialectic to describe the creation of things. He uses the notion of a universal Being which assumes certain pre-existing unities. The Hegelian-based notion of a dialectic of difference is thus based on figuring models of representative thought based on dominant models of being (see Malabou 2004). Deleuze emphatically rejects the notion of a universal subject, and the notion of the representation of that subject. Rather, in the cinema books, Deleuze adopts the method he laid out in *Difference and Repetition* in order to speak of the thinking of difference as 'the state in which one can speak of determination *as such*' (Deleuze 1994: 28, original emphasis; see also Williams 2003: 57–58). The cinema books continue Deleuze's Kantian critique against the determining values espoused in the Cartesian cognitive and *perceptual implications* that support the determination of 'I think' and the assumption of being (able to think, able to conceptualize, able to judge, able to imagine, able to remember, and able to perceive). As Deleuze says in *Difference and Repetition*, '"I think" is the most general principle of representation' (1994: 85; 138). This point is useful for wresting epistemological representational analogies, judgments, conceived identities, imagined likenesses and differences away from images (*ibid.*: 138).

The Deleuzian ciné-dialectic is used as a method for *differentiating*, for the purposes of describing and comparing the same entity, in order to find out differences in kind. In the cinema books, Deleuze continually reminds us of the relations between structures of thinking and of images; of the determination and indetermination of the structures of situations, and the behaviour of characters. As he describes with the *perception-image*, the *a priori* relations that we have with *things* in the world tend to lend shape to the ideas we have from film images, and indeed, determine *how* images are formed. The poles Deleuze names in the Cinema books include: the classical and the modern, natural and realist, the objective and subjective (of the *perception image*; of *montage*; C1: 71), empiricism and metaphysics, darkness and light, vertical and horizontal, psychological and analytical temporal expressivity, the organic and the crystalline forms of duration, degrees of zero and infinite spatial modalities, the *a priori* structure and the 'undifferentiated abyss' (Deleuze 1994: 28). These poles do not pose 'problems and solutions' for the cinema, rather Deleuze uses the dialectic as a *diaphora*: a transport, or passage of movement for intensive fields, aleatory encounters of unconnected parts, 'anomalies of movement' – that form relations 'as external to their terms' (C1: ix, x). The cinema's organization functions through the creation of such fragments, such poles of thought, by the affective intervals created between movement and within time, dialectic movements productive of mutations of form. Deleuze's theory of the cinema directs us to pay attention to the openings that fragment, empty or crack forms; where pure situations of rhythmic bliss or chaotic or controlled violence or intensive potentiality alter the screen set, reconfiguring the very imperceptible site of consciousness and its 'pure possibility' (Sitney, quoted by Deleuze C1: 233–234n 24). So, in the consideration of screen-based forms, Deleuze's cinema dialectic is neither Hegelian nor Socratic, nor is it geared toward achieving antimonies, rather Deleuze engages the dialectic for its binomial mechanism: its devise of thrust and reversal, the way that a dialectic argues from different modes or poles of energy. In this movement, the action of the cinema engenders different styles and forms of film: the movement engenders the differentiation of form.

In terms of the form of the two-volume system, the Second World War is a marker that is often invoked to describe the distinction between Deleuze's two cinema books, but again, the terms of this separation lie within the components of the elements of the war invoked. We can observe that these books are separated by extensive vectors, one concerned with movement, the second concerned with time. This break is often described historically (in terms of key 'moments' in cinematic history, such as the advent of Italian neo-realism), but actually it is less an epistemic separation than an expression of the aesthetic (and stylistic) poles of the same event. As we shall further explore, Deleuze invokes the notion of a pole frequently in the cinema books, and uses it as a signal for *movement*: a *caesura-reversal* that enables critical perception of 'caesura points' and ensures that there are no distinctive limits for the image to be thought (C1: 34).

The Function of the Deleuzian Ciné-system

When we see or hear images or sounds as they move across a screen, they interact with our body of already determined knowledge, perception and experiences – this is what we can call the aesthetic domain of screen participation. What we think we already know, or what we imagine can be confirmed or shifted, augmented or reduced by what we see and hear. Deleuze's system argues for an awareness of the processes and forces of an internally regulating entity that operates as an organism that relies upon certain systems to keep it functioning. Deleuze describes his system in a number of ways. Discussing the intensive forms that different films' content will focus upon (which he describes in terms of the large form and collective knowledge and the small form and vectorial points), Deleuze likens the body of the cinema to both mathematical planes of calculated movements and organic paradigms of life. Overall, the cinema books depict a cine-system that functions rather as a human body functions, in that it requires a respiratory system, a circulatory system, and a nervous system – each part of which contributes to the cine-system in singular and collective screen circumstances. As Deleuze described in an interview published in *Libération* in 1980, 'A system is a set of concepts. And it's an open system when the concepts relate to circumstances rather than essences' (Deleuze 1995: 32). So this cine-system is not THE system, rather it is a processual system – an open-ended practice of making concepts.

The Deleuzian system is designed to be to be used, abused, extended or reconfigured. It offers a number of discipline-specific pedagogic and intellectual avenues – for fields of film, media and communications studies, philosophy, education, sociology, political theory. The existing literature on Deleuze's cinema books demonstrates this breadth of possible applications and extensions. Specific authors have picked out parts of the system that are relevant to the work that they are interested to make or engage with. In the English language, Steven Shaviro published *The Cinematic Body* in 1993, providing an account of the implications of some of the genetic terms of cinematic thinking provided in the Deleuzian system – such as the terms of 'molecular sexuality'; D.N. Rodowick focussed on the arguments of the time-image to describe the terms and possibilities of Deleuze's 'time-machine' (1997); Barbara Kennedy provides a close reading of the terms of the affection-image, looking at Deleuze's affect-image in relation to a set of specific case studies (2000); Ronald Bogue in *Deleuze on Cinema* (2003) looks at the core arguments of Deleuze's Bergsonian-influenced taxonomy of cinematic signs; David Martin-Jones wrote a book based on this system that focuses on the concept of 'national identity' (2006); Anna Powell has used the system to look at horror films and 'altered states of consciousness' achieved through experimental cinemas (2005; 2007).

What the Deleuzian approach to cinema provides is a platform that enables and encourages a more considered and holistic approach for analysis of the moving sound-image. Instead of privileging a cognitive, analytic, sociological, or historical method, Deleuze's system draws us to attend to first the forms of production and then the affective forces at work that contribute to the types of forms, and thus content, that are created or re-presented on screen. Within the Deleuzian system, notions such as 'history', 'knowledge', 'gender', 'subjectivity' or 'nation' are rejected as being constructed determinations that are often as inadequate in their ability to articulate ideas on screen as they are static. Such notions are of course not without value, but it is in their application to the moving sound-image that Deleuze's cinema books frame.

Rosi Braidotti noted that Deleuze's emphasis on the 'activity of thinking differently' throughout his work, together with his 'emphasis on processes, dynamic interaction, and fluid boundaries' is an approach that is entirely suited to understanding the methods, limitations, and potential of our contemporary culture (Braidotti 1994: 111).

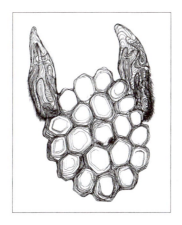

2

Movement: the *Movement-image*

Deleuze begins his investigation into the cinema in terms of its movements in two arenas: the philosophical and the technical. Deleuze argues that movement informs our understanding of the formation of worlds in terms of the types of information it selects and generates as new forms. The cinema creates many different types of movement-images and Deleuze describes six key types: the perception-image, the affection-image, the impulse-image, the action-image, the reflection-image and the relation-image. Drawing on the concepts of philosopher Henri Bergson and film theorists André Bazin, Noël Burch and Jean Mitry, the point that Deleuze argues is that the screen image is a relational whole which changes, either through movement or through temporally mediated events that have altered the situation of the moving-image. From this perspective, he argues that the image equals not agree with Bergson's appeal to Zeno's paradoxes in *Creative Evolution* as a way of discussing the cinema as merely 'the reproduction of a constant, universal illusion' (C1: 2). Rather, Deleuze looks to Bergson's earlier work, *Matter and Memory*, which he reads as a crucial work of critical theory for the cinema, with its discovery of the movement-image (C1: 2).

The Function of Movement

How the cinema works is through 'false movement', says Deleuze; movement may have 'instants in time' but they are never immobile. The cinema 'immediately gives us a movement-image', observes Deleuze (C1: 2), because the cinema has filmed movement – however imperceptible – it has filmed a duration. To think of an analogue state of projection is to miss the point of the movement image, as it reduces the cinema to its merely mechanical function, and ignores the release of images of time, no longer dependent upon a chronometric movement (see chapter 10 Time). D.N. Rodowick discusses this aspect of Deleuze's film-philosophy in relation to Chris Marker's 1962 *ciné-roman La Jetée* (1997: 4). Thus, for Deleuze, the cinema 'does not give us an image to which movement is added', rather: 'It does give us a section, but a section which is mobile, not an immobile section + abstract movement' (C1: 2), and this is what we see in the sections of movement in Van Sant's *Elephant*. We can call these mobile sections little plots of time, but what is clear is that these movements are but sections of the whole movement. This does constitute a set, as Bergson discusses in *Creative Evolution*, a closed system and a finite set, but, as Deleuze in his second commentary on Bergson clarifies, this is *'an infinite set'* (C1: 59, emphasis added). Explaining his point further Deleuze notes, 'despite some terminological ambiguities in Bergson, it is not an immobile or instantaneous section, it is a mobile section, a temporal section or perspective' (C1: 59; see chapter 5 Perception).

After we have seen the whole film of *Elephant*, we can appreciate the senses of infinite that Deleuze employs here in two distinct ways. First, there is the terrible social sense of the boundless repercussions of events as depicted in

Elephant (and similarly with films that address specific events[4] in tumultuous public social histories: *La Bataille D'Alger* (*The Battle of Algiers*; dir. Gillo Pontocorvo, 1966); *11'09"01– September 11* (Prod. Alain Brigand, 2002); for critical commentary on cinematic affects of violence and war, see Shapiro 2009). The events of such films describe how singular incidents actualize the existence of things, drawing in both the new and a pre-existing assemblage of things, and then how that assemblage becomes transformed anew through that singularity (Stagoll 2005: 87). Second, with this statement (the infinite set) Deleuze challenges the false problem of the operations of a movement-image as a closed set by mathematically based philosophy. (Hence his flag concerning *false movement*.) Under Deleuzian image (atomistic) theory, Aristotelian-based theorems of cinematic movement, space and time pose problems that are often false problems because they are incorrectly framing known physical laws of the universe. There may be issues of narrative equilibrium to be achieved that 'motivate' movements of cause and effect within a certain style of film, but when dealing with events in the world, resolution of any kind is a decision enforced by the closed sets of factors such as genre or production. Extending Deleuze's diagramatization of the event, we can observe that the infinite set in film constitutes an actual real 'event' that can be 'a vibration with an infinity of harmonics or submultiples such as an audible wave … [f]or time and space are not limits but abstract coordinates of all series …' (Deleuze 2001a: 77).

The 'vibration' of an event – an instant in time – and the infinite ripple affect causes the type of movement that is the subject of the second and third of Bergson's theses on movement, and Deleuze's on the movement-image (and this movement is to be further understood in Deleuze's discussions on *relations* and *perception*). As the boy in *Elephant* bumps into Alex the gunboy in the cafeteria, the gunboy is annoyed enough to write down the other boy's name in his record of who to kill. This instant in the film (second thesis) creates a movement-image of change (which is the third of the Bergson theses). The instant is one formed in a response to an environment, 'a transition of one form to another' (C1: 4), such as we see the dance movements in films where performers respond to their environment and incorporate it in their movements (Deleuze references the action movements of actors Fred Astaire and Charlie Chaplin (C1: 7)). This *relation within* is the second thesis on movement – what Deleuze terms the 'privileged instants and any-instant-whatevers' (C1: 3). This thesis on movement is critical for film analysis, as the cinema shows us that properties of the instant that are made through the *qualitative* (relating to inherent, distinguishing properties) as opposed to quantitative (relating to measurable properties) types of movement. This 'instant' in *Elephant* is both poles of movement: privileged and any-instant-whatevers, not unique, but an instant of movement within the continuous movement of the film. Deleuze gives us the example of Russian director Sergei Eisenstein, whose focus is always directed toward such instants as pivotal moments of a film. The moment in *Bronenosets Potyomkin* (*Battleship Potemkin*, 1925), for example, when a mother is shot standing at the top of a staircase and her baby in its pram teeters at the top of the Odessa steps, is a chilling image of war. This is undoubtedly a climactic moment in the film's narrative, but in describing the movement of this moment of the image, says Deleuze, we should not confuse this as a moment of an 'actualisation of a transcendent form' (C1: 6; see chapter 4 Montage). Although Eisenstein's cinematic subjects are marked by 'moments of crisis' – the 'pathetic' points of scenes – such 'remarkable instants' are 'still any-instants-whatevers' and these can be 'regular *or* singular, ordinary *or* remarkable' (C1: 5–6, original emphasis).

Again Deleuze enters into a philosophical debate with his peers on this point, providing a primary lesson on the 'modern scientific revolution' (C1: 4–5). Alongside the developments of modern astronomy, modern physics, modern geometry, and the differential and integral calculus (after Newton and Leibniz), where does the advent of cinema sit with its own relational engagement with time and movement? Initially regarded as an 'industrial art', '[cinema] was neither an art nor a science' (C1: 4; 6). What the cinema does, says Deleuze, following Bergson's cue, is provide us with new questions about 'reality' (C1: 8). Ancient philosophy regarded those false instants of time as immobile and productive of the 'eternal'. Cinematic mobile instants produce 'the new' (C1: 7). And Deleuze underscores what, for him, is the essence of cinema: its production of a new ontology, he continues, 'that is, of the remarkable and the singular, at any one of these moments: this is a complete conversion of philosophy' (C1: 7; for critical work on the Deleuzian 'production of the new', see O'Sullivan and Zepke 2008).

The term 'conversion' is precisely the basis of Bergson's third thesis on movement: 'Movement always relates to a change, migration to a seasonal variation' (C1: 8). Through the introduction of new matter to a situation, an insertion of a new section into a whole, then the whole has changed, altering its configuration forever, and enabling us to see the notion of an infinite whole (C1: 10).[5] This movement and change, as Deleuze goes on to explore through his cinema books, is defined through relation, perception, affection, time, space, sound, action, direction, speed, and thought itself. Consider the divergent images of movement through change in *Drugstore Cowboy* (dir. Van Sant, 1989), or in *Lola rennt* (*Run Lola Run*; dir. Tom Tykwer, 1998). When Deleuze considers thought and the movement-image in *Cinema 2*, he demonstrates that change does not have to be translational, as in a variation of a set of things through physical movement, but may constitute a conversion of thinking by non-translational movements, moving transversally, or ceasing movement altogether. When cinematic movement enters into the world, movement has an even more pervasive force upon perception and thus philosophical practice. Following Bergson, Deleuze describes the assemblage of executed and moving images as a mechanism of the universe – a 'metacinema' (C1: 59). Deleuze stresses how we can consider every single image that we can imagine – and those we cannot – as made by movement, movements of 'interatomic influences', atoms, molecules, our bodies, brains, eyes, as all pervasive, and which shape 'an infinite set' (C1: 58–59). In other words, the image is a dynamic entity, as he shouts at us in 1983, 'IMAGE = MOVEMENT' (C1: 58, original caps).

Deleuze says a film may be comprised of multiple kinds of images, but has one type of image as its dominant one: active, perceptive or affective. Then the relations produced through each of these types of image form the impulse-image, and as we shall see, the limits of the action-image in its crisis of movement (C1: 68; 70). Deleuze brokers a discussion on how to 'extinguish'

in this pragmatism any special effects of post production), Deleuze argues
that the polar of such *quantitative data* is the *qualitative* data made through
movement. Both aspects have implications for processes of creating meaning.
The physical mobility of the camera – its 'primitive' capacity for moving, is
the false movement that Deleuze investigates – arguing that while the image
that is movement, but the 'shot' the camera creates 'is the movement-image';
a 'mobile section of a duration' (C1: 22). This is an important point for analysis of all information generated by technologies of all types, not just screen
media, and here indicative of how the arguments concerning temporal shapes
that Deleuze explores in his cinema books can be extended to other and future considerations of all media. It is not 'sufficient', notes Deleuze, to merely
distinguish 'concrete' or 'imaginary' properties of something, dependent upon
whether it is within the spatial frame of the shot, or out of the shot (C1: 17).
Rather, the frame carries within it the possibilities of a far more complex
set of processes which function: 'As Bergson says, although he had not seen
its application to cinema, *things are never defined by their primitive state,
but by the tendency concealed in this state*' (C1: 25, emphasis added). Film
theory that analyses its material by determining whether or not something
is 'in or out of shot' can often overlook this inherent tendency or nature of
something, as equally as it can neglect the technical aspects that might be
generative of types of image properties.

Developed for screen by writer Peter Handke, the story of *Falsche Bewegung* is based on Johann Wolfgang Goethe's novel *Wilhelm Meisters Lehrjahre*
(Goethe [1795–96] 1917). Goethe's novel is a narrative of the process of apprenticeship, where the travel topology canvassed is a pedagogy of life experience: change through movement. The relationship between travel, movement
and perception is a philosophical theme that Deleuze repeatedly returns to in
the cinema books (see chapter 5 Perception). Yet Wenders's film takes not only
the pedagogic nature of 'the passage of life' as its plot, but also examines the
passage itself – as physical and as metaphysical (relating to the constitution
of being) movement-frames. This is a common trajectory in Wenders's films:
how movement comes to constitute and consolidate the tracing of pathways
of existence, the desire to experience things, and how histories are created

– not just by humans, but by things and places and events, as in *Der Himmel über Berlin* (*Wings of Desire*, 1987). The themes of apprenticeship and peda-gogy no doubt appeal to Deleuze, who had already made a lengthy study of the notion of apprenticeship through the search for love, carried out in his book *Proust and Signs* (2000).[1] To access any new system (language, love, culture), specific semiologies must be learnt (signs and their meanings) – this is the nature of an apprenticeship of any new arena or paradigm. Yet certain axiomatic ethics of pedagogy are involved in any apprenticeship, therefore, as once one part of the system is learnt, then others are engendered, and this has consequences for the system – in terms of knowledge, perception and aesthetics. One can only see what one is trained to see: even the most 'objective' of framing is affected by the style and manner of an apprentice-ship (however Deleuze will describe how the cinematographic *cogito* alters this fixed perception in his account of the *perception-image*). The 'relatively closed system' (C1: 12) of the cinema, thus provides a 'material universe' (C1: 59) of a contained system of apprenticeship, enabling a 'becoming' (C2: 145) of situations, conditions, characters or things. This closed system is open to change (and this is not to be considered a paradox) – as a process articulated by what Deleuze terms Bergson's 'infinite set' (C1: 59). In the context of its cinematographic use, the closed system to which Deleuze refers is in fact the detailing of how a film takes shape. In this technical process, regulated by what Deleuze and Guattari called the '*machinic processes*' of social formations, a self-affective transformative 'metacinema' arises from the cinematographic shot, cuts and framed composition (Deleuze and Guattari 1987: 435, original emphasis; C1: 59). Deleuze's thesis is this: it is the inherent nature of this socially coded technical process – the cinematographic layout itself – from which the whole of the movement-image arises. This is the machinic nature of the cultural assemblage of a film: machinic not in the sense of the mecha-nist dimensions of the cinematic, but in the sense of the cinematic body as a social, living system (*l'agencement machinique des images-mouvement*) (C1: 59; Deleuze 1983b: 88). This is a position of defining film as formed through process; a '*machinic assemblage*' (*ibid.* original emphasis).

What are the Frame, Shot and Cut?

Any discussion of the frame and shot, framing and cutting, plunges into the technical aspects of filmmaking which determine the creation of an image, the construction of scenes: a film. Framing seems simple, but is not: decide what object to film, and point a camera at an object. Do you zoom in to fill your frame with the texture of its surface, its materiality? Or do you frame the object sitting in situ, providing context through information about the scale, physicality, relativity of the object to its surroundings, but lose important details? There are important issues of choice that are raised by this complex activity of framing and shooting. Films are often remembered through the recollection of a particular framed scene – an arrangement of things, a colour, sound, or dialogue, a close-up of some thing or person – which may be intense, absurd, revelatory or excessive. These technically created facets of the cinema generally operate within already existing paradigms – those axiomatic systems of knowledge that are instantly 'recognizable' – as regulated by cultural conventions and economic controls.

Shooting and cutting will affect the way that the framed object appears. Holding the camera on the object for one continuous shot (a *long take*) (X number of minutes of chronometric time mapped with screen-time) will convey a different perspective of time and place, for instance, than a sequence comprised of two or more shots cut together at certain time intervals, with or without sound information either transitioning across or interacting with or matching the image in or out of frame. The action of splicing (*collure*) involves the literal splicing together of celluloid sound and images. While a literal physical cut was used for film stock such as 16mm or 35mm (common stock in the twentieth century), digital editing of shots employs a similar process of using units of image and sound in post-production editing. Cutting individual shots and sounds together that were filmed or made in different space-time axes so that they present a continuous sequence (a whole) is a technique commonly referred to as *montage*. Sound can operate at various levels of montage against or with the image (see chapter 4 Montage).

The pace and rhythm of intercutting shots, either with aspects of the same scene or with discontinuous spatial scenes, affects the image in a number of ways. Established connections, the sense of continuity, and the idea of chronometric time are transformed by the length and pace of shots, thereby altering the breadth and quality of information conveyed by the frame (see chapter 4 Montage). Even if an image is the result of an immobile camera (a fixed shot), the shot provides a temporal perspective on continuous information (C1: 24), provided by other connections in movement, such as sound, preceding frames, the character or topology of the scenery, and so on. For example, consider the opening shot of the landscape with its frenetic alien sounds in *There Will be Blood* (dir. Paul Thomas Anderson; dop. Robert Elswit, 2007). This shot is held for a determining length of time before it is cut to a contrasting shot below ground, an industrious silent frame of misanthropic activities as yet buried under the petroleum sediment hills. Contrary to such marked cuts of time are the shots of Wilhelm in *Falsche Bewegung* held as long as the tedium of life shows itself in the framed image. In each movement-image, created by the cut shots, conceptual and economic choices have been made about aesthetic and generic formations. As Deleuze will describe, the length of the shot and the decisions about the lengths of movement between cuts results a movement-image that shapes dimensions into multiplicities.[2] Rather than situating his analysis of the shot and cut just at the cardinal level of counting frames and lengths of shots (which results in the naming of something already resolved), Deleuze will focus on the kinds of translations in the on-screen circumstance-generated conditions.

In the French language the camera 'shot' *plan* implies a number of different meanings, including the sense of a geometric plane, something which Deleuze will play off in his discussion of the image as an *ensemble*. In philosophical terms, Deleuze describes the plan in terms of its affective organizational (and political) terms of the planes of immanence and transcendence (Deleuze 1988a: 128). Although the Spinozist sense of the hidden dimensions of social power or what Deleuze terms as the 'theological plan' (*ibid.*) are completely underplayed in the cinema books, the word *plan(e)* provides a rich vector for film philosophy and for screen analysis. In cinematic terms, Deleuze draws upon Burch's discussion of the geometry of the French etymology of plan, but with qualifications (Burch 1980). The geometrical organization of the plan is used in the measurement of distances between the camera and its framing of an object or body for the name of the shot – a *plan américain*, for example, a term used to describe a group shot of characters from their knees up (a 3/4 length shot). A shot can also be named after its lens type – a zoom (lens) shot, a wide-angle (creating distortion, for example scenes in *Pierrot le fou* (Godard, 1965), the deep-lens shots constructed by Gregg Toland for Orson Welles for *Citizen Kane* (1941), and then developed in the *The Magnificent Ambersons* by Welles and Stanley Cortez (1942). Bogue details Deleuze's use of the *plan* and *plans* as encompassing all possible senses and techniques of the shot – whether close-up (*gros-plan*), long shot (*plan d'ensemble*), or a tracking shot, and so on – in terms of Deleuze's address of a 'unity of movement' (C1: 27) which 'brings together a multiplicity of elements' (Bogue 2003: 45). In terms of framing and cutting the shot (*cadrage et decoupage*), Deleuze also mines the etymology of this word for his discussion. *Cadrage* is the framing in ciné-terminology, but to speak of the *cadre* is to address the framework of something and to speak of the environment. The activity of cutting – *découpage* (*découper* = to cut into pieces) – is not the same as in the English adoption of this word meaning an act of cutting and reassemblage, but in the French film industry, *découpage technique* refers to the process of the construction of time-space blocks of film, the act of shooting script, of editing length to film duration and spatial qualities to the limits of the frame, of throwing things into relief through cutting, interweaving images (Burch 1980: 3–16). The English-speaking film industry has no single word that encompasses this sense of *découpage*). This point should be considered when drawing from Deleuze's descriptions of montage and the action image as a result of instances of *découpage* and affective framing of particular conditions and qualities.

How Deleuze Uses the Frame, Shot and Cut

Considering the effects of the framing and movement of shots in images is a method of topological philosophy. As used by Deleuze in the Cinema books, it continues the type of critical epistemology Deleuze presents with Guattari in *A Thousand Plateaus*, where their study of geometric *physicality* enables a framing of qualitative material (Deleuze and Guattari 1987: 361–364). Here, Deleuze and Guattari use this method of 'descriptive geometry' – such as Deleuze will employ to describe camera shots and movements across a frame – as 'a minor science' and a 'mathegraphy' (*ibid.* 364). This approach provides a methodology for the taxonomy of film concepts as Deleuze's interest in the frame, shot and cut/edit of the film is not for technical reasons – although he takes time to explain some of them – rather he is interested in what concepts and forms these types of activities might enable.[3]

In *Cinema 1*, Deleuze says Jean Epstein comes the 'closest' to the concept of the shot as a 'mobile section, that is, a *temporal perspective or a modulation*' (C1: 24). Deleuze cites Epstein's description of 'the nature of the shot as pure movement', a 'descriptive geometry' (C1: 23, translation has modified Epstein's citation slightly). In his discussions of specific films, Deleuze argues for attention to the product of the shot construction and its form of modulation. Deleuze constantly draws his taxonomy back to the notion of *the false*, which he will address in *Cinema 2* as a 'power' (C2: 126). The false power can transform cinematographic elements. Over the chapters that engage elements of the shot, montage and narrative in cinema, Deleuze describes how different sequences of images 'enter into relative continuities' (through sequence shots where different images are rejoined to the whole), or are formed through 'false continuities' (where what is outside of the frame, which Deleuze refers to as 'the Open', draws into the image) (C1: 27–28).

Cinematic consciousness is produced by the different types of *framing of the image*, and the ways in which that image has been constructed by what Deleuze explains in terms of kinetic and chronic regimes, where a movement of duality also produces false and true continuities (C2: 126–128). Thus the shot construction and its form of modulation work to form the 'two poles of existence, the connections that determine a continuity *and* discontinuous appearances to consciousness' (C2: 302 n1). Deleuze charts examples (in the films of Hitchcock, Godard, Ozu, Syberberg, Mankiewicz) where attention to the framing of the image, and the dis/continuity of parts within a shot work to construct different screen arrangements, but also new images (C1: 12–13; C2: 126–127). The unity of the image, or what Deleuze sometimes refers to as its whole (*tout*), is created through the movements of different sets (*ensembles*). We see the closed system of framing an image as in the transformation of Wenders's characters of Alice or Wilhelm, or in Dutch director Marleen Gorris's 1997 film *Mrs Dalloway*, or Stephen Daldry's 2002 film *The Hours*, where the interconnections and changes brought about through the system enabled by 'Mrs Dalloway' reveal the process of subjectivity to be about the levels of becomings, changes through movement.[4]

In all senses of the shot, Deleuze says, the shot holds a dual unity, a 'dual requirement' (C2: 27). This in no way refers to the 'shot-reverse-shot' of classical Hollywood cinema, although this is a type of shot that, when employed, contributes to the type of unity to which Deleuze refers. The unity is one achieved through movement, for example where a shot engages a singular moment through its framing, and its correlation to other shots, either sequenced before or after it, with which it may enter into multiple relations. It may produce an open or closed system.

The various ways in which a movement-image is framed, shot and cut together has the effect of fusing all possible narratives in a film, resulting in the 'coalescence' of multiple images (such as in images in Wenders's films) (C2: 127; see chapter 10 Time). The assessment of the meaning of the film is thus *not* made in terms of the links between narrative and stylistic continuity, as is the case with much formalist film theory. Deleuze's ciné-system focuses on how and what variations of images produce: 'As in mathematics, cuts no longer indicate continuity solutions but variable distributions between the points of a continuum' (C2: 121). Deleuze develops the *incompossible* in terms of a 'crystalline' temporal mode and 'false' narration of movement (see chapter 12 Topology). Such complex domains are inferred when he simply states: 'The shot is the movement-image' (C1: 22). But, as Deleuze addresses with his notion of the movement-image, there are two aspects of movement to first consider: sets (closed) and wholes (open). The shot is 'the intermediary' between the set and the whole (C1: 19).

What is a set? Within individual films the type of narratives, the range of information given, the places, time and people created are contingent and controlled by the type and style of frame, shot and editing (cutting technique, speed, rhythm). These technical considerations are what distinguish the qualities and functions of things and bodies in film. Deleuze addresses the production of a film through this technical formation of a set of things: *'everything which is present in the image* – sets [*décors*; scenery], characters and props – *framing'* (C1: 12, original emphasis). Each of these parts that comprise the set of a frame are the 'elements, which themselves form sub-sets' (C1: 18). Each *set* (notably, the word Deleuze uses in the French is *ensemble*, which is a mathematical set, but also invokes the notion of an *assemblage*) produces a finite set of things – a closed system – determined in space and by abstract conceptions of time, by their framing.

Sets are thus different to the *wholes* of duration (Bergson's third thesis; see chapter 4 Montage) but both comprise the movement-image. Extending Bergson's thesis, Deleuze takes 'three levels' of this framing to consider the technicalities of how it is possible that the discreet parts of the (closed) sets in a scene/film (individual objects, people, sounds, etc.) operate to create a whole that forms an *infinite system*, where that assemblage of images keeps on producing more and more variation of meanings (the influence of Spinozan thought on Deleuze here is worth further consideration (cf. Negri 1991; Gatens and Lloyd 1999). The three levels he names are:

1. sets;
2. the 'movement of translation' and 'modification' of the objects within sets;
3. the duration or whole which changes 'according to its own relations' (C1: 11).

Describing the first level – a set that frames things – Deleuze directs us to consider how the technical stresses of the cinema produce paradigms for

forms (and herein lies the influence of philosopher Henri Bergson, but equally
that of film theorist Noël Burch). Identifying the process of camera framing as
'limitation' (C1: 13), Deleuze states: 'Framing is the art of choosing the parts
of all kinds which become part of a set. Within this set, there may be sub-
sets which provide further degrees of information. The main set is a closed
system, *relatively* and artificially closed' (C1: 18, emphasis added). Useful for
film (and all moving media) analysis are the five characteristics that Deleuze
describes as comprising the 'first level' of this closed system (or closed sets)
of the framed image. In each film, choices concerning elemental details for
shooting and cutting provide: (1) *information*, which is relational to (2) the
limits of the frame, (3) the *topology* of that framing, (4) the *point-of-view*
of the shot, and the inference or interference of (5) any *out-of-frame* (*hors-
champ*) material (C1: 14–15).[5]

The second level describes the shot and movement formed by shot and
cutting techniques which cause a translation of movement and modification
'of their respective positions' (C1: 11). In films each shot works to construct
a specific *cinematographic consciousness* through particular types of movements: creating the mobility of the cinema's duration, creating the type of
topological dimension for the image. This dimension can be thought of as
the spatial orientation of the image, but the physical movement of the camera, explains Deleuze, is what offers situational points for analysis of shifts
in perception, mutations, changes; variations and image-becomings, where
change or endurance is apparent by the modifications of the situation shown
through movement (C1: 23). Deleuze discusses this conscious change of the
shot through its movement in relation to Hitchcock's film *The Birds* (1963).
The Birds is often referred to in film studies for its cross-cutting editing technique of increasing speed between edited shots of bird attacks, their victims
and the onlookers, where the editing rhythm creates a pace for the action
(cf. Bordwell and Thompson 2003: 224–225) However, Deleuze is following
film theorist Noël Burch in looking at *The Birds* to see how 'shot transitions'
(Burch's terms) 'can give rise to patterns of mutual interference' (Burch
(1969) 1981: 12). This approach directs film analysis to look at the arithmeti-
cal affect in addition to its pace. Deleuze discusses how this technique of the

movement of the elements of the scene can be analysed in terms of: (1) the resonance of the 'relative movement' of a director's screen signature, (2) the dynamism and geometry of specific movements, and (3) the 'distributions between elements' (C1: 20–21). The first two points are elements that Burch would come to dismiss as pointless formalism (Burch 1980: vi). However, it is the third point that distinguishes Deleuze's cinema system, in its articulation of the variation of elements – of the contradictory and complex elements of a situation – as they coalesce over time. Each of these divisions of the elements that make up the whole of the set of a shot offers insight into both the construction and the division of the elements which makes up the scene. This is the 'dividual' of what avant-garde artist Jean Epstein referred to as the *'perspective of the inside'* of an image (Epstein cited by Deleuze C1: 23, original emphasis; C1: 221 n20). Whatever kind of shot, says Deleuze, it 'always has these two aspects: it presents modifications of a relative position in a set or some sets. It expresses absolute changes in a whole or in the whole' (C1: 19).

The 'third level' of Deleuze's Bergsonian inspired thesis of movement is the determination of the whole and the expression of duration (C1: 20; C1: 29; see chapter 4 Montage, chapter 10 Time, chapter 12 Topology). With regard to this level, Deleuze describes how the topology of cinematographic consciousness is never static – it is one of movement and change (Bergson's third thesis), even in a set of 'vacant interiors' (C1: 12). When he writes: 'the whole is the Open, and relates back to time or even to spirit rather than to content and to space' (C1: 17), Deleuze is describing how the whole (sets of images) are shaped in image (in film), through the internal relational movements (such as modes of montage) of sets. The framing of an image (key for Deleuze's cinema system) provides the paradigmatic framework where difference – *the dividual* – causes change, through introduced elements of time: 'This is Ozu's thinking: life is simple, and man never stops complicating it by "disturbing still water"' (C2: 15). Taking Japanese director Yasujiro Ozu's implication of this image of life – as one of perpetual movement – this image records the event of a disturbance to water, whether it is in the view of the camera and explicitly recorded, inferred through off screen sound, or noise dialogue. The shot is what provides a map of an image's movement, a particular filmmaker/

cinematographer/director's 'signature' style of filmmaking (C1: 21) – such as the beautiful and tragic consciousness that Ozu's style conveys through human interaction with the elemental worlds and vice versa (see Ozu's film *Akibiyori* (*Late Autumn*, 1960)). In the Deleuzian sense, the term 'shot' refers to the camera as a dominant consciousness: a cinematographic consciousness that will determine the forms of filmic universes that are framed, a provider and selector of levels of participation to information.

The Function of the Frame, Shot and Cut

Deleuze's discussion on the frame and shot orients itself through the mediation of specific directors whose work excelled in showing the limits of the camera and of human ability for perception and action within a system of their own devising, or their reaction to an elemental system beyond their control. The choice of what is framed determines how something is perceived (see also perception-image). To frame, a physical or abstract 'centre' is invoked. To find a centre, or even an asymmetrical 'acentre' of an image for the purposes of framing and shooting, x number of elements, objects and functions come into interaction. This is the aspect of differentiation (and dedifferentiation – the loss of specialization in form or function) that Deleuze addresses with numerous examples from the cinema to show what happens.

The centre is *physical* in images where a specific actor's style – Deleuze mentions Gene Kelly, Fred Astaire, Jerry Lewis and Alain Masson – effect a 'degree zero' (C2: 61). Behaviour and gesture have generated the situation, modified the genre, and created a new or different image. We can also note that the framing of the image (its arrangement within the set), its shot and cut (spatial and temporal), is also a result of decisions on the production and arrangement of the elements within the image (including the actors body), how they are cut together in a shot. However, as Deleuze argues, it is the movement of the cinematic world that affects the mobility of characters, to the point where an infinite mobility is engendered by its very limitation by the frame (C2: 59).

Deleuze constructs the technical terms of the screen's topology to focus on the *information* that a framed set – or shot will offer. Analysing the complexities of information provided in film and in media spaces is a theme that runs throughout the books (cf. C2: 268–269), and Deleuze chastises us for not assessing the image properly in its framing, 'because we do not know how to read it properly; we evaluate its rarefaction as badly as its saturation' (C1: 12–13). Saturation has been one of the dominate features of Contemporary Hollywood cinema particularly since the advent of 'MTV' culture (1981) and digital editing styles where 'rarefaction' of the image is the tendency of the movement-image toward the simplification of the image, through a stress on a dense singularity. In Jarmusch's *Stranger than Paradise* (1984), a singular sound, such as the repeated refrain of the song 'I Put a Spell on You' performed by Screamin' Jay Hawkins, or a singular frame when the image is cut to a black frame in between scenes, acts as a decrease in information of the frame. But at the same time this rarefaction invokes its polar – as a density of the frame, a saturation of black references, Hawkins' expansion of the genres of blues and rock, and Jarmusch's use of 'I Put a Spell on You' as a sound-image. Deleuze engages with this aspect of the extreme 'affective framing' in terms of the temporal and spatial implications (compression or dilation, rarefaction and saturation), and close-up of an expression or event in a later chapter on 'the affection-image' (C1: 102, see chapter 6 Affect). The sound ('I Put a Spell on You') and the image (black frame) change the whole scene when heard or seen. These frames re-shape the meaning of the (whole) image through an 'accent' on a 'single object' (the example Deleuze gives is the famous glass of milk shot in Hitchcock's 1945 film *Spellbound*, where the entire frame becomes filled with the white density of the milk). Deleuze references Burch on this point of a black or white screen frame, saying this type of change in the framing of an image constitutes a change in the 'structural value', rather than just serving as 'punctuation' (C1: 13; 219 n2). Whether tending toward a saturated image as in Hitchcock, or when the set itself becomes emptied, as in one of Ozu's 'vacant interiors' or Michaelangelo Antonioni's 'deserted landscapes', the meaning of the image is formed through its framing (see for example *L'Eclisse* (*Eclipse*) 1962; C1: 13). 'Saturation' is to be considered in terms of 'the multiplication of independent data', in terms of a collapse of spatial organization (Deleuze's example is director William Wyler – think *Roman Holiday*, 1953 or *Ben-Hur*, 1959) and the hierarchical arrangement of information (Deleuze's example is Robert Altman – see his films *MASH*, 1970, *Short Cuts*, 1993 or *Gosford Park*, 2001. All of Altman's extras have as much part to play as 'the stars', and equally there is little differentiation between focal and background objects) (C1: 12). What the camera does, says Deleuze, is frame, shoot and cut together, or montage events in such a way that the internal situation of the event is revealed.

Using examples of a specific shots from films enables Deleuze to quickly make a distinction between the modes of time, the qualities of space, and thus importantly, the political conditions that the camera movement fixes under action-images, or will invoke as thought portals as a time-image. Does the movement of the camera in a film track you across a physical space, or does it plunge the action into the depths of time? These are the criteria Deleuze will use when addressing the technical *stresses* that are in play by the operations of filmmaking, which he continues further in his investigation of the type of movement generated by the activity of *montage*.

4

Montage

Deleuze looks at four schools of montage – American, French, German and Soviet – and divergent directions taken during the first era of cinema. This chapter will address each of those directions and how Deleuze situates montage in relation to the movement of time. In the Deleuzian system, montage is the 'determination of the whole' of the image, achieved through the techniques of cutting (editing) and creating continuities. Montaged images create sets of images – it is the whole of the political and aesthetic spectrum of the production of thought, of commodities, of modes of address. Montage creates movement which in turn produces specific modes of time that are not fixed, but situational events that are contextually reproduced over the passage of chronometric time, as different people interact, intervene, and encounter things in divergent ways.

American director Todd Haynes made a film about folk singer Bob Dylan en-
titled *I'm Not There* (2006) in which six disparate actors of different shapes
and body types 'perform' six different episodes descriptive of a component
of phases in Dylan's life. In Deleuzian terms each of these images come together to make a whole life that depicts a life of multiple facets, whose final
form is in perpetual movement. In a conversation on how the production
of ideas occurs, Deleuze refers to the poetry of Bob Dylan as exemplary of
the 'long preparation' required to produce work (Deleuze and Parnet [1977]
2002: 6–7). Deleuze describes how things are made after an 'encounter' with
other things, people, but also after encounters with 'movements, other ideas,
events, entities' (*ibid.*). Dylan's lyrics on this nature of the processual formation of thought – in 'a-parallel evolution' are repeated in Deleuze's position
on the function of montage in the cinema: montage is a producer of forming
consciousness (*ibid.*; C1: 20). Film is comprised of a number of different
kinds of images, and Deleuze calls this image-assemblage montage. Through
connections as yet un-thought, un-named, but intuited through things already 'manifested' in forms and the performance of those intuited senses,
montage makes possibilities take new forms. What might represent life most
of all is not a mimicry of life, but a practice that shows how life shapes itself
by chance and through contrived connections. Through this movement, and
through these circumstances, events, fissures and forces, and political and
thus aesthetic positions are formed. Similar in its aesthetic ideals to the
anti-hero journey movies of *L'Avventura* (*The Adventure*; dir. Antonioni,
1960), *Little Dieter Needs to Fly* (dir. Werner Herzog, 1997), *Stranger Than
Paradise* (dir. Jarmusch, 1984), *Im Lauf der Zeit* (*In the Course of Time*,
commonly known as *Kings of the Road*; dir. Wenders, 1976), *Into the Wild*
(dir. Sean Penn, 2007), or *Scott Pilgrim* vs. *The World* (dir. Edgar Wright,
2010), *I'm Not There* demonstrates how different encounters generate multiple images and perspectives that modulate the whole (the components
of the image) into a specific consciousness of something. As Deleuze will
argue, the image is a product of 'the sensory-motor schema', located in the
'hodological space' of the screen (C2: 127). To understand the composition
of the image, Deleuze looks first at descriptions of things, then the forms

of 'continuity' that the type of film sets up (logical, continuity shots or sur-realistic connections).

To recap the *movement image*, the three levels of Bergson's thesis on movement that Deleuze ascribes are: (1) the creation of a closed system (by a screen situation), (2) the movement that occurs between each component in the system (a scene/character/situation/film's internal relations), and (3) the changing whole (the mode of montage) engages in *kinetic migration*; as ideas and things circulate, their movements 'enables each to contain or prefigure the others' (see chapter 2 Movement; C1: 29).

Operating as the third level of Bergsonism comprising the *movement image*, montage types engage images in and out of the frame in different ways. Dependent upon the type of montage, there are a range of political and aesthetic implications for the images produced. Montage will create certain forms of the movement-image, and this is the reason why Deleuze pinpoints this technique as fundamentally one of epistemology, where the screen engages in a pedagogy of perceptual formations. Scene by scene in turn, images give rise to signs (as we shall read with regard to the Peircian semiotics Deleuze draws upon in chapter 8 Transsemiotics) of meanings of all types, including the signs of the process of creative formation itself: this is montage.

What is Montage?

Considered within the domain of twentieth-century modernist art movements, montage was a radical practice that caused a reassessment of vision in cognitive and perceptual terms. Montage refers to a technique of putting together different things, and has various specific names for that technique, according to the media platform being used: photomontage for photographic images; collage or montage for the plastic arts of sculpture, painting, drawing, or sound; montage for screen work. Modernist painters such as Natalya Goncharova (for example her painting *Linen*, 1913) and Juan Gris (*Still Life with Open Window, Rue Ravignan*, 1915) made famous their vernacular technique with their practice of the collection, collation and collage of disparate images and things from their everyday situation. James Joyce's novel *Ulysses* (1918–22) exemplifies the work of the modernist artists' who were trying to visualize the dynamism of everyday life, the processes of change, and the scale and terms of movement, the dimensions of speed and slowness. Their method engaged the principle of self-reflexivity where the hook-up of process and examination of the object becomes a part of the final work. Visualization in whatever medium is recognized to be concerned with investigating the types of relationships generated from forms (abstract and representational), sound, colours and movement-images. Through this epistemological investigation of vision, the question of representation of life is in itself critiqued. This era, says Deleuze, 'was the search for a kinetics as a properly visual art', which was to be seen in the silent cinema of the era, as well as the plastic arts and music (C1: 43).

In relation to screen forms, montage generally refers to the joining of cinema shots (with sound being a component part of any shot). Montage can serve either or both of the primary movement-image functions, either to perform a cliché or metaphor of sound-imagery, or to engage in creative or destructive aesthetic-political ends. Montage thus serves to disrupt *or* standardize the schemata of standard sensory-motor perception and provides a different/ normative vision of the world. In this sense the critical consideration and analysis of montage is an encounter with the specific *pathologies of movement* that a particular director, producer, actor, financier, chooses to engage.[1]

As a process, the activity of montage creates an image of time and determines the particular mode of time of a film. Montage is movement, whether mechanical activity (mobility of the camera (C1: 24–28) or in the edit suite) or movement within perceptual processes, and this movement is what will create a cinematic whole: the film itself. Technically speaking, there are many different types of montage that a director/cinematographer/editor/sound engineer-producer may intuitively, deliberately and/or accidentally choose to use for the purposes of filming.

Deleuze names a number of different types of montage, via their function in terms of the creation of forms, through their dialectic of difference (see the discussion on how Deleuze uses the ciné-system to engage a screen-dialectic of form). The editing together of disparate and like things, whether as music enfolding a single shot, or whether as two or more places cut together, produces a range of effects and affects. Deleuze concludes at the end of *Cinema 2* that montage is one of the most significant components of image production and the cinema. Ultimately, the non-extensive, internal (or immanent) 'perpetual exchange' of actual and virtual image is what Deleuze will define: the production of the autonomous image (C2: 273). Deleuze describes this further in relation to the time-image, but for now we must continue with the taxonomy of technical details.

In his system, Deleuze notes three forms of montage:

1. 'the alternation of differentiated parts';
2. montage of 'relative dimensions';
3. montage of 'convergent actions' (C1: 31).

The technique of montage enables the relational variation of the movement-image to express multiple positions in space and show how these may vary, or depict how images might change in what we understand as historical, cultural, geo-physical or chronometric time. Through montage, divergent aspects of an image are brought into proximity, are linked together, through direct and indirect cinematographic techniques (of which matters of perceptual capacity are just as important to consider as formal techniques). The result of which is the 'whole' that Deleuze speaks of – meaning the specific type and form of relational *consistency* of the whole of a filmic world.

In filmmaking terms the key names for montage techniques of the early twentieth century are the Russian film makers Lev Kuleshov, Dziga Vertov and Vsevolod Pudovkin. To construct his argument, Deleuze draws on the filmmakers who use and discuss montage – Eisenstein, Vertov, Pasolini, Jean Epstein (C2: 36). Deleuze also looks at the work of directors whose films rely on the perfection of certain types of montage – Luchino Visconti, Welles, Hitchcock, Resnais, Rouch, Perrault, Godard – and the film theorists who discuss it – Bazin, Jean-Louis Schefer – and the philosophers who attended to the kinds of forms that were produced by modes of dialectical movement that montage produces – Aristotle, Kant, Hegel.[2]

How Deleuze Uses Montage

For Deleuze, montage is a form and technique that is the primary way that the movement-image and its varieties are composed. Deleuze is speaking of analogue methods of montage, so techniques are different for digitally compressed images, but the morphological process of montage remains the same for all types of screen image. In *Cinema 2* Deleuze poses the following chicken-and-egg question: 'Which is first, montage or movement-image? The whole is produced by the parts but also the opposite: there is a dialectical circle or spiral, "monism" (which Eisenstein contrasts with Griffith-style dualism)' (C2: 159). Deleuze has already answered this question in *Cinema 1*, in his third chapter on montage, where he describes montage in the Bergsonian terms of duration: the movement-image is expanded from within as more montaged images dilate the whole. This durational whole, says Deleuze, is expressive of 'the indirect image of time' (C1: 29). In this Bergsonian sense, Deleuze radically alters and extends how we can approach the techniques of montage.

The discussion of montage lends itself to a number of core concerns for the Deleuzian ciné-system. Screen montage is the cinematic equivalent of philosophical problem-framing. The image identifies the issue and then contrasts it within its world, or with other elements that either challenge or complement it. Deleuze always has his philosophical problem of difference in mind, arguing that the forms that Eisenstein creates make him 'a cinematographic Hegel' (C2: 210). Devoting a large chapter to the subject of montage enables Deleuze to flesh out some of the problems of the differential method he employs to articulate the movement-image. Philosophical debates concerning the 'singular' and 'the infinite' are engaged in his discussion of the 'any-instant-whatevers', for example, as part of his address to Plato's question on the composition of the transcendent moment (or sublime) and relational ontology in Forms. In describing how the 'alternation of differentiated parts' (instead of an image composed by dialectical opposition) (C1: 31; 45) leads to different types of montage wholes, Deleuze also gives examples of what he terms the 'relation-image' (cf. C1: x; C1: 215). Deleuze notes that 'the techniques of the image always refer to a metaphysics of the imagination: it is like two ways of imagining the passage from one image to the other' (C2: 58). In this sense, a *dialectic of movement* (which we can see as a component of the montage) is where time can be defined in relation to movement (C1: 31–32). Time can be considered as a whole, as an interval, or indirectly produced through montage (C1: 32). Over the duration of the film, *I'm Not There*, for example, the lived eras of Dylan as subject become simultaneous images through the montaged alternation of the differentiated parts of each image. Other kinds of relation-images arise when time is not produced by movement and mental images that arise through relations: (1) natural relations and the mark, (2) abstract relations and the symbol, (3) free indirect relations and the opsign and sonsign (see chapter 13 Thought).

Montage is an essential component for the indirect time-image to occur, the result of a motor-sensory movement (see chapter 10 Time and chapter 12 Topology). The physics of movement on screen are the montage-event that Deleuze addressed from the first chapter of *Cinema 1*: 'the cinema is the system which reproduces movement as a function of any-instant-whatever, that is, as a function of equidistant instants, selected so as to create an impression of continuity' (C1: 5). In calling attention to the ways in which films dramatize their internal and external organization, Deleuze draws our attention to the kinetic processes of the screen – how ideas are played out, but also how characters or situations take form, or are engaged in what Deleuze calls the process of becoming (see chapter 11 Politics).

Deleuze divides the variations of montage into what he views as the 'four main trends' that can be distinguished by their culturally specific concerns – however different their technique or style (C1: 30). Thus he names four 'schools' of filmmaking of the early twentieth century that engage distinctive practices of montage: American, Soviet, German Expressionist and Pre-war French (C1: 30). Deleuze will qualify this grouping of 'national' productive characteristics of cinematic groupings, making the observation that as with any group, in terms of shared communal 'themes, problems and preoccupations', they provide 'an ideal community … to found concepts of schools or trends' (C1: 30). When referring to Deleuze's concept of a 'national' cinema, it is a definition that is not guided by a determining territory, or geographical site, but is marked by its mode of dramatization of the circulating ideas and the forms they may manifest in various states of transition and motion that are produced in specific countries' conditions (see chapter 11 Politics for ways that Deleuze engages different nationally produced cinemas).

Deleuze characterizes the style of montage from each named national cinema in the terms of this sense of community, testing out some of his claims in other parts of his argument. Although this might seem like a simplifying rule for classification, Deleuze argues that the only 'generality' about montage is its function means that it places 'the cinematographic image into a relationship with the whole; that is, with time conceived as the Open' (C1: 55). By this, Deleuze refers to his overarching conception of the movement-image as duration in the Bergsonian, vitalist sense; as an ever expanding living thing.

Deleuze names, after Kant, two main modes of movement created by montage as two kinds of the sublime: the mathematical and the dynamic (C1: 53). Each have different functions. These are movement-images of the mathematical – as in the work of Abel Gance, and his film *Napoléon* (1927) (C1: 46), and the movement-images of dynamic composition (via montage), such as we see in F.W. Murnau's silent film *Sunrise: A Song of Two Humans* (1927) and *Nosferatu* (dir. Murnau, 1922) (C1: 46–53). Deleuze will invoke the sublime when describing indirect time-images, that have gone 'beyond' the movement-image, yet which require movement to figure their composition (C1: 53; C2: 238; chapter 13 Thought).

The Function of Montage?

Montage reveals that the formation of an image is through the movement of the coalescence of the two sides of the actual perception of the virtual object (C2: 68). The dialectic of the virtual actual is the premise of the law of this paradigm. Godard offers Deleuze access to one of the technical methods that a film maker uses to convey the wholeness of time, for example in his specific montage techniques in works such as his *Histoire(s) du Cinéma* (*Histories of*

Cinema, 2007), or *Notre Musique* (*Our Music*, 2004), or in direct dialogue, such as from *Nouvelle Vague* (*New Wave*, 1990): 'The past and the present that they felt above them were waves of one and the same ocean.'

The type of fragmentation to a continuum, caused through cutting different shots together, creates what Deleuze calls (in relation to the fragmentation employed in French director Resnais's films, cf. Resnais 1948; 1950; 1955; 1968) 'a technical stress which is essential in the cinema' (C2: 120). In other words the type of montage engaged determines, through intensive means, the form of reality or thought-image created by a screen image. Further, Deleuze stresses that this technique of fragmentation, which produces a continuum of fragmentations, is 'inseparable from the topology, that is from the transformation of a continuum' (C2: 120). New and different forms of 'reality' are created through transformations of forms. Montage is a technique for change: a form of self-producing machine, particularly visible on screen where situations and events work to reconfigure individuals and communities. For example, consider the range of intensive forms of community created in scenes in the following films: *4* (dir. Ilya Khzhanovsky, 2005), *Code 46* (dir. Michael Winterbottom, 2003), *2046* (dir. Wong Kar-Wai, 2004), *Er shi si cheng ji* (*24 city*; dir. Zhang Ke-Jia, 2008).

What montage does, according to Deleuze, is achieve the 'determination of the Whole' (*la détermination du Tout*) (C1: 29). This is different to the *realization* of the Whole, which is, according to Deleuze, a process that only *thought* can achieve, evidenced through actions (see chapter 13 Thought). Different forms of montage draw up the internal, external (non-localizable), and peculiar variations of movements of life. For example, Deleuze describes hacked montage (*montage haché*) as a process where fragmentation alters the topology of the image (C2: 120). Deleuze also discusses Bazin's idea of the 'law of the "forbidden montage"' (C1: 153). This is a useful concept to keep in mind for screen analysis. When there is a scene with simultaneous terms to be held as an 'irreducible simultaneity', where montage or shot-reverse-shot are not appropriate, then the filmmaker engages this mode of composition. Deleuze refers to this as the 'third law' of 'organic composition', made common in American genre cinema (C1: 151–152). Van Sant's film *Last Days*

(2005) – a sound meditation on the final forty-eight hours of rock star Kurt Cobain's life – has many examples of this forbidden montage. Like *Elephant*, single shots are held in a fixed frame – no cuts – and either pull back or track forwards at an infinitesimal pace to enlarge or reduce the information in the frame, degree by degree, so that the situation is highlighted and drenched in a continuous, simultaneous sound. The subject must be enclosed with its surrounds and no cut-way, no *hors-champs* (out of frame) can be allowed.

In *Cinema 1* Deleuze says montage is 'the determination of the whole (the third Bergsonian level) by means of continuities, cutting and false continuities' (C1: 29). In *Cinema 2* Deleuze states that montage is 'the principle act of cinema' (C2: 34). In regarding the act of cinema as its 'determination of the whole', Deleuze extends the standard discussion of the construction of the plane of composition of a screen scene in terms of *continuity or discontinuity* (Godard's infamous jump-cuts, against the rules of classical Hollywood's 180-degree line of composition, for example). What Deleuze is stressing is against analytic cinematic theory which takes analysis of the moving image back to its shot by shot analysis, removing the movement of the living image, and often applying a critical methodology that is better suited to a (still) photographic image. Screen-based images move and change. Thus, in stressing the 'whole' that is created, and continually created out of *variations* of shots, it is important to recall that Deleuze considers those component parts as living entities. In this, Deleuze is drawing on Bergson's vitalist philosophy for the creation of new things, and on Nietzsche's affective theory where 'forces' are substituted for the old philosophies of 'judgement' (C2: 141; chapter 6 Affect).

Deleuze argues that the type of articulation of movement-images is the fundamental act of the cinematographic – which marks its difference from the photographic still, for example, and that which enables the formation of all kinds of distinctive types of films and movement images. Deleuze argues that montage is 'primary' to the shaping of both the cinematic whole and its component images (C1: 29, 55).

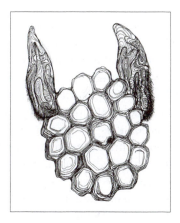

5

Perception

Perception is one of the ways in which the screen-image engages attention. Exactly what or whose perception is being framed? Film theory often invokes the notion of a 'spectator' or 'participant'. Philosophy discusses the 'phenomenology' of the activity of perceiving something. Both approaches often neutralize or make assumptions about the racialized, gendered, sexualized and thus political position and physical body of that perceptual activity. In the Deleuzian ciné-system, perception is an element of a movement-image. The perception is a form that presents images of a framed perception of things, and the perception in things.

'*Esse est percipi*, to be is to be perceived' (C1: 66). This idea is one that Deleuze reiterates throughout the cinema books. The act and activity *of being* is a perception and a perspective. Film dramatizes this perception, making images that demonstrate and perform things, and thus creating new aesthetics and new perspectives. Deleuze points out that existence is empirically contingent upon the subject that is doing the perceiving. Significantly, this subject is not a human subject, rather it is the perceptual capacity of the subject of matter produced through technological platforms that enable perception (for example, within a *mise-en-scène*). For the film theorist, the difficulty of this idea rests with the description of *esse est percipi*: the actual articulation of the technical and philosophical production of this notion, which Deleuze describes as the perception-image. Deleuze draws his example from Samuel Beckett's silent film, *Film* (dir. Alan Schneider, 1964), where actor Buster Keaton embodies the perception-image; he creates images that are the subject and the object, and the cinematic perception, showing consciousness to be a matter of being (*ibid.*).

Taking the famous film by the Lumière brothers of *L'Arrivée d'un train à La Ciotat* (*Arrival of a Train at La Ciotat*, 1896), we see that the perception of movement is done by the camera, recording in one shot a steam train arriving at a train station with people milling about. The camera notes details about the materials and forms of the time of filming (Gunning 1995). *L'Arrivée d'un train à La Ciotat* is a silent film, and any subsequent overlaid sound-track has the effect of re-framing and dramatizing the moment. This is a perception-image produced by and in the camera, and functions as any technological platform functions: as a recording device of images.

However, Deleuze's argument is that in addition to cinematic perception, there are two further fields of perception to be accounted for: those created by the subject or object of the camera, and then how the whole of cinematographic perception is productive as an autonomous form. The whole is comprised of different types of perception image, which are formed through different types of movement. The second type of perception is easily figured through subjects that are framed by or which acknowledge the presence of the camera. A train travels towards a camera; an actor performs in front of a camera; an actor might even directly address a camera; an animal may run towards or away from a camera. An example of this subject/object perception is to be found in Leslie Harris's film *Just Another Girl on the I.R.T.* (dop. Richard Connors, 1992). In the opening sequence of the film, the main character Chantel (played by actor Ariyan Johnson) stops her journey, turns, shaking her head at the camera trailing her, and in direct address to camera she talks into it and to the audience – just as she has had to engage with the various perceptions and perspectives of others who have engaged her on her journey (Jerry the model who picks her up at the train station, an older man who gives her a 'don't enter my space look' and moves away from her reading over his shoulder in the train, a boy in the street who engages her private trajectory, and who calls out to her as she walks past). Chantel tells her cinematic stalker: 'I'm a Brooklyn girl [...] I don't let nobody mess with me. I do what I want, when I want'. The dialogue is in contradistinction to the elements of the plot that subsequently unfold, and Chantel's 'control' over her own subjectivity is seen to be a false notion that she holds, as constituted within her world. Chantel's direct address to the camera works by providing another perception-image to the set of previous montages of movement-images. Rather than explain these types of perception-image in terms of the 'mediation' of the technology, Deleuze argues for a philosophy of difference here, an interjection to examine how something has changed between images. This offers a way of considering how differentiation of perception occurs by and in the image. While 'natural perception' engages 'fixed points or separated points of view' (the phenomenological position of Chantel at that moment), Deleuze describes how the function of 'cinematographic perception' is something that 'works continuously' to form the movement-image (C1: 22).

As we saw in the last chapter, what is in the image is a useful term to approach the shot and frame. What is in image is the camera's perception-image; all of the component parts that will comprise the image – 'sets, characters, props – *framing*' (C1: 12, original emphasis). However, when the image is 'reflected by a living image' it becomes what Deleuze says and 'is precisely what will be called perception' (C1: 62). This creates the third field of the perception-image that Deleuze discusses – the creation of a whole.

For example, in *Der Himmel über Berlin* (*The Sky over Berlin* also known as *Wings of Desire*; dir. Wenders, 1987, dop. Henri Alekan[1]), the shots after the title frame are connected by point-of-view of the camera, modified by the rhythmic axis of the movements it sees: the sun is shrouded by clouds shining thinly over the 1980s cityscape of Berlin, graphically matched with a full screen eye of an angel, an aerial shot of the view that that sun-eye sees above the city of Berlin, shots of children who see this sun-angel looking at them, back to what is above – a bird, the angel, a plane, the angel on a plane looking at a child looking back – until the camera's frame is pulled by another consciousness and it picks up Peter Falk's character, until his thoughts, audible for the complete film image but not for the film world, and his musings continue until he mentions the name Berlin, at which point the camera frames the outside of the plane again, those same clouds swirling above the city as the plane descends towards the ground. Languorously controlling the pace of the music that has lent continuity to this entire opening sequence, the mobile camera's framing through the plane-window point of view is distracted by the sounds of radio transmissions from a radio tower emitting the signals of multiple stations from Berlin. The sound is a murmur that swells and ebbs throughout the entire film – that of thousands of voices, of thoughts controlling, directing, perceiving, observing, as the humans and angels continue in their existence. The camera leaves the plane and pursues these sounds of life, and the duration of the life-sound watchers – the angels, whose framed perception of the material history of the city provide the film story. The film oscillates between the two perception-images of the framed perception and the perception within. These are the key elements of Deleuze's perception-image: observing a passage between subjective and objective, and seeing the perception-image change its modes as it constitutes a different set of images.

Wenders' film-thinking about the perception of a specific thing leads us to the heart of Deleuze's discussion of the perception-image, and the limits and possibilities of perception-images.[2] For on the ground in Berlin we have numerous, in fact multiple, other perceptions of that same city's history; how to account for these is a question cleverly framed in *Królik po berlinsku* (also known as *Rabbit à la Berlin*; dir. Konopka, 2009), where the perception-image reveals a pocket of human interval in land control – rabbits who were able to freely breed and live in some of the pockets of the no-man's-land space between the Berlin wall of eastern and western Berlin. This perception-image is contingent upon the duration of the living land and of its perception.

What is the Perception-image?

Screen images and sounds give form to thoughts and ideas. Screen images and sounds create worlds. In order to make sense of images, we place things into known categories of genres and style conventions, as determined by political and aesthetic cultural practices. Screen-based media materializes *perception* of these conventions and their complex, transitional and variable connections and relations, through movement which renders temporal conditions visible and audible to certain audiences, and obscures, censors, excludes and complicates situations for others. Perception of the moving time-based image is a function of the cognitive and intellectual abilities of the perceiver of that image, and of the perception-image, but, with the Deleuzian perception-image there is a second aspect where perception is to be understood as formed by a *'double system, of a double regime of reference of images'* (C1: 62, original emphasis).

Perception as a double regime of reference of images refers to a 'complementary' movement that takes place in the movement-image (C1: 62). 'The image [image 1] reflected by a living image [image 2] is precisely what will be called perception', notes Deleuze, and further, these two aspects result in the 'perception-image' (C1: 62). For example, using the film scenes discussed above, our perception of the moment on the train station is in relation to the start of the Lumières' film and its durational movement of images until the end. Within that short space (approximately forty seconds), the image of the train (image 1) has come together through movement-images of the train (+ image 2, the living image); we recognize an action-image, it produces a certain affect where the arrival of the train causes the passengers to move, which in turn gives rise to a perception-image. Or, if we take the example of the rabbits of *Królik po berlinsku* living in the site between walls in Berlin (image 1, situation), from their perception, an action (existence) was affectively enabled by the non-threatened environment (image 2, life/affect), providing a perception-image of Berlin's historical site. Chantal (image 1, situation) in *Just Another Girl on the I.R.T.* perceives herself (image 2) as being in control, her actions and statements leading to a perception-image. In each of these examples (and there are many more that could be engaged to demonstrate the procedures of perception[3]) the perception-image is something that is formed by an arrangement of the elements in the screen image; it is an 'image reflected by a living image' (C1: 62). As Deleuze describes it, there is a doubled system of images at work here, where we have an image (train/rabbit/Chantal) referencing its own lived/living image through the site of the screen. Deleuze describes the form of this 'living image' as 'the centre of indetermination or black screen' – as we shall discuss, this refers to the movement of the perception-image (*ibid.*).

The transformation of forms by the images produced by the camera provides Deleuze's focus. To engage the arguments of the creation of philosophical Forms (as we discussed in the chapter on the movement-image) and further look at the elements of the set of movement-images, Deleuze divides the perception-image into three phases of perception forms:

1. the two poles [of perception], objective and subjective;
2. liquid perception;
3. gaseous perception.

First, the subtractive phase of the perception image is produced by polarized movements of objective and subjective (i.e., *we perceive the thing minus that which does not interest us*). Deleuze takes what he calls a 'nominal, negative and provisional' definition of perception, noting that the image as comprised of a set can be seen by someone who is either internal or external to that set (C1: 71). Deleuze notes that there are 'sensory', 'active' and 'affective' factors that will be contributed to the image (set) by the perceiver (either internal – a character, animal, or situation within the screen – or external to the screen). The perceiver's either subjective or objective perception of the image this contributes towards its formation.

In order to describe this 'difficulty' of relating how a cinematographic perception and external subjectivity or 'cogito' is formed and informed through the movement of the camera, Deleuze develops the notion of the '"being-with" of the camera' that French film-theorist Jean Mitry engaged in his book *The Psychology of the Cinema* ([1963] 2000). Deleuze notes that Mitry points out that a shot-reverse shot scene on screen has the effect of throwing into doubt the position of the perception of the image as subjective or objective. Deleuze does not take the same route as Mitry in solving this form, although Mitry's discussion certainly has left an imprint on how Deleuze continues his argument on perception, including the following points: Mitry describes the difficulty for the film theorist, in engaging with the description of things through language; Mitry compares filmmaking to other art forms, describing the limitations that each media's structural properties hold for expression; Mitry notes that film signification is 'organised in terms of images'; and finally Mitry describes the 'active' 'unity of identification being-with its object' ([1963] 2000: 54; 83). Reproaching Mitry for his 'partisanship' in condemning Vertov's montage forms, Deleuze rejects the phenomenological position of 'knowing' that Mitry ultimately takes, and instead argues that the activity of the doubled system of perception as a 'being-with' the camera is productive of a 'cinematographic *Mitsein*' (C1: 72; 81).[4] Modifying Mitry's invocation of the largesse of a *Mitsein* to a Bergsonian position of a non-unified consciousness – a multiplicity – Deleuze invokes his mantra of perception that he repeats throughout his work: 'We perceive the thing, minus that which does not interest us as a function of our needs' (C1: 63). This holds as a useful proposition to consider and test against all screen works. Deleuze describes this tendency toward a subtractive perception as 'the first material moment of subjectivity' (C1: 63). The next two material aspects, as 'avatars' of the movement-image, relate to the action-image and the affection-image (C1: 65).

The problem that Deleuze identifies is how to extend the discussion of 'perception' beyond the poles of objective and subjective? Experiencing the 'cinematographic perception-image', notes Deleuze, has always engaged a 'specific, diffuse, supple' degree of perception that must be thought of in terms of the type of mobility it engages (C1: 72). Where is the camera in relation to the characters that it is filming, for example – is it waiting in anticipation, is it following them, is it tracking them in shots, does it offer itself as a cinematographic point of view? In these terms, we can use the cinematically produced perception-image as a subtractive phase for both analysis and production of images.

Reminding us of associated problems with the linguistic interpretation of images, Deleuze engages Italian film maker and theorist Pasolini's and Mikhail Bakhtin's respective theories of 'free indirect discourse' in order to describe the aesthetic consciousness of the perception-image, as engaged by certain schools of style (Pasolini 2005; Bakhtin in Voloshinov 1973). Deleuze notes that the camera in fact engages 'an assemblage of enunciation', that produces 'two inseparable acts of subjectivation simultaneously ... there is no mixture or average of two subjects, each belonging to a system, but a differentiation of two correlative subjects in a system which is itself heterogeneous' (C1: 73). Taking the terms of Pasolini's account of the aestheticization of style that a film director imposes on an image, Deleuze considers how the two poles of subjective and objective are useful for describing how the movements in perception images are not just doubling, but engaged as in a duel. By imposing other images and actions upon characters, images are transformed – this is Pasolini's notion of 'free indirect subjective', created by the 'free indirect discourse' that the camera produces (C1: 74–76). In this, Deleuze directs our attention to thinking past the subjective or objective to look to the 'pure Form which sets itself up as an autonomous vision of the content' (C1: 74). Extending his critique of *Difference and Repetition* that refuted the way that ideas are compared from external differences, Deleuze then questions the differential forms that the perception-image takes within the heterogeneous elements of screen worlds (cf. Deleuze 1994: 39).

The second phase of perception-image Deleuze describes is 'liquid perception'. Deleuze enlists examples from French directors from the early part of the twentieth century: Jean Epstein, Marcel L'Herbier, Abel Gance, Jean Grémillon and Jean Vigo. Deleuze addresses Epstein's 1923 film titled *Cœur fidèle* (*Faithful Heart*). This silent film montages together fixed-camera shots of a couple in a centrifugal carnival ride and flashback scenes, providing 'an amplified movement' of the lovers' moment (C1: 77). Fixed points disappear with graphic cinematography and post-production editing, but Deleuze then turns to contrast the earthiness of the Vichy-led, German-occupied French nation (1940–44) to describing a common motif of this era of French cinema, water, and the ways in which aquatic movement has the effect of displacing any sense of a central point. Deleuze's film examples include Grémillon's *Remorques* (*Stormy Waters*, 1941) and Vigo's surrealistically styled *L'Atalante* (1934). The 'liquid element', says Deleuze, is one that holds the possibility of a 'grace' of movement that does not occur on the land (C1: 79; see chapter 11 Politics).[5]

The subject of the screen image rarely holds its own agency, and discussion of a perception-image in Deleuze's terms must consider the 'material universe' of the entire production of the screen situation and the multiple dialectical levels this creates (C1: 40). Underwater, we see Jean (played by actor Jean Dasté) in *L'Atalante*, or on top of the body of water we see Juliette (actor Dita Parol) trying to walk across the boat in *L'Atalante*. Each actor's body offers contrasting perceptions and affections by their milieu; through movements each create different shapes on screen (forms) and different action-images. The specific location of the bio-technical body (camera, spectator, participant in screen culture) already has an individual culture that provides agency for the action and form of the perception-image.

Third, Deleuze provides an account for non-material perception-images in the gaseous phase. Beyond the solid and the liquid is to reach 'another' perception, which is also 'the genetic element of all perception' (C1: 85). Deleuze looks at examples of where motor-sensory perceptions are replaced by images of 'pure auditory and optical perceptions' that make perceptible the 'molecular intervals' (*ibid.*). The molecularity Deleuze invokes here is in relation to the 'microperceptions' of the processes of things changing over duration – the terms of 'becoming' (Deleuze and Guattari 1987: 248–249, 292–294). Difference is not just difference in form, as Deleuze points out with the perception image, but difference at levels of molecularity. Molecular perception is something that is 'peculiar to a "ciné-eye"', but is also specific to cognitive, hallucinatory, sensory functions of the body' (C1: 79–80). The 'ciné-eye' to which Deleuze refers here is the 'kino-eye' of Vertov's *Chelovek s kino-apparatom* (*Man with a Movie Camera*, 1929) (C1: 82). Deleuze notes that Vertov's dialectic is 'in matter and of matter' (C1: 83). Deleuze considers the marine perception to hold even a 'clairvoyant function', but for the most extensive aspect of perception, a fluid perception, then in considering 'the genetic element of perception' Deleuze notes that there is a change in 'camera-consciousness' (C1: 85). Deleuze contrasts the movement-image of 'aquatic lyricism' of the French Impressionist cinema of the 1920s with the 1960s and 1970s American experimental school's gaseous perception. Of the latter, Deleuze mentions Michael Snow's film *La Région Centrale* (1971), Stan Brakhage, Jordan Belson, Ken Jacobs and Owen Land's *Bardo Follies* (1967). Although a very brief discussion is given, Deleuze's method of looking at differences of perceptual phases provide for a useful method for discerning difference beyond technological or mechanical points. Deleuze takes Snow's description of the convergence of camera and machine as productive of a 'Nirvanic zero' (Snow, cited by Legge 2009: 74), enabling a 'gaseous state of perception' where the image is defined by its 'molecular parameters' (C1: 84–85).

How Deleuze Uses the Perception-image

Deleuze discusses perception in the *movement-image* in relation to the types of variation that the movement of perception forms. Extending and testing the thesis he expounded in his book, *Bergsonism*, Deleuze takes the 'problem' of perception and solves it in terms of time, rather than space ([1966] 1991: 31). Through movement, certain new forms are created, and the perception-image is where the material of the cinema changes into a 'new dimension', and moves into a 'degree zero' – where the image is expressive of the 'relation between movement and the interval of movement' (C1: 35; C2: 31). Where the affection-image is something that happens in that interval, perception-images are produced in the time-based relations and the movement between the two. Deleuze looks at the type of aesthetic values generated by the movement of the cinematographic medium, in its differentiation of the 'signaletic material' of the movement-image – that Deleuze defines as modulation of the image through sensory means, 'kinetic, affective, rhythmic, tonal, and even verbal' – and duration as a method which reveals the qualities inherent in things (C2: 29).

The question of 'perception' is one that Deleuze focuses on through his system's objectives, asking how is cinematographic consciousness created? As we have seen, Deleuze engages the arguments of the creation of philosophical Forms, the significance of film form, and the question of the technological platform of cinema itself. In addition, the political ramifications of the creation or mutation of forms, perceptual construction, their address and their affective capacity as produced in cinematographic consciousness is also an issue Deleuze considers (see chapter 11 Politics). The context in which Deleuze qualifies the cinematographic *cogito* differs from that of his peers. For example, Foucault describes the modern *cogito* (self) as an historically bound self, limited by its contemporaneous modes of surveillance and control (Foucault [1966] 1977: 309ff). Deleuze discusses how 'moi [me] = moi' (translated as 'ego = ego'), but the connotations of ego/me are different from the Foucaultian self (C2: 153, 199). Deleuze's cinematographic self is not the brain, as he notes, the 'brain is certainly not a centre of images from which one could begin, but itself constitutes one special image among the others' (C1: 62).[6] Deleuze rejects the idea that consciousness or perception is *of something* (C1: 56–61). Instead of describing a generalized account of 'the perception' of 'the viewer' or 'a character' in the cinema books, Deleuze addresses subjectivity as a component of all potential elements that come to constitute that self or subject by and in cinematographically generated consciousness. Subjectivity is an element of the image (see also chapter 11 Politics). Deleuze argues that 'the sole cinematographic consciousness is not us, the spectator, nor the hero; it is the camera – sometimes human, sometimes inhuman or superhuman' (C1: 20). Cinema is not an illustration of 'something'. Films do not 'do' philosophy, they 'make'; they generate images and concepts and react upon those made images. Things are 'luminous by themselves' (C1: 60), different to the phenomenological sense of 'sensing' or the illumination of something (this is the argument of intentionality).[7]

He writes:

> An atom is an image which extends to the point to which its actions and reactions extend. My body is an image, hence a set of actions and reactions. My eye, my brain, are images, parts of my body. How could my brain contain images since it is one image among others? External images act on me, transmit movement to me, and I return movement: how could images be in my consciousness since I am myself image, that is, movement? And can I even, at this level, speak of 'ego', of eye, of brain and of body? Only for simple convenience; for nothing can yet be identified in this way. It is rather a gaseous state. (C1: 58)

In his chapter titled, 'Second commentary on Bergson – the movement-image and its three varieties', Deleuze begins by stating: 'The historical crisis of psychology coincided with the moment at which it was no longer possible to hold a certain position. This position involved placing images in consciousness and movements in space' (C1: 56). Deleuze refers to the historical crisis that philosophers such as Maurice Merleau-Ponty found themselves in in relation to the topic of phenomenology.[8] Merleau-Ponty advocated the need for extending the cognitive reconstruction of experienced visual fields by incorporating sensorial awareness (1964: 48–50). As we have discussed, rather than follow the phenomenological position (such as Merleau-Ponty's or Husserl's notion) that consciousness is of something, Deleuze follows Bergson's position, which is radically opposite to phenomenology, and describes 'me' as being an element of the image (C1: 58–61). Deleuze explains creative expression and his philosophical rejection of the 'transcendental subject' by the philosophical terms of Bergson's 'living image' (C1: 62) and Spinoza's 'planes of composition' (Deleuze 1988a: 128–9). The 'plane of immanence or the plane of matter' is the place where the doubled system of the perception-image exists (C1: 61). While encouraging attention to the material constitution of all bodies (not just human ones, but bodies of water, molecules, the earth, animals, etc.), Deleuze opposes the phenomenological 'natural' point of view, as he argues that perception of the materiality of the image is contingent upon a set of elements, and is not always determined by movement. Of the latter point Deleuze notes, 'in the adult world, the child is affected by a certain motor helplessness, but one which makes him all the more capable of seeing and hearing' (C2: 3).

The Function of the Perception-image

Deleuze describes how differentiated images, subjects and ideas, and other activities of consciousness (the perception of layers of recollection, memory and sound, for example) are able to create a perception-image as an aspect or sign of a movement-image (C1: 68).

Watching, or participating in screen works, the form appeals or repels the participant on a number of levels. One important aspect of screen cognition is the position of consciousness, how and where it is situated, manipulated or stimulated by the screen-based activity. Commercially oriented films are careful to frame and thus direct the consciousness of the viewer through the screen event, ensuring that a certain degree of conscious 'satisfaction' is achieved, in relation to the market value of the experience.

Experimental films, on the other hand, often tend to push the perceptual boundaries of an image, forcing the viewer to question a number of different planes (and thus forms) of existence: for example *Meshes of the Afternoon* (dirs Maya Deren and Alexander Hammid, 1943); *Free Radicals* (dir. Len Lye, 1958–79); *Window Water Baby Moving* (dir. Stan Brakhage, 1962), *Spiral Jetty* (dir. Robert Smithson, 1970); *Je tu il elle* (*I you he she*; dir. Akerman, 1974), *Chunguag Zhaxie* (*Happy Together*; dir. Wong Kar-Wei, 1997), *Inland Empire* (dir. David Lynch, 2006). There are points in these films where perception becomes a time-image, not just a motor-image of the material world.

The critique of the possible perception of something and the recognition of something are central for Deleuze's argument for how the movement-image is different to the time-image. Through movement we come to find the indeterminate centre of the image, and this varies according to the type of movement-image (a centre is a conceptual point in Deleuze's system). In terms of the polar coordinates of every movement image, the centre might be thought of as a mobile point of reference within the trajectory of a movement. If we think of a literal camera movement, as Deleuze does, following Bazin's discussion of the camera in the film *M* (dir. Lang, 1931), the protagonist is posited as the centre of the image, which we only realize when the camera ceases to follow his movements within the closed set of the screen frame, and instead 'arcs off'. But the centre may also be the interval (Jarmusch's black attitude), a rupture or break that conceals the middle, or the essence of things and people, such as the driver at the centre of Kiarostami's camera in *Ten* (2002). 'The essence of a thing never appears at the outset', writes Deleuze, 'but in the middle, in the course of its development, when its strength is assured' (C1: 3). In his discussions of the cinema, Deleuze will always focus on how movement is made in relation to an acentre of the image (the 'signaletic material' (C2: 29)). This 'middle' to which he refers is a quality that arises from the forms and actions of a particular kind of (directorial/cinematographic) movement. 'The image reflected by a living image is precisely what will be called perception' (C1: 62). In defining the perception-image, Deleuze draws upon a number of strands of philosophical debate, as he begins to qualify the terms of his taxonomy further and develop the different aspects of cinematic modulation between movement and time, and make comments about the philosophical understanding of the creation of Forms.

6

Affect

The affection-image is one of the three core varieties of the movement-image in the Deleuzian ciné-system. Deleuze situates affect as a potential force that holds consequences for not only the composition and expression of movement, but directs, controls, and situates the metaphysical movement of the creation of difference through the virtual to form a whole, a complex entity that is open, in infinite movement.

In Charles Laughton's 1955 intense expressionist film, *The Night of the Hunter*, a most poignant scene arrives. Two little children, who have been orphaned and terrorized, have run away from their current situation. Pursued by an enraged man, the Preacher Powell (played by actor Robert Mitchum), they spend the night in an open row-boat, moved down the river by its current of black and silver water. The film maps the movement of these children as they negotiate a short, but intensive period of their lives, and the affects of the movement of other bodies that they encounter upon their own directed-becoming. Tracking them, the Preacher rides his horse alongside the river, humming a sinister word alongside the musical score of darkness and folly (music by Walter Schumann). There are several shots that comprise this scene, where camera frames and situates the children alongside and from the point of view of the animals they pass in the night: a gleaming spider's web, under which their boat passes, a bullfrog puffing up as if to sing. The camera shots present the animals in close-up, providing intervals to the shots of the man on the horse, his shadow, and the children in the boat (dop. Stanley Cortez). The girl's sweet voice reigns over the scene: 'One night these two pretty children flew away/Flew away/Into the sky/Into the moon'. In following scenes we see more animal life: the dilated eyes of an owl on the prowl, an awkward and ancient tortoise, a pair of quivering rabbits, some bleating sheep. These shots of animals are affection-images, they serve as images that bring into focus the actions of the human-nature of adults: the hunter's agitation of hatred of youth, a world-weary woman feeding a gathering of children and treating them as useless livestock to be half-tolerated. Repeated shots of the boat and the water's surface shows it to be an image produced through an 'intensive series' of affection-images, and to also be an image of a face (as the clock face): 'a receptive immobile surface, [a] receptive plate of inscription ...' (C1: 87). The boat is but their hapless shelter from the nightmare of life as it must pass through these affection-images of their world – these are images that present what Deleuze will term the 'genetic' and the 'differential' signs of life (C1: 110; C2: 33). In this we see that the affection-image is what Deleuze terms an extensive '*movement of world*' (C2: 59, original emphasis). Referring to *The Night of the Hunter*, Deleuze will note that this film shows the movement of the world: 'The frightened child faced with danger cannot run away, but the world sets about running away for him and takes him with it, as if on a conveyer belt' (C2: 59).

In this way Deleuze discusses the affective nature of the expressionist film as extensive to movement, noting that the abstraction of space of the scenes of this type of film has the affect of 'potentializing' space, 'making it something unlimited' (C1: 111). An affection-image is thus a sign that expresses a specific aesthetic that will situate an image, event, body or thing outside of 'actualized' spatial paradigms, yet within time, even as it performs crucial movements; as Deleuze describes, an affect is an 'entity' in itself (C1: 95–101; C2: 32–33).

We see this actualization of the virtual nature of the affect-image in many different situations, often best utilized in horror, suspense or mystery gen- res. For example, in *Gwoemul* (*Monster*, also known as *The Host*; dir. Bong Joon-ho, 2006), an affective intensity is generated through the screen-time's lengthy search for a missing child (actor Ah-sung Ko), who is in mortal peril. In *Das Cabinet des Dr. Caligari* (*The Cabinet of Dr Caligari*; dir. Robert Wiene, 1920) the missing Cesare (actor Conrad Veidt) generates an anxiety-affect for the other characters. In *Shock Corridor* (dir. Samuel Fuller, 1963), another type of anxiety-affect pervades the simple *mise-en-scène*, affecting a change in all bodies present. A reverse plot of another narrative of social affects upon bodies occurs in a film from French director Agnés Varda, such as her *Sans toit ni loi* (*Without Roof or Rule*, also known as *Vagabond*, 1985). Rather than approach analysis of these disparate forms of narrative suspense as engen- dered through emotive manipulation of the screen story, as a universal plot technique of a countdown to life or death, Deleuze's device of the affection- image enables us a more extensive analysis of the discreet screen images. In charting the kinds of critical points and pathways that affective-images cre- ate, the type of screen analysis Deleuze's system now engages focuses on con- tent created structures and the styles of their critical construction. Further, through the development of the affection-image, Deleuze provides the criteria by which we might comparatively evaluate the effectiveness of the political and perceptual communication by one particular screen image over another.

What is Affect?

The affection-image is the image that will provide the requisite force to move the perception-image into the state of being an action-image. As a reactive facet of the cinematographic movement-image, the affection-image is a 'power-quality' that plays and 'anticipatory role' for screen events (C1: 102). Deleuze's discussion of the affection-image and screen affect sets about explaining this apparent paradox of an image that is pre-image or an anticipatory image.

In these terms of the affect-image, the camera is as much a body of interactivity as an actor's body, or the body of a landscape, or the body of a director's work, or as we say, the body of a film genre. Affect is what will cause the movement from one state to another. The movement and subsequent mixing between any animate or inanimate bodies produces affects: on screen it could be an entity like rain, or the sound of an animal, a computer-generated monster or a particular space or colour. The affect is an intensity that will produce a dynamic expression in a body causing it to alter its composition and its potential trajectories. This is different to a screen effect, which concerns the technicalities (stylistic and technical) of how to render that affect. Technicalities in themselves can produce further affects. Deleuze discusses these in the larger sense of the complexity of the singularities that will connect or disconnect on screen, thus contributing to the range of possible qualities and powers that the affect offers.

Deleuze will describe the sensations and ideas generated through these filmic bodies as movements of forms of screen intensity. Deleuze will argue that intensity, or sensation, is the product of the potential power of an affection-image, or often a series of action-images. A movement (or action) occurs, giving rise to an affect, in turn generating a reaction and perception of both the affect and the action. Although montaged images might be involved, Deleuze is describing something different from the narrative or stylistic manipulation of the shot, such as the intensity garnered through a shot reverse shot countdown to some kind of incident (C1: chapters 5–8).

A screen situation's potential intensity is converted from moment of anticipation to realization through many methods. For example, a rush of sound or movement may occur, or a wave of emotion or expression may be realized in a body or across a face on-screen, or a morphological shift might occur between disparate objects or sentiments to produce a compounded or synergesic affective power, and thus affection-image. Deleuze begins his discussion of the affection-image by inviting us to consider the proposition that the 'affection-image is the close-up and the close-up is the face' (C1: 87, original emphasis). Continuing his engagement of Bergson's discussion of the nature of movement, Deleuze will explain this curious statement over two chapters of *Cinema 1*. Another clue is given from Eisenstein, who understood that an iconic image of something (for example, a religious symbol, a revolutionary colour, a scream of terror) could provide an 'affective reading of the whole film' (C1: 87). An affection-image thus engages the two components of movement and intervals: if we imagine the image of an (analogue) clock, for example, we have hands that take 'micro-movements' with 'intervals', with the movement forming part of an '*intensive series*' (C1: 87, original emphasis). This intensive series of movement, continues Deleuze, 'marks' and 'prepares' the way to 'a critical instant', a 'paroxysm', a 'momentary independence' (C1: 87, 89). As always in Deleuze's system, this image is of 'two poles' (C1: 87); to analyse an image, one must consider both sides of which it presents. What possible variations in affective outcome can an image engender? Off screen, in the minds of viewers, the affective outcomes of screen-based media are infinite. On screen, the affect of movement contributes to the whole affection-image; it is a '*reflecting and a reflected unity*' (C1: 87, original emphasis), while the affect of critical forces generate an infinite processual quality for the film. Deleuze points out that this 'quality' is 'common to several different things' – object/body/idea – this is a point of argument that he continues in looking at the construction of a cinema of thought and the thought-image in *Cinema 2* (C1: 90; chapter 13 Thought). New things may be incorporated at further viewings of a text, for instance, events that had not yet happened when the film was made, but subsequently impact upon the way it can be viewed. There may be a momentary autonomy of intensity, but affect is never independent (cf. Massumi 2002a).

Deleuze's affection-image is drawn from Spinoza's theory of potential – the potential some thing or body has in its movement and mix with other bodies or things (Deleuze 1988a: 122–130). How the prince can become a frog and can become a prince again, and to what effect, on screen, is the concern of Deleuze's attention to the concept of affect. It is to this internal, inherent quality of the screen image that Deleuze refers, when he says: 'Affect as immanent evaluation, instead of judgement as transcendent value: "I love or I hate" instead of "I judge"' (C2: 141). In *Cinema 2* he provides further discussion of this conception of how we can critique a film by tracing the affective conditions – the phrase 'affect as immanent evaluation' leading us to evaluate affect diagrammatically. Deleuze gives examples of this, discussing the difference between 'affective fusion' and 'affective composition' created by Eisenstein's montaged images (C2: 160–161).

How Deleuze Uses Affect

As Deleuze will describe it, the affection-image of the screen is not a representational image, such as the action of an impact upon a body, or the reflection of an emotion upon an actor's face – such images are action-images. Affect is the *intensive power* that propels extensive actions. In Deleuze's philosophy this intensive power is what gives the cinematographic its ethical agency. In his chapters on affect, Deleuze looks at how images hold a certain 'quality of a possible sensation, feeling or idea' (C1: 98). By this he means that the image holds within it a certain value that can be deployed in a number of ways. This occurs through:

1. propositional affects (the expression of states);
2. actualized affects (expressed relational affects, for example, sound, or different types and forms of montage). (C1: 97–99)

The difference between an active series of movements and an affective series of images is that movement has to 'go beyond the state of things' (C1: 101). Deleuze's reference is to Wenders's 1982 film *Der Stand der Dinge* (*The State of Things*) (see chapter 2 Movement). On screen we are often shown situations where a body is trapped, immobilized and at the mercy of its environment. The screen situation requires that perception of this situation be registered through action, but to get to that movement, some form of impetus must be provided. The affection-image registers a process of interval that occurs in between perception and action; the juncture where *something happens*. Deleuze often refers to this point of change as the site of an *encounter* – one encounters something and things change – I meet you on the street and we decide to go and do something together. If I did not encounter you on my journey, I will have undertaken a different course (cf. C2:1, 157). In terms of the screen, Deleuze describes how watching a film takes the viewer into 'the domain of the perception of affection' (C1: 67). This place, this domain, this juncture, this encounter, are all sites where the affection-image creates a change – this may be chemical, sensorial, structural, durational, intellectual, cognitive, perceptual – a relational affect. Following Bergson, Deleuze will refer to the affection-image as genetic and differential – unlimited. Any screen image that has provided an encounter with something that then opens a new domain provides explication of the affection-image: 'We are in the domain of the perception of affection, the most terrifying, that which still survives when all the others have been destroyed: it is the perception of self by self, the *affection-image*' (C1: 67–68, original emphasis). This is the domain of the topological affect. Affect is what causes perception to move into action, and as such, an affect is a potential power, an energy, a force. It may be actualized anywhere in the range from sad affects (grief, pain, destruction, loss, death) to joyful affects (happiness, pleasure, life).

Deleuze's use of affect in the cinema books extends his discussion of Spinoza's concept of affect (*affectus*) as a mode of thought (Deleuze 1978; 1988a; 1990a). Spinozist affect refers to the types of knowledge one can infer through the movement of bodies and how through that movement, interactivity and encounters occur that alter the dimensions of each body. Using this Spinozist sense of affect as movement, knowledge and the intervention into the modes of perceptual power that knowledge brings, means that Deleuze will engage the terms of a cinematic image in a different way to standard cognitive or psychologically based screen theory (although there are some aspects of 1970s standard film theory that we see Deleuze employ in his cinema books).

When translated into the cinematographic, Spinozist affect and affection-image convey the 'quality' of a possible 'state of things' (C1: 98). Deleuze stresses this aspect of potentiality; the affection-image '*is not* a sensation, a feeling, an idea, but *the quality of a possible* sensation, feeling or idea' (C1: 98, emphasis added). Such qualities have no concrete forms in themselves, but in culturally produced and politically controlled forms such as art (film, music, literature, fine arts), qualities are actualized, signalled, signposted through symbolic means, such as the device of culturally specific fetish objects or religious iconography. In a larger sense, then, affective images register at the level of forces, such as we see in the different social forces that impact upon the duration of life in *The Host* or in *Vagabond*, or in the series of *Iron Man* films (dir. Jon Favreau, 2008; 2010) or narratives concerning the affects of all types of conflict upon communities such as *Aguirre, der Zorn Gottes* (dir. Herzog, 1972), *Au Revoir, les Enfants* (dir. Louis Malle, 1987); *Sometimes in April* (dir. Raoul Peck, 2005), or *The Bridge to Terabithia* (dir. Gabor Csupo, 2007). As Deleuze will discuss, a singular affect as an expressed entity in a specific cultural and spatial temporally controlled domain thus becomes a particular type of complex 'proposition' (C1: 105). Deleuze gives the example of the change in community attitude from proposition to actualized affect as registered in the face of Joan of Arc in conjunction with her surroundings in *La passion de Jeanne d'Arc* (*The Passion of Joan of Arc*; dir. Dreyer, 1928) (C1: 70).

In these terms, affect can be understood in Deleuze's consideration of the Foucauldian terms of power relations (Deleuze 1988b: 70; cf. Foucault 1977). There is an 'internal' power-play being enacted in the image, and this must be understood as different from the action-image where 'real relation(s)' between components is maintained by the camera (C1: 106–107). Deleuze also invokes writer Charles Péguy (influential for Deleuze's *Difference and Repetition*) and Maurice Blanchot in these pages to underscore the affective politics at work in these types of images, understood as exercises 'in power' that are expressed in the image as an affective quality, thereby evoking connections that can be made through the intersections of things (Deleuze 1988b: 71; C1: 106; cf. Blanchot 1992; cf. 'Clio' in Péguy 1958).

For this kinetic idea of the affection-image and its description, Deleuze draws on C.S. Peirce's definitions of sign-images and then extends these for the cinema. The affection-image draws from the Peircian notion of 'firstness', as Deleuze says, 'something that only refers to itself, quality or power, pure possibility' (C2: 30; cf. Deledalle 2000). The affect is not immediately 'knowable' to the elements within the set that it affects. Deleuze gives an example from Peirce that further exemplifies this 'quality' of an affection-image: 'You have not put on your red dress', where the colour red provides the quality, the affect of the image (C2: 30). In films, colours are frequently used to indicate affective qualities, wherein the affection-image provides the cumulative perceptual push over into an action. For example, consider the activity incited by the colours of Mao's revolution in Godard's *La Chinoise* (1967), or the time-image of the grief of loss and embrace of life in Krzysztof Kieslowski's *Trois couleurs: Bleu* (*Three Colours: Blue*, 1993), or the political affect invoked in Lars von Trier's *Zentropa* (1991), where the poles of both movement and time are forced through the colour washes of red stain make the images pass through all modes of movement.

The affective-image thus arises from style, situation, object and movement and time-images of all forms (including action, perception, thought, reflection, relation, etc.). Deleuze gives examples of the range of affective treatments by directors; 'Hitchcock's suspense, Eisenstein's shock and Gance's sublimity' (C2: 164) to 'quantative mediocrity' or 'blood-red abritrariness' (C2: 164) or the 'hallucinatory' visual style of Ozu or Antonioni (C2: 129, 204–205), and the eidetic cinema of Viking Eggeling (1924), Norman McLaren (1948; 1949; 1955) or George Landow (C2: 214–215).

The Function of Affect

Deleuze's discussion of screen affect provides a further discussion of an aspect of the movement-image and an extension on Bergsonian form. Deleuze uses affection to develop an answer to the problems of the phenomenological tendency toward sensorial answers, arguing: 'Affection is what occupies the interval, what occupies it without filling it in or filling it up. It surges in the centre of indetermination, that is to say in the subject, between perception which is troubling in certain respects and a hesitant action' (C: 65; see chapter 5 Perception). The affection-image describes an account of the variability and how it occurs on screen, drawing on the richness of life itself as 'a quality or a power' (C2: 32). The affection-image comes prior to an action, it is the intensive 'Power' by which a body can express a 'more radical reflection' of a particular 'Quality' (C1: 90). In the Spinozist sense that Deleuze uses the term, power is indicative of an essence of something, not always realized (Deleuze 1990a: 93). For example, in his short film, *Sans Titre* (*Untitled*) commissioned as a postcard/teaser film for the Cannes Film Festival's fiftieth anniversary in 1997 and his preparatory work on his 1999 film, *Pola X*, French director Leos Carax inserted *The Night of the Hunter* riverboat scene, amid a montage of films where children are under threat, being or have been killed. It is a montage technique of homage, where the debt to other cinema is acknowledged. While some film theory discusses this form of inter-textual referencing as 'postmodern' or 'remediation', we can also recognize this as the *cogito* of the cinematographic at work, actualizing the qualities of a specific screen affect for various stylistic and historical ends.

This scene and sound from *The Night of the Hunter* through its combined action-perception-montage *moves us* as an affection-image. In this sense our consideration of an affective film is in terms of the movement-image, the question of mobility: the tortoise and the hare. When King Kong draws the tiny body of his captive female close to his face and we wonder what the next move will be (*King Kong*; dirs Merian C. Cooper, Ernest B. Schoedsack, 1933; *King Kong*; dir. Peter Jackson, 2005). In extension to the perception and the trajectories of the never completed, yet made real through the thought of possible outcomes, we might recall something about the essence of a film in terms of a completed action, a gesture, a glance: the final kiss, the last twitch of a dying body, the song that hangs over the closing credits of a film – these are actions whose affects become immanent to those action-sound-images. The affect is the dynamic force produced from an action which in turn becomes embedded in that image of activity. The association between action and affect can easily be shifted, manipulated, augmented or reduced through the tricks and techniques of screen media. And therein lies the pleasure and the terror of the screen, holding the capacity to alter and create.

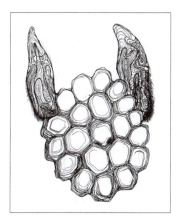

7

Action

The action-film has a universal currency and is one of the most popu-
lar at the box-office. Deleuze notes three main forms for the action-
image – the small, the large and the trans-morphological. In the ciné-
system the action-image is a key figure in the philosophical argument
concerning Plato's philosophy of Ideas and Forms. Deleuze will argue
that film can engage and produce the ideas that give rise to forms, just
as it can reproduce harmless or inept copies of ideas. Although Deleuze
describes the action-image in terms of actors and imbues the action-
image forms with a vitalist, respiratory movement, he contrasts the
action-image against a 'cinema of the body' – a body that will create
thought.

Action films: *The Navigator* (dirs Donald Crisp and Buster Keaton, 1924); *Scarface* (dir. Howard Hawks, 1932); *Ladri di biciclette* (*Bicycle Thief*; dir. Vittorio de Sica, 1948); *Shichinin no samurai* (*Seven Samurai*, dir. Akira Kurosawa, 1954); *Cléo de 5 à 7* (*Cléo from 5 to 7*; dir. Varda, 1962); *Jaws* (dir. Steven Spielberg, 1975); *Mad Max* (dir. George Miller, 1979); *The Terminator* (dir. James Cameron, 1984); *Tetsuo* (dir. Shinya Tsukamoto, 1989); *Point Break* (dir. Katherine Bigelow, 1991); *God, Construction and Destruction* (dir. Samira Makhmalbaf, 2002); *Children of Men* (dir. Alfonso Cuarón, 2006). Action is a movement that exists in every film. Examine the various types of action-images created in the above list of films of the past 100 years, from territorial wars to a school lesson. Through the arrangement of things on screen we see; we hear; we sense; we imagine the state of things, the situation and its affective impact. In combination of elements, through their interactivity, they embody an affective connection which, in turn, produces a dynamic image, an action in movement. The resultant image is the set of the movement-image – the action shows the modified situation, but embedded in that situation is the process of modification, the process of that dynamic transference of energies. Deleuze's action-image looks at the type of forms that action takes, describing the method of this movement, the reactions of the elements of the action-image and what these things produce in image.

Action-image: Canadian director Bruce LaBruce and Rick Castro's 1996 film *Hustler White* follows the cruising scene of boys on the Santa Monica Boulevard in Los Angeles. The physical action of the film tracks all ways up and down this specific territory, the strip acting as a topological figure of reference that holds a range of orienting qualities for all of the elements of the film. If we consider these qualities as elements produced by the action-image, we can determine that the figure of the strip is not only a geographical locale, but a sign of possible transformation of any form that engages with it. LaBruce and Castro's film offers story arcs that appear to have certain narrative resolutions but in fact work to create unresolved forms that are generative of a certain perspective, with no absolutes offered. It is a formula LaBruce repeats in all of his films: take as a central aspect the life of a character in a specific situation, submit that character to certain activities and then reexamine that character

through an on-screen *re-casting* of the staging of the elements of that character by its social, historical and geographical actualization. Or, as Deleuze says
of the types of reworking that Howard Hawks brings to bear upon the action
genres of Noir and Western cinema, the knowledgeable director is engaged
in 'deformations, transformations or transmutations' of forms (C1: 178). The
kinds of matter-of-fact action around the tracked scene in *Hustler White*, and
LaBruce's later film *The Raspberry Reich* (2004), are the action-images of the
film, sourcing documentary genres and forming new types of social realism
and comedy. LaBruce shows us things – people, ideas, objects – and then
carefully traces and repeats the movement around those things for us to see
how they come to be constituted through on-screen trajectories that modify
them. His method is to make action-images that are a physical comedy of
errors, chances and expectations, as the film acts out the perception and
consequences of the *idea* of action-images. *Hustler White* directly references
the action images of Hollywood fame, where these films' journeys are also
psychological as well as physical in the determination of their staged paths:
in Hollywood stories such as *The Wizard of Oz* (dir. Victor Fleming, 1939),
Sunset Boulevard (dir. Billy Wilder, 1950), *Easy Rider* (dir. Dennis Hopper,
1969), or *Taxi Driver* (dir. Martin Scorsese, 1976) (C1: 242 n14). LaBruce
channels the prescient direction of Luis Buñuel's biting social commentary in
L'Âge d'or (*Age of Gold*, 1930) or Kenneth Anger's attitude in *Scorpio Rising*
(1964) or *Kustom Kar Kommandos* (1965). LaBruce's territorial commentary can also be compared with the social irony and social environmental
activity presented in Park Chan-wook's 2006 film *Saibogujiman kwenchana*
(*I'm a Cyborg, But That's Ok*), or *Black Sheep* (dir. Jonathon King, 2006) or
the telling of historical becomings in Mikhail Romm's *9 dney odnogo goda*
(*Nine Days of One Year*, 1962), *Aguirre, der Zorn Gottes* (*Aguirre, Wrath of
God*; dir. Werner Herzog, 1972) or *Die Bleierne Zeit* (*The Leaden Time*; dir.
Margarethe Von Trotta, 1981).

Through a disparate range of scenario producing realities, these types of
narratives share a film form constructed through the action-image. They are
films that provide us with examples of the action-image, which 'do not merely
designate forms of action, but conceptions, way of conceiving and seeing "a

subject", a story or script' (C1: 178). Describing the action-image, Deleuze will indicate the theme or genre (the song style or the journey) of the film at this point in his taxonomy, but considers how content is produced by the creation of forms by certain kinds of images. In other words his system is charting not so much what the films are about, but how cinema produces different kinds of 'aesthetic and creative evaluations' by its different forms (C1: 178). As he has argued from the beginning of *Cinema 1*, the action-image has a certain kind of 'functional reality' (C2: 4). However, it is in examining the types of function that movement plays (or the differential relations engaged) to produce the form of the action-image, that Deleuze will, by the end of *Cinema 1*, distinguish between the forms of movement-image of the habitual nature of the action-image (sets of clichés, the established terms of 'reality') and the action-image created through the mental image, that produce, often by virtual means, new forms for thinking, such as we see in a film like *Rope* (dir. Hitchcock, 1948) (C1: 200; chapter 10 Time).

What is the Action-image?

The action-image forms part of the movement-image system. The action-image is always part of movement, a reactive motion around a perception: action comes after perception (perception is produced by affection). One of the infamous scenes from Buñuel's 1930 film *L'Âge d'or* (*The Golden Age*): the Man (played by Gaston Modot) sees a certain type of dog. It embodying all he abhors, and the affective qualities of that perception (he feels annoyed/ frustrated) engender an action and he kicks the dog. Perception and action are locked into a duelling catalytic movement on screen. The action-image feeds the vortex of energies, initiating further images. The Man's body is already imbued with affects and impulses and they are actualized by the actions he takes. 'Qualities and powers' writes Deleuze, 'are no longer displayed in any-space-whatevers, no longer inhabit originary worlds, but are actualized directly in determinate, geographical, historical and social space-times' (C1: 141). In other words, the action-image is a movement-image that shows us the immanent constitution of an image: after perception, we fill, or the perceptive conjunction is filled by, a constitutive affect, which propels perception into activity. On screen this translates as the action-image: something happens and an action actualizes a response, creating a change in the screen situation. Hours of screen-time are produced using this formula.

Different qualities of the action-image describe issues that the action-image raises in consideration of the larger system of the movement-image. Using C.S. Peirce's classification of signs – but with qualification – Deleuze considers the conditions of how the action-image works to modify the situation on screen (see chapter 8 Transsemiotics). The idea of 'secondness' (a term from Peirce) applies to the action-image to describe the way that the action-image is produced in conjunction with another type of movement-image, as a 'duel of forces' (C1: 98, 142). As Deleuze discusses, this is not a simple 'mirroring' of images, but a movement of images, two very distinct things. The action-image shows how the cinema reveals the movement of all things to be an inevitable component of the path of universal variation. 'What is called action, strictly speaking, is the delayed reaction of the centre of indetermination' (C1: 64). The centre of indetermination is the 'living matter' with 'receptive organs' as framed (relationally, physically or as cognitively inferred) although compromised, affected by various speeds of encounter or perception of the action (C1: 65–66).

Deleuze divides the action-image into three main forms: small, large and trans-morphological. He discusses them with interlocking, but distinctive terminology. Deleuze comes up with conceptual formulas that can be applied to any screen situation in order to describe the type of action-image:

1. large form: the screen situation or film will have a *mise-en-scène* that displays a situation (S), an action (A), then a modified situation (S') = (SAS') (C1: 143–147);
2. small form: will have a *mise-en-scène* that displays an action (A), a situation (S), then a modified action (A') = (ASA') (C1: 160–164);
3. trans-morphological forms: 'deformations, transformations or transmutations' (C1: 178).

In the dialectic logic of the movement-image, the action-image *shows how* the operative properties that contribute to the creation of stories and the pre-existing structures of culture and socio-political states (actual and imaginary) from which they draw, can solidify, change, or create new states, things, or people: new forms of movement-images. This dialectic produces a different type of image, form and idea to that of images produced by a logic of relations – which is the time-image. Deleuze further distinguishes between different domains where the small and large forms manifest on screen. With the small form, the movement from action *to* situation is facilitated by a vector, which Deleuze says is exemplified in film forms that express 'the physico-biological domain which corresponds to the *notion of milieu*' (C1: 186, original emphasis; see chapter 9 Signs (Vector)). With the large form, the movement is from situation *to* action, which Deleuze relates to 'the mathematical domain which corresponds to the *notion of space*' (C1: 186, original emphasis; see chapter 12 Topology).

To test out these ideas and look at the variables of this logic, consider any film that might be termed an action genre; perhaps a monster action film such as *Alien* (dir. Ridley Scott, 1979) or *Pulgasari* (dirs Chong Gon-Jo and Shin Sang-Ok, 1985), or a war film such as *Battle of Algiers* (dir. Gillo Pontecorvo, 1966) or *The Hurt Locker* (dir. Katherine Bigelow, 2008). Like the western, the war or monster film as a genre has always been invested in the action-image. Even when the sights and sounds of war or monster film are unseen and unheard, and indeed unimaginable, the action-image engages a specific event – activity – that of the duel. A power struggle, a power relay where sides switch, and the terms of life and death are rapidly interchangeable. The duel encompasses all the literal torsions of power movements. Pause for a moment and think of what a duel on screen might encompass – gun slinging, Clint Eastwood, words, romance, family, institutional relations, power struggles? Herein lies the essence of Deleuze's action-image in every sense of the word 'duel' – the struggle, the fight, combat, contestation, the challenge – 'action in itself is a duel of forces ...' (C1: 142). As Deleuze describes, through this actualization: 'The action-image inspires a cinema of behaviour (behaviourism) since behaviour is an action which passes from one situation to another, which responds to a situation in order to try modify it or to set up a new situation' (C1: 155). Deleuze describes the 'incurving of the universe', the sense of how 'a character' can actualize themselves in an image and modify the situation they find themselves in (C1: 65; 141). In the case of the action-image, this is done through sets of images that contain certain qualities and forces, or powers, being determined and actualized by the movement around a centre.

Describing the range of complex behaviours of the actor's body and its ability to demonstrate the 'condition of the development of the action-image', Deleuze begins to account for how the actor's body succeeds when it engages the conditions of the construction of the image it infers – in a self-conscious way (C1: 158). This argument is further fleshed out when Deleuze discusses the *thought-image* at the end of *Cinema 2*. Deleuze demonstrates how interested he is in the concept of 'subjectivity' by his fascination with actor's bodies, their modes of playing characters and the types of qualities they bring to the screen. The discussion on the action-image also extends to account for directors such as Luchino Visconti, whose work focuses on the 'autonomous, material reality' of things – which have a way of modifying the action-image and the characters within the scene (C1: 4; cf. Visconti 1960).

In his discussion of the action-image Deleuze will give as his examples directors from the German expressionist period – Fritz Lang and Georg Wilhelm Pabst – Swedish director Victor Sjöström's *The Wind* (1928), and early Hollywood classics: *Scarface* (1932), King Vidor's films *The Crowd* (1928), *A Street Scene* (1931), *Our Daily Bread* (1934), *An American Romance* (1944). Deleuze will name a significant number of actors of the twentieth century whose work demonstrates this *condition of the development* of the image, as a part of the action of behaviourism that engages (in various ways) with other bodies, things and situations. These actors include Orson Welles, Maria Falconetti, Greta Garbo, Stanley Baker, Alain Delon, Klaus Kinski, Charlie Chaplin, Jerry Lewis, and Chantal Akerman.

Similarly, this logic of cinematographic behaviourism extends to all action-images where a force of nature and/or manufacture interferes and interacts with the daily actions of people or cultures: *The Wizard of Oz* where Dorothy (Judy Garland) suffers a psychosomatic response-action to the elemental as: 'the dispersive situation, the deliberately weak links, the voyage form, the consciousness of cliché, the condemnation of the plot' (C1: 210, original emphasis). These changes came about in cinema in various ways, and Deleuze's discussions relate to specific national cinemas throughout the cinema books (see chapter 11 Politics). Ultimately, German national cinemas play a large role in Deleuze's overall thesis. In his discussion of the action-image, Deleuze focuses on the situation and forms of American, Italian and French comparative works. In these, Deleuze positions the action-image as a 're-examination of the sensory-motor schema' (C1: 210), through the tactics of 'parody' (Altman; C1: 211); 'mutation' and 'breaks with tradition' (French new wave cinema; C1: 211, 213); Italian style's 'dispersive and lacunary reality' (Rossellini, DeSica, Fellini; C1: 211–212). It is only in these transmorpological forms that Deleuze sees any potential for the multiple pathways of 'hodological space' to offer ways out of 'concrete space' by the processes of differentiation (C2: 128–129; see chapter 12 Topology; C2: 28–9). Deleuze describes this (differentiation) as the determination of the 'virtual content of the Idea [form]' in terms of 'the consequences for the cinema' (Deleuze 1994: 209; C1: 178). Deleuze needed to produce a philosophical model that would describe the movement of cinema as a model that charts the shifts in the history of things and people. Literally, this larger sense of what film encompasses emerges not by its 'representation' of history, but through the discussion of the different determining qualities of situations and forms – productive of Ideas – of various times (Deleuze details this process in *Difference and Repetition* 1994: 209). Buster Keaton's 'burlesque', for instance, has the effect of changing the forms of the action-image from within his 'trajectory gag' and 'machine gag' in films such as *Our Hospitality* (dirs John G. Blystone and Buster Keaton, 1923) and *The Navigator* (dirs Donald Crisp and Keaton, 1924), which are inflected with certain characteristics that are action-images with a 'minoring function' (C1: 173–176; chapter 11 Politics).

The perceptual and behavioral capacities of a body (including molecular bodies, the elemental bodies, the body of the character and the cinematographic body) are in turn productive of a particular kind of affective response determined by those limitations, productive of a reaction. For the actor on screen, for example, there are some things that their body or mind cannot or will not do, and others that the law will not allow, as in the case of child actors (cf. *Lolita*; dir. Adrian Lyne, 1997). Similarly with non-human bodies or with animals, there are some physical and logistical impossibilities for bodies: dogs cannot fly and mountains do not move. Actions on screen are a realization of perception and affection. Deleuze's approach is to take the central and the peripheral body in action.

The Function of the Action-image

Deleuze says the action-image is situated in the actual place and time of a history and society, as a product of the relation between the 'mileux which actualize [the screen environment] and modes of behaviour which embody [the realism of this environment]' (C1: 141). Thus, the action-image is the moderator of the form that screen-produced 'reality' will take. This raises a point central for film-philosophy, which is an examination of the relationship between ideas and forms. With the capacity of film to create things, and to use the principle of continuous creative growth of concepts, the question of what ethical paradigms engage the Platonic index of the question of judgment is one of the underlying narratives of the cinema books. The question of form, and how and what type of structure arises, becomes the content – the story on screen.

The action-image is unthinking in Deleuzian terms, however it *is* an image that charts the behavioural reaction to 'living matter' (C1: 64). In following Bergson here, Deleuze flaunts a philosophical 'behaviourism' that can be considered to be a category mistake in philosophy. It is an image that provides the sensory motor situation that might then lead to a body encountering and interacting with other bodies. Deleuze describes the action-image as a respiratory act, literally imagining how life forces are breathed into an image through the various forms of action. Deleuze's description of the action-image and its forms of transformation offers film analysis a distinctive way of articulating historical consciousness of an image, thereby addressing Plato's position on *and Guattari in A Thousand Plateaus – a combination of the ideas of a range of thinkers of language systems: Hjelmslev, Kafka, Proust, Beckett, Godard, Pasolini, Herzog. In the Cinema books, Deleuze diverges from the linguistic philosophy of de Saussure's approach to the sign as a substitutive system for classification (as was commonly used in film theory of Deleuze's time of writing), and instead utilizes C. S. Peirce's non-linguistic approach, combining this theory with insights from a range of thinkers, including Barthes and Pasolini, to make apparent that the range of sound-image relations on screen are produced through non-representational expression.*

In fact, [Godard] made a science fiction film with the Rolling Stones [*One Plus One*]. He had his camera track slowly through the Olympic Sound Studio in Barnes, as Kubrick tracked a camera through space. The head of Brian Jones moves quietly across the screen like only one other thing in your memory: the space ship in *2001* that appeared at one side of the screen and, in a galactic silence, drifted across the field of vision.

Wenders [1986] 1989

After our participation in a screen-event, we ask 'what is that?' as Wenders does after viewing Godard's film *One Plus One* (*Sympathy for the Devil*, 1968) at the Electric cinema, London.[1] In joining together apparently disparate worlds – the head of musician Brian Jones (of The Rolling Stones) and images of the Black Panther movement – Godard changes the expression and content of both. It is a highly problematic film in many ways, derided by critics at the time of its release, for taking images out of their context of everyday production and abstracting them to a degree where their generative political and cultural contexts are masked (cf. Debord 1969).[2] Yet this abstraction reflects the processes of music creation; where the impulses behind a seemingly 'radical' song are swallowed in the production and consumption of the form. What do we see and hear in *One Plus One*? The possibilities of the organization of a black syntax, minor forms of political activism (graffiti, student protests, critique of popular culture), the creative process behind a famous song, an historically famous recording studio, gender suppression and control (simplified images of the roles of black women in the Black Panther movement; white 'virginal' sacrificial tokens; disturbing on-screen games with Godard's wife of the time, Anna Wiazemsky, playing the character 'Eve Democracy'; a woman controlled), all mapped by an hypnotic cinematography (by Anthony B. Richmond). The tracking camera creates a new continuum of a clear-cut montage through the conjunction of *and*, and one plus one equals x?[3] In fact Godard's films from the 1960s – such as *Les Carabiniers* (1963), *La Chinoise* (1967), *Week End* (1967), and *One Plus One* (1968) – present an index of images on the topic of each film's themes, speculating not only on the nature of cinema itself (as in *Bande à part,* 1964), the themes that cinema takes on (as in *Le mépris* (*Contempt,* 1963)), but also the alignment of images with politics, and a questioning of how this sound-politics and image-politics – produced by the image – can be articulated. The conditions of conjunction prove to be a pressing question arising from the critique that Deleuze takes up in the cinema books, against the linguistic basis of semiology, instead advocating an image-based method.[4]

Deleuze looks to the components of the sound-images that are generative of meanings informing our aesthetic processes. Film theorists call this type of analysis film semiology or film semiotics (Barthes 1967: 9; Metz 1974a; Stam *et al.* 1992; cf. Buckland 2000). What Deleuze does in the cinema books is devise his own semiology, comprised of components of an image (including sound). Deleuze creates an open-category semiotics, produced through his method of 'a taxonomy, an attempt at the classification of images and signs' (C1: xiv). For the main terms of his analysis, Deleuze engages the work of C.S. Peirce, whom he champions as a semiotician (C1: 69; cf. Deledalle 2000; Ehrat 2005: 13–14.), but engages only as far as his nomenclature of signs. In addition to C.S. Peirce (C1: 198), Deleuze takes up film maker Pier Paolo Pasolini's call for a study of the conditions of the principles of reality that cinema engages (Deleuze references Pasolini's book, *Heretical Empiricism* (1972) 2005; C2: 286 n.8), together with Henri Bergson's reminder of the 'modulation' of the object through its movement (C2: 27).

Throughout his entire oeuvre, Deleuze is critical of the restrictions of semiotic analysis, which he argues against because of its structuralist methodology (cf. Deleuze 2004: 170–192; Surin 2005: 24). Deleuze engages, but differentiates his work from that of theorists including Edgar Morin, Christian Metz, Roland Barthes and Umberto Eco in the cinema books to construct his political polemic against linguistic-based theory from analysis of the image. Earlier in works such as *A Thousand Plateaus* with Guattari, a critique of Bertrand Russell and Noam Chomsky is engaged and the type of accounts of the limits of language and thought's ability to express a singular position are discussed (Deleuze and Guattari 1987: 148). In his book on *Foucault* ([1986] 1988b; usefully read as a supplement to the cinema books), Deleuze continues to offer ways in which the notion of subjectivity can be conceived – not in any sense of a structuralist semiotic construction, but in the terms that Foucault indicated – as an historical archive of folded layers of selves, of cracks and fissures of time that are multiple and 'co-extensive' (1988b: 118; see also chapter 5 Perception).

Deleuze describes how a taxonomic approach – that we refer to here as the transsemiotic method[5] of the ciné-system – can assist in our apprehension of film's conceptual practice. Deleuze seeks to account for the image not through 'codifications' or 'resemblances' (as many semiotic theories do), but through the image-in-process. Deleuze's account describes the political constitution of an image, the ontology of an image, and how, through repeated viewing of an image, the participant notices that it is never the same. We can thus characterize Deleuze's transsemiotics as an account of a *becoming-image*: that is an account of the image as always in process, as always being reconfigured. We see this, for example, through different types of cinematography, and post-production editing and stylization (for example think of different types of animation, the forms of which inform the content). These differentiating factors and the ways in which the image reveals or envelops the modulation of these factors, as Deleuze writes, 'nourishes' the relation between object and images through its own terms of modulation – whether an indirect and direct image (C2: 27–28; C2: 266 n5; Barthes 1968: 51–54). With all of these elements, Deleuze negotiates the complex field of film theory in the early 1980s, and develops a non-linguistic semiotic that attempts to account for how every time we watch a film we see another thing, and in the most basic of epistemological terms, one plus one does not equal two.

What is Transsemiotics?

Semiotics is one of the most powerful tools for analysis of all kinds of texts. Semiotics is the study of signs: things that stand in for something else. The ways and means that different semiologies are used for the critique and discussion of screen-based works have figured some of the most highly charged political positions for screen-based theory and philosophy. One of the most famous film semioticians was Christian Metz, who produced an analytic method that would examine the components of the story to see how they worked. Metz drew from an earlier theorist, Ferdinand de Saussure (Rushton 2009: 266). De Saussure's system argues that a sign has value by virtue of its place in a system, and that the substitution of elements within that system means that it can still function. This type of semiotics focuses upon images and symbols or signs, which are termed the semiotic expressions. These are the language and words that we apply in order to describe any given thing produced by a complex system such as screen image (which are a result of teams of people producing creative and technical work. See Barthes 1967: 30).

In film analysis semiotic systems have been developed for use by film theory and film philosophy to deconstruct and describe the constituent functions of objects and the relations and actions of and between characters and things on screen (cf. Lotman 1976; Johnston [1973] 1977; Metz 1974a; Monaco 1977; De Lauretis 1984; Buckland 2000). Articulating the ways that cinema can be 'read' or 'worked through' uses a particular theoretical framework to articulate a certain type of 'reality'. Film semiologies developed from the work of Metz, Barthes, Lacan, or de Saussure are reworked and expanded after the period of 1960s and 1970s when theoretical investigations based on postcolonial, feminist, and economic live world developments revised many of the ways in which film histories record the polyphony of images. Cinema and film theory incorporated elements of these debates into theories that seek to account for the technicalities of film signification, as well as the other processes at work, for example, through investigations into cognition (cf. Bordwell 1985), emotion (cf. Tan 1995), the systematization of genre theory (cf. Williams 2007), gesture (cf. Bellour 2000), music (cf. Rose 1994); the politics of language (cf. Shohat and Stam 1985), race (cf. Minh-ha 1989), reception theory (cf. hooks 1996; Jenkins 2000:165–182), or sexuality (cf. Rich 1998: 368–380; Williams 2008) (this is by no means a definitive list). Feminist philosophy has been at the forefront of revisions of epistemology of the subject, later engaged by film theory; Butler 1999; Hendricks and Oliver 1999).

In Deleuzian terms, semiotic methods are inadequate as a tool for analysis. Primarily, as Deleuze and Guattari noted, 'language is a political affair before it is an affair for linguistics', and thus no 'general semiology' (1987: 140) can be applicable in theory (see also the arguments in Pearce 1997). The main problem with semiotic approaches (such as a pure structuralist, historical, cognitive or psychoanalytic methodology) is that they rely on what Deleuze and Guattari describe as 'pre-signifying regimes', where one 'signifier' takes control over an expression (for example, of people: imposing gender role demands; of places: imposing territorial nationalist controls; of cultures: music, dance, rituals; of politics: the assumption of previous economic directions, etc.), thereby abstracting local inflections and ignoring the content of the local expression in favour of a power-label for 'analysis' (1987: 137).

In addition to the study of the basic elements of language signs are other political and cultural indicators that predetermine with what the system of signification is comprised. For example, language systems are generally quite arbitrary, and the words and sounds of words are often unrelated to the thing that they stand for. How does the word 'film', for example, relate to a film we see? It does in the sense that 'film' used to consist of a strip of celluloid coated with a 'film' of chemicals, but that word does not describe anything of the nature of film, although it does indicate the historical origins of its photographic process of production. For the most part, language is arbitrary – the word 'girl' in English totally different to the word for 'girl' in French, or in the Japanese language. How the word 'girl' is linked to an actual girl is through other elements. What semiotics attempts to do is *describe that linkage*. Feminist critiques have demonstrated how such paradigmatic systems maintain gender biased values even in exchange systems (cf. Irigaray [1978] 1985: 170–191). Similarly, Deleuze and Guattari's critique of semiotic systems is that descriptions can merely re-ascribe or transfer interpretation to another place, not really changing anything (1987: 138). The de Saussurian model has limited application in cinema, because while the screen produces images that may invoke signs of, or 'be representative of' something, all kinds of films engage different modalities of signification that are indicative of certain things – and all images have a political as well as aesthetic position that they signify.[6]

Instead of the structural linguistics of the semiotic methods, Deleuze and Guattari propose a 'pragmatics' of a 'transsemiotic' (1987: 145, 136), a method that Deleuze continues to investigate in the cinema books in terms of its 'generative' and 'transformational' application (*ibid.*: 139). This method builds upon the semiotic approaches of Peirce and Louis Hjelmslev by using Guattari's transversal technique and Deleuze's schematic use of mathematic philosophy (Deleuze and Guattari 1987: 43; Hjelmslev 1961). The transsemiotic method that Deleuzian film philosophy brings is the ability to undertake a differentiating expressive model, enabling discussion that performs not only a critique of the conditions of expression, but, as feminist critique has also arrived at (following a not dissimilar pathway), the possibility of cracking apart regimes of control that suppress expression (cf. Deleuze and Guattari 1987: 140; Braidotti 1994; Mohanty 2003).

How Deleuze Uses Transsemiotics

How do we articulate and write about different screen conditions? We must use a constructed language, but one that it is not at all equivalent to the cinematic 'language system of reality', which, as Deleuze points out, 'is not at all a language' (C2: 28). Engaging the Deleuzian system for screen analysis, we might observe that *One Plus One* appears to depict the form of dual point of view Deleuze describes in the large form of the action-image (SAS'), where we see situations (S) altered (S') after an action (A) occurs. By the end of the film, we can observe that a situated image enters into a 'perpetual exchange' with itself, and the restricted action of the camera and the events being recorded are contained within the circuit of the cinematography. In this way, the film transforms this movement into a time-image through the system of different signs that comprise the conditions of the film. In his description between the differences of the components of the signs and images of movement and time image, Deleuze takes a clear position on the semiotics of images and signs, and addresses the problem of the 'relations between cinema and language' (C2: 25). At first we might assume that he is addressing the problem of describing one medium (the moving sound-image) with another (written or spoken language). However, the 'problem' for Deleuze is the methodology of linguistic philosophy, semiology or the science of signs, as it is applied to film analysis. Screen semiology is a contentious and disparate method at the time of Deleuze's Cinema books in the early 1980s (cf. Hawks 1977: 123–150). In *Difference and Repetition* Deleuze challenges the prevailing linguistic philosophy (such as Rorty 1967) by presenting cases for the limits and the creative powers of language through the work of Raymond Roussel and Charles Péguy, which leads Deleuze to a discussion of the heterogeneity of signs and the ways in which movement and pedagogy can alter that sameness (Deleuze [1968] 1994: 22–24). In *Proust and Signs* ([1972] 2000), Deleuze sets out the concept of literary machines where signs are never singular but multiple. In turn these concepts are extended in *A Thousand Plateaus*, where Deleuze and Guattari set out a scathing argument against semiotics as the 'scientific' study of language, invoking an extensive range of supportive evidence, including Foucault's critique of the historicity of described structures, and devoting two plateaus (chapters) to the 'postulates of linguistics' ([1980] 1987: 75–148) and the 'regime of signs' (*ibid.*: 111–148). One of the main propositions running through *A Thousand Plateaus* describes the workings of the war machine as an organizational force that corrals its subjects into obeying through the order-words of signifying regimes, including language. Deleuze and Guattari contend: 'A rule of grammar is a power marker before it is a syntactical marker' (1987: 76).

The Deleuzian transsemiotics focuses on the image. Just as Deleuze approaches the description of the categorical structures that a screen-based perception-image creates with qualifications, when describing the signs of the image, Deleuze is careful not to be prescriptive about the types of realities, or the 'cognition' of the different worlds that screen-based experience creates. Instead, he comes to describe how certain types or genres of films tend to create, reconfigure and occupy certain categories of meaning through the type of cinematic sign they employ.[7] Signs can signal or switch, envelop or open different forms of screen ontology. In the cinema books Deleuze describes two main signs – one for movement, and one for time. This is how he sees cinema as organizing itself, and he disagrees with theorists who discuss film and ignore either of those two aspects (and he argues why). Deleuze names the main three movement signs: the perception-image, the affection-image, the action-image. He then invokes several other movement-signs, including the impulse-image, the reflection-image, the relation-image. These movement-signs are then qualified, and can be given further forms and content through description of the range of signs that organize them. Further, Deleuze describes different temporal signs including (but not limited to): opsigns, sonsigns, tacitsigns, mnemosigns, onirosigns, hyalosigns, chronosigns, noosigns, lectosigns, qualisigns, crystals, seeds. These names are indicative signs for when types of forms change and alter things on screen. Each of these signs can be qualified by further signs, and Deleuze's system (as an open and 'trans' (across) system) can be technically difficult to follow. Some of the terms drawn from Peirce can become confusing, as Deleuze engages them for different ends to Peirce's project (C2: 30–34). For example, if we look at a division of the signs of movement-image, into affection-image, into icon-image, into describing a close-up shot of a face on screen, and its emotive reaction to a range of affects, Deleuze describes this face as a 'set of the expressed and the expression' (C1: 97). This set becomes an 'icon' – a 'sign of the bi-polar composition of the affection-image' (*ibid.*). The icon sign can be further divided into other signs that articulate the type of icon sign it is; this is the process of *differentiating* that Deleuze speaks about through the books – not a comparison, but a qualification of the types of transformations or translations that the form has taken, thus generating new kinds of signs. The movement-image and its 'modulation' of 'an object' (a reality) come *before* the sign that we use to label it (C1: 27). Bogue has usefully mapped out the main signs of the

Deleuzian system (2003: 70–71). Although complex, Deleuze's method gives us licence to invent our own names for signs, as Deleuze clearly demonstrates an open-system, and signs are useful for detailing and qualifying the meanings and contents of different screen forms. For example, Kara Keeling describes the signs of an 'image of common sense' in her discussion of some of the cinematic epistemologies and ontologies of race on screen (2007), engaging a Deleuzian method to examine some of the overlooked issues of the image. Developing some of the implications of an anti-semiotic (and thus anti-psychiatric) approach, Ian Buchanan and Patricia MacCormack have argued for a 'schizoananalytic' method for screen studies interested in Deleuze and Guattari's anti-semiological work (2008). Deleuze's open-system method thus is valuable for extending film studies and qualifying significant changes to film practice; for example, just as 'genre' theory qualified 'auteurist' theory (cf. Gledhill and Williams 2000: 222), so can a Deleuzian transsemiotics qualify practices of cognitive semiotic film theory and film philosophy. This is by no means a 'master theory', but a philosophical approach that Deleuze takes, engaging a rhizomatic method (some would term 'post-structural') in order to engage with the ontology of film and the embedded epistemologies screen images create.

As Deleuze is classifying images not according to the terms of 'so-called classical narration' (C2: 26; cf. Bordwell 1985), any sense of narrative that we ascribe to the 'what is it?' question is derived from different forms of movement-images and the compositions and different types of time-images. So when Deleuze begins to summarize his approach to the relationships generated by screen sound-images (in chapter 2 of *Cinema 2*) he begins with some qualifications about the use of the semiotic classifications. In work previous to his cinema books, Deleuze had already critiqued the political outcomes and philosophical limitations of structuralist work (Deleuze [1967] 2004: 170–192; Deleuze [1969] 1990: 50; cf. Lecercle 2002). In Cinema 1, Deleuze engages Peirce's classifications of the image as relational stages. Deleuze uses Peirce's system for the classification of signs and images, using Peirce's numerical values through which certain qualities can indicate differences in kind, and the image can be classified as relational stages (cf. Bogue 2003: 67–69). To this he adds a measure of Bergson, in order to figure in the registration of the different states of the movement-image. Specific examples of films also qualify Deleuze's meanings. In Deleuze's system, they are the states of: (1) 'ze-roness' (perception-image), (2) 'firstness' (affection-image), (3) 'secondness' (action-image) and (4) 'thirdness' (relation-image) (C1: 98; C2: 30). Deleuze also engages Pasolini's notion of 'free indirect discourse', which is a form that describes the cinematic image in similar terms to Peirce's triadic system (C1: 72–73; see glossary, the *perception-image*). However, where Peirce's theory of the sign is the sign as an image that stands for another image (its object) through the relation of a third image (interpretant), this three-way move-ment ultimately returns to its linguistic measurable sign. Pasolini's system of free indirect discourse 'testifies to a system which is always heterogeneous, far from equilibrium' (C2: 73). In his text and in the dense footnotes of the cinema books, Deleuze invokes a number of theorists of semiotics, includ-ing Mikhail Bakhtin, Barthes, Umberto Eco, Julia Kristeva (C2: 26; Kristeva 1980). In particular, Deleuze engages works of three of the most famous French film semioticians of his era – Metz (with particular reference to his work *Essais sur la signification au cinéma* (1964–68), translated as *Film Language* (1974a)), Raymond Bellour's *The Analysis of Film* (2000), and Morin's work *The Cinema or the Imaginary Man* (2005). However, Deleuze reads the work of these film theorists not as film theory but as film philosophy. Deleuze argues why Metz 'and his followers' 'remain Kantians' (C2: 286 n8), and why their theories are less appropriate for his system than the type of Bergsonian approach to the image that he has thus far taken.

The question of 'reality' plays a fundamental part in Deleuze's approach throughout his entire oeuvre. The construction of a particular epistemology of truth, and the 'pedagogy of perception' that film theory creates, provide im-petus for Deleuze as a philosopher to address the details of the structures pro-ducing and shaping this reality. Following his summation of 'signs and images in the cinema' (C2: chapter 2), we can see that Deleuze rejects film theory that presents the terms of a prescribed narrational framework, where the questions and answers already have a phenomenologically prescribed content.

American ordinariness helps break down what is ordinary about Japan, a clash of two everyday realities which is even expressed in colour, when Coca-cola red or plastic yellow violently interrupts the series of washed out, unemphatic tones of Japanese life. And, as the character says in *The Flavour of Green Tea over Rice*: what if the opposite had occurred, if saki, samisen and geisha wigs had suddenly been introduced into the everyday banality of Americans ...? (C2: 15)

Objects and spaces of a certain hue and materiality are framed by the cinematography (by Yuuharu Atsuta) in certain ways that convey an array of information. The information is presented by way of the modes of encounter through the camera, which Deleuze describes in the terms of the transsemiotic crack: *break down*; *clash*; *violently interrupts*; *suddenly*. The subjective and objective quality of the images is given weight through their situating placement in chronometric time, communicative of a sense of ethnic place, but not one of space. Information about things is given in terms of epidermis, wigged, sedated by rice wine, a physical presence through their singular and combined sets of shots. To take the analysis further, we can look at each of these signs individually, as vectorial points, where the movement between object and image ceases and enters into a degree of a time-image. Deleuze's approach to the image-sign, whatever sort it may be, is vitalistic: for example, what he looks for in the image are indicators of this philosophy: 'It is clear that the image gives rise to signs' (C1: 69). He continues, 'For our part, a sign appears to be a particular image which represents a type of image, sometimes from the point of view of its composition, sometimes from the point of view of its genesis of formation (or even its extinction)' (C2: 69). As we have noted above, one of the problems with semiological models is that they can rely upon linguistic structural platforms for their methodology, and Deleuze strongly rejected structuralism for its deterministic reliance upon some form of 'transcendental' signifying position (Deleuze 2004; Stivale 1998: 253). Instead, Deleuze develops a semiology that places the image as its central sign, and signifier of not just meaning, but of ontology – of life itself. 'Language is not life; it gives life orders' (Deleuze and Guattari 1987: 76).

Deleuze's screen semiotic is the crucial aspect of both cinema books. It is the blood supply for the skeleton and neural network. It provides us with the means to interpret unwieldy and obvious screen texts (cf. Kennedy 2000; Powell 2007). Commercialism aside, screen-based forms do have the potential to perform as a creative art. However, as Deleuze describes, the transformative powers of syntactical and semiotic rearrangement remain firmly grounded in pre-existing power arrangements that even the screen medium may not overcome. What can alter is our thinking about the ways in which we record, articulate and analyse the perception-image; as Deleuze notes, 'Godard says that *to describe* is to observe mutations' (C2: 19, original emphasis).

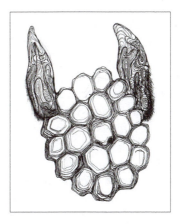

9

Signs (Vector)

In the Deleuze's taxonomy, over twenty different signs generated by the movement-image and over a dozen from the time-image are charted. The way that the ciné-system works, by infinite generation, means that there is no limit to the number of signs that cinema can produce. A taxonomy is reliant upon signs for the terms of its classification process. In semiotics, signs are things that stand in for something else; in Deleuzian transsemiotics, signs are topological figures that affect change.

Rather than present a cursory account of each of the named signs in the Deleuzian ciné-system, and speculate on the myriad of possible growth signs, this chapter focuses on just one sign in order to demonstrate the richness behind each and every taxonomic classificatory term that Deleuze produces. Ronald Bogue's table of images and their corresponding signs provides a useful reference tool for seeing how images are composed through their corresponding signs of composition and genesis (Bogue 2003: 70). This chapter looks at the 'vector' which, in Deleuze's system, is a sign of genesis. This means that when it appears, it signals and can enact creation or destruction. As Bogue reminds us, Deleuze's taxonomic system is more Bergsonian than Peircian, and thus Deleuze's focus on the notion of genesis should not be too surprising (Bogue 2003: 67).

A vector is a geometric modelling tool that we are using to describe the capacity of screen space. In the Deleuzian ciné-system vectorial points create, map and modify intensive moments and the behavioural conditions of screen spaces. Understanding the vector as a sign, and its difference from an edit or montage, is crucial for the development of interpretive practices for film studies. Quite distinct from an allegorical reading of film, the vectorial defines the internal relations of a film and how their connections impact upon the film's style and form. The vector creates a skeleton-space, a screen space composed through broken and indirect connections made up of heterogeneous parts.

Consider the *extent* of Deleuze's description of the following scene from one the key vampire films of the twentieth century,

> It is the hour when it is no longer possible to distinguish between sunrise and sunset, air and water, water and earth, in the great mixture of a marsh or a tempest. Here, it is by degrees of mixing that the parts become distinct or confused in a continual transformation of values. (C1: 14)

Deleuze refers to German director F.W. Murnau's film, *Nosferatu, eine Symphonie des Grauens* (*Nosferatu, A Symphony of Horror*, 1922). Like all films of the vampire genre, it contains its fair share of overtly theatrical spooky scenes, but *Nosferatu* remains unsettling even through its melodramatic staging. Deleuze describes *Nosferatu*'s cinematic composition in terms of sensory reaction and atmospheric movement. His literary tone echoes that of one of the foundational European film theorists, Béla Balázs, who similarly noted that the emotive atmospheric disturbances of *Nosferatu* resonated with 'the glacial draughts of air from the beyond' (Balázs cited by Eisner 1973: 97). Both Balázs's and Deleuze's descriptions focus on the *dynamic conditions* of the film. Both address the film in terms of the energy and movement of the screen. Both undertake to translate into words this movement on screen, as shifts in emotive space registered by cinematic bodies. Deleuze's description, however, takes us into the very *formula* of atmosphere in *Nosferatu*. Deleuze tells us *how* those types of dynamic fluctuations create specific forms of the action-image through points of physical change on screen. Deleuze's words do not just describe a film style, but convey how the film world's (diegetic) fluctuations – here called marshes or tempests – alter the film form through a specific switching of meaning. This modification causes movement in terms of on-screen time, space and subject meaning. In turn, this movement creates change on screen – in terms of the technical dimensions of the film, the visceral sensate forms produced by these physical connections, and the modification of thought of the sound-image. The term Deleuze uses to describe this transformation of form in cinema is 'vector'.

As one of the earliest vampire films, *Nosferatu*'s power lies in its unsettling characterization of a bone-chilling fear of change and fear of otherness. *Nosferatu*'s disturbing narrative encompasses the plague, infected blood and soil, sexual chemistries, genetic reordering, strange personality traits, organic transmutations, journeys, strange weather patterns, social mores, fears and nightmares. These often unrelated elements are united by what Deleuze describes as vectors, by providing links in the screen circumstances. These *vector-links* are often disjointed – their connections made on screen by zigzag, tacit or irrational means. The vectors transform the scene disturbances into a series of joined incidents that operate in discrete temporal and spatial realities. Re-combined they create screen situations of incredible intensity such as we see in *Nosferatu*. Deleuze describes this type of action-image as the 'small form' and a 'cinema of behaviour (behaviourism)' – evident in the vampire film, the military, or western film, historical films, noir-style melodramas and thrillers – where filmic 'reality' and meaning resides in the creation of closed and intense worlds such as those by directors like Hitchcock, Anthony Minghella or Sofia Coppola. It is *the structure and style of filmic behaviour* that film theory (and to a lesser extent, film criticism) seeks to describe in its writing. This behaviour is inspired by the on-screen action and 'engendered' by screen situations (for example brought about by acting styles, or socially imposed gender rules), says Deleuze, 'since behaviour is an action that passes from one situation to another, which responds to a situation in order to try to modify it or set up a new situation' (C1: 155).

What Is the Vector?

The vector is a term used to indicate the concept of agency, a sequence, or used to represent spatial coordinates, direction and magnitude of a quantity. The vector is a model employed across a range of disciplines – medical, biological, aeronautical, computational and mathematical – used to describe real and abstract qualities. In film vectors actively reconfigure the quantitative dimensions of a scene – affecting the whole of the film's final form. The vector is the point at which things change on screen.

First expounded in his pursuit of 'the image of thought' through critique of the notion of 'representation' in his 1968 thesis, *Difference and Repetition*, the vector and vector field are terms Deleuze uses to indicate *how things move and are thus transformed* according to the physics of the forces that determine the situations of forms and their trajectories. In 1980 in *A Thousand Plateaus*, Deleuze and Guattari use the term vector as a way of differentiating between the forms and conditions of what they term an 'abstract machine' or 'machinic assemblage' – forms and conditions of which we can see demonstrated by cinema (1987: 145). In an assemblage there are two vectors, say Deleuze and Guattari: one vector is concerned with distribution and organization of things and territories (stratification) and the other vector works to re-orient the form and content of an assemblage to deterritorialize its stability (smooth space) (*ibid.*: 144–145, 474–500). In *A Thousand Plateaus* the types of movement that occur within an assemblage from stability to dynamic form and back again are discussed in relation to speed vectors (drawing on Paul Virilio), but it is not until the Cinema books that the differentiations of vectorial movements are further explored and applied (cf. Deleuze and Guattari 1987: 396). In both *Cinema 1* and *Cinema 2* Deleuze draws on the mathematical utility of the vector in order to express how the physical cinematic system is able to convey fluctuations of relations of all kinds, and retain the *conditions of spaces* (curved, three-dimensional, flat, surface or virtual) through the transformation of things (such as we recognize in *Nosferatu*).

Deleuze draws our attention to the *structure of behaviour* of cinematic form, in part from Merleau-Ponty's discussion of the relation between cinema and psychology (Merleau-Ponty 1964). The structure of cinematic behaviour is created in films like *Nosferatu* through vector points that act as connectors that Deleuze describes, after Bergson, as the 'sensory-motor' links (Bergson 1994: 42–43, 231; Merleau-Ponty 1996: 10, 91, 159). These links create a cinematic performativity that marks out *Nosferatu* as one of the formative vampire films through the iconic situations of *über*-vampirism that are affectively enacted by all on-screen elements in the film (such as the weather, people, horse and carriage, or ethical shifts). Through sensory-motor disturbances in the screen situation, the *vector points* of the action-image transform and alter the fabric of the communities that they contact (both on and off screen). For example, in the passage quoted at the start of this chapter (from *Cinema 1*), Deleuze's description of the emotional and ethical changes in *Nosferatu's* filmic world is styled by the words *marsh* and *tempest*. This choice of words connotes not only the sense of a connection of the elements through a disturbance (tempest) or congestion (marsh) of air and water, but also invokes the emotional conditions on screen created by those mixtures. In his use of the word *tempest* Deleuze writes his own vector – as a *quality of measure* – into his description of the on-screen vectors communicating the sensory-motor screen properties. Like Balázs Deleuze conveys how we might translate our screen experience into a manner of language that will have some resonance with the moving medium. Be aware of that hour of *mixing*, Deleuze writes, for it is here that vampiric vectors work their dark magic.

In Deleuze's cinema system vectors are simply the 'signs' of the variable dimensions of forces that operate to bring a screen situation to life. The 'tempest' is such a force: a sign of the vector. As we have seen with the movement-images, all images are immanent in the larger forms directing them as they convey a meaning beyond material existence. For example, an index might constitute the generic elements of a particular screen world. The eccentric movements, cloaks and long fingernails of actor Max Schreck's performance as Count Orlock in *Nosferatu* set a standard index for generic discussion of all somnambulists and vampires-in-disguise. Equally the décor and cinematographic framing of *Nostferatu* marks an indexical territory as a (spooky) screen form that continues to be strategically utilized by the genre (cf. Powell 2005). The use of the term 'index' thus enables Deleuze to signal (and simplify) the complexity of the cinematic operation comprised of multiple signs, including the vector. It is important to note that, as the vector indicates the variation in the whole, it is what Deleuze describes as 'an index of lack': that is, where there is a gap in the narrative the vector makes the connection (either elucidating or mystifying the situation in the example of a noir film) (C1: 160). Vectors are the sign that a *modification* has occurred on screen.

Focus on the vectors in film analysis requires us to pay attention to any number of singular elements, which may form the evaluative relationship between modelled forms (all aspects of the *mise-en-scène*, sound and cinematography) in the screen space. In addition to considering the conditions that come to constitute an image, Deleuze asks that film analysis acknowledge the concrete terms of the screen through the laws of physics. Vectorial elements produce meaning through the creation of new connections between things. In between those connections made by the visual, sonic or haptic vectors of the image are further spaces – vector-induced moments of 'vertigo' between edits (C2: 180; see chapter 12 Topology). Always attentive to the physicality of language, Deleuze invokes a signpost phrase from novelist Dashiell Hammett (author of the book, *The Maltese Falcon* (1930)) to describe the physicality of the vector sound-image as something that puts 'a spanner in the works' (C1: 164). Noted examples of this *spanner-vector* (as disruptive or constructive heavy-handed shifts in situation) are obvious in classical Hollywood films such as *The Big Sleep* (dir. Hawks, 1946) and *The Maltese Falcon* (dir. John Huston, 1941). This style is continued in contemporary noir, such as Frank Miller's *Sin City* (dirs Frank Miller and Robert Rodriguez, 2005). As noir-thrillers the divisive plot twists and turns of these films rely on vectorially produced atmosphere, revelations and concealment of physical and emotive images. As we have already observed – thinking of *Nosferatu* – the screen vector is what styles the *transforming* of a scene's action *and* the vector provides the imaginary or theoretical nuances of a script, *and* the physical and intellectual situation of the *mise-en-scène* (C1: 178–179). In other words the vectorial point can generate both physical and conceptual movement. In Deleuze's film theory analysis of the type of vector contributes to the critique of cinematic practices, knowledge that will enable our better apprehension of the kinds of *living relations* the cinematographic creates through its perception of the world.[1]

On screen the vector marks an incidence of change. Thinking with vectors cues us to the *organization of sensory stimulation* on screen through systemic shifts in the direction and quality of things in the cinematographically constructed world. A vector can occur with the introduction of a certain sound or the use of a physical motif to indicate a shift in temporal or spatial dimensions. As we have discussed, the vector signals where a difference in the conditions of the screen *transform*. This transformation is not to be confused with moments of a switch in a situation of a scene in terms of a sonic or graphic match between sound and imagery: for example, the matching of the infamous bone cut to same shape spaceship in Stanley Kubrick's film *2001: A Space Odyssey* (1968), or the fluid formal correlation between ejaculation cut to ultrasound gel squirt in Catherine Breillat's film *Romance* (1999). These are instances where contrast or comparison is injected in the film situation through editing methods and are what Deleuze refers to as Eisensteinian montages (C1: 36; chapter 4 Montage).[2]

Rather than just think about the graphic cut between sound-images, Deleuze insists we pay attention to the type of form of transformation that takes place – the type of vector. In addition to any allegorical correlations to be made in analysis of a film, first explore the internal structure of motor-sensory links on screen. How, and with what, is the film's internal structure composed? What are the film world's limits in physical terms? What types of internal focuses or gathering points are created by those boundaries? What are the vector points? The vectorial form is to be considered and expressed through the following five interrelated aspects of screen composition. These are implicit and intentional aspects of scene construction:

1. the constitution of the sound-image through the physical organization of the screen (or what Deleuze terms 'gestural' and 'motor' structures);
2. the sensory qualities/behaviour of a change in screen situation;
3. what type of impact these variations have on localized situations;
4. the overall form of the film (in this case, small);
5. how this form creates a particular type of space (skeletal) by the temporal distances between vectors.

The *vectorial points of change* within a screen's continuum can be both *abstract* (for example, the range of elements and concepts conveyed by the 'vampire') and/or *physical* (the designated narrative, stylistic attributes and sensorial qualities of the film/scene). The vectorial moments are such moments of intensity on screen and the vector is the *carrier* of those forces and sensations.[3]

How Deleuze Uses the Screen-vector

The vector provides Deleuze with a physical term to describe the *relational changes* between two or more specific screen elements, such as cinematography, acting modes, lighting, editing, sound, post-production film effects, and any other technological situations where forms are altered, through human and elemental means. In altering technical aspects of the film, such as lighting, or in scene edits, the vector is a micro 'vertigo' space, a 'between' that engenders micro worlds, and a macro space for thought.

As a practical component of the calculus, Deleuze uses the vector for the description of the representation of all manner of what he called 'local' (meaning particular) screen situations and actions. However, he will also account for the sensory terms of the sound-image's specific conditions of construction. This sense of the *local-vector* is seen in documentary, historical films, noir genres, comedy, costume dramas, the neo-western genre, in the films of Godard, and in television. All contain instances of where a *local condition* situates the sound-image. As we have already discussed, the *spanner-vector* of the transformation of situations is representative of an obvious vector situation. However, one of the pleasures of cinema (whether mainstream or 'arthouse') are those nuances of change in situation that can be slight and so subtle that they are not realized until some time after viewing. For example, consider the films of Chinese director Zhang Yimou or American director Orson Welles. Both create films that focus on the conditions created in restricted environments – *local-vectors*. For example, in Yimou's films such as *Raise the Red Lantern* (*Da hong deng long gao gao gua*, 1991), and the blockbuster *Hero* (*Ying Xiong*, 2002), or in Welles's *Citizen Kane* (1941) or *The Magnificent Ambersons* (1942), the films' conditions create controlled settings. These settings describe specific historical conditions that provide core *censorial, gendered, and racial vectors* for accessing knowledge of the respective politics of Chinese or American cultural policies. Yimou describes the tight controls of Chinese social behaviour, generating screen ethics made by intense colour and sound treatment. Welles does the same. Recognition of this vectorial form can be used for analysis more or less universally across films where a certain form of *militarism* rules that filmic world.

Other examples of screen situations that create instances of localized 'realities' reference the very relation between the screen and its construction. The dramatized link between the sensory and the motor perception of cinema reveals the medium to us as one that is a 'world which becomes its own image' – as Deleuze comments in his remarks on 'the identity of the image and the movement' (C1: 57). Such moments of cinematic construction, which we can term *method vectors*, are to be found in a wide range of film styles. Contemporary mainstream films often acknowledge the world of their film's production through extra-diegetic (external to the film world) devices: for example, the use of a contemporary soundtrack in period films such as Ang Lee's film *Brokeback Mountain* (2005) or in Sofia Coppola's film *Marie Antoinette* (2006). *Brokeback Mountain* and *Marie Antoinette*'s respective *mise-en-scènes* are set in their historical pasts (Wyoming, 1963, and Paris, 1780s), and like the many variations in productions of vampiric-vectorial forms reveal much about the era of their production through their subject focus which creates a small form cinema.

Like the political films of Godard or Lars von Trier, the films of Yimou, Lee and Coppola operate as political allegories. Just as Pasolini's film *Salò o le 120 giornate di Sodoma* (1975) engaged localized situations to attend to the transformation of forms created by larger (global) forces, each of the above examples enact their vectorial form through local levels. Broadly speaking we could also characterize this sense of a local situation as an appeal to a cinema of 'allusion', as Noël Carroll once described (not to be confused with the 'post-modern') (Carroll 1981). However, to speak only to the 'allusions' these forms of cinema raise would miss one of the momentous specificities of the physics of cinematographic perception: *the detailing of close range*. What a vector enables us to articulate is *how* a moving image can convey situational aware-ness and change. A screen will produce a sound-image of a form of localized knowledge. Changing that sound-image by combining it with other images, sounds, movements, colours and bodies will alter the dimensions of that first image, thereby changing what we grasp to be the *situation* of the image. The vector thus causes an associative function to occur by embedding a thought (through various means) or by enacting a change in screen elements.

Put simply, attending to the vector points on screen enables Deleuze to follow changes within the moving image – the very processes of modelling the dynamics of the multiple dimensions of the screen. Deleuze plays on this no-tion of 'the small form' of the image (as opposed to the large form, discussed in chapter 12 Topology), where the tiniest of physical movements that might enable an abyss-sized trajectory of thought is preyed upon by cinema. The small form can be created by any component of the screen. Consider the figure of *Nosferatu* himself, as rendered by Herzog's 1979 version of Murnau's film, where actor Klaus Kinski's body is 'caught in uterine regression', according to Deleuze's description of this film's visual geometry of scale as 'a foetus reduced' (C1: 185). Deleuze's allusion to the metaphysical womb asks us to question the physiological style of the screen situation, rather than analyse the psychoanalytical constitution of the actor/character's mind.

Thus the vector might take the form of the tone, accent or pace of delivery of an actor's dialogue, it might be the colour of the actor's skin or eyes or hair texture, it might be the type of camera movement used between images (hand-held, tracking, swing ellipses), or a close-up, or it might be an object used in a situation to segue the realism of the screen situation. To conceptualize the power that such 'small forms' hold, Deleuze also refers to the small form of cinema as the *skeleton-space* of the screen situation. As a skeleton-space, a whole space (of the film) is composed through broken and indirect connections made up 'with missing intermediaries, heterogeneous elements which jump from one another' (C1: 168). This has implications for further thinking through the 'temporal distances' that are created in such a space (for example, between material and organic objects or historical concepts, etc) (*ibid.*, see chapter 10 Time). In this sense of shaping the screen's totality vectors provide the quantitative links required for recognition to occur between the infinite ranges of physics of the moving image worlds on screen. The skeletal space of the vector provides an 'empty' site for *chi* (Chinese for *the breath*); it is an encompassing space.[4]

Vectors are thus those rhetorical or geometric ellipses on screen, the individual points that enable an action on screen (A) to 'disclose' a situation (S), catalytic for a new action on screen (A') (where A' equals a modified action) (C1: 160). According to Deleuze this form – ASA' – has multiple possible configurations of movement dependent on the type of screen sound-image and style of action. The ASA' is modification of a situation through movement. Deleuze describes this form using the Riemannian sense of elliptic space, with his discussion playing on both senses of the word as the geometric field and the rhetorical 'gap': ellipse and ellipsis. Generic descriptions are rhetorical indices for Deleuze – they are formed through what he terms 'a reasoning-image' such as 'the famous image of the train, whose arrival we only see from the lights which pass across the woman's face, or the erotic images which we can only infer from the spectators' (C1: 161). The rhetorical sense of such a screen ellipsis has enabled a cinematic perception of events and objects, beyond everyday perception, as the logic of objects (and their temporal and spatial impression) are disclosed, modified and trigger off a further action.

In the second geometrical sense of the ellipse, the vector enables Deleuze to delineate the descriptive movements of the screen components. The screen vector is a form that will effectively provide access to a screen situation in thinking of apparently discontinuous entities, by asking the screen participant to consider two positions by way of a third form (the vectorial point or space) that holds a differential quality or singular difference (C1: 187, 239; Duffy 2006c). Deleuze wrote of the vector form: 'It is as if an action, a mode of behaviour, concealed a slight difference, which was nevertheless sufficient to relate it simultaneously to two quite distinct situations, situations which are worlds apart.' (C1: 161). The vector does not denote a type of seamless exchange or transportation of information. Rather it is a specific function that articulates the magnitude and 'change in direction' of 'an obstacle' or 'the power of a new impulse', creating a specific screen form, as Deleuze says, 'in short, the subordination of the extensive to intensity' (C1: 51).

The Function of a Vector

Employed by Deleuze as a formal term, a 'vector' is a practical concept for the consideration of the physical and sensory dimensions of screen spaces and situations created through those narrative, stylistic and technical processes of filmmaking that involve the *transformation of forms*. In *Nosferatu* a vector space is the point where the relationships of elements begin to transform, as Deleuze writes, so that by *degrees of mixing* (quantities of assimilation) *the parts become distinct or confused*. Of course *Nostferatu* engages in expression of a certain type of dramatic mood that such films never fail to impress upon their viewers, and in this sense provides an easy illustration of a vector. However, the vector is not just a category of the expressionist film (cf.

The Cabinet of Dr. Caligari; dir. Robert Wiene, 1920), just as it is not to be confused as a term that describes the *mise-en-scène*. As Deleuze explored, the vector is a physical arrangement (*agencement*) that provides a necessary facilitation for the abstract machinery of filmmaking to cohere. That ensemble is created through associational means, through what Deleuze calls the vector, or 'line of the universe' – the 'broken line which brings together singular points or remarkable moments at the peak of their intensity' (C1: 218).

Vector-fusions form the series of incidents that create the intensities of *Nosferatu*. Deleuze gives another example – the *vector-pause*, seen in Vertov's use of the intertitle – as a restoration of 'intervals to matter' (C1: 81). This screen interval is not so much a gap between sound-images; rather it creates a hiatus that provides a 'correlation' of images, a 'properly cinematographic enunciation' (C1: 82). Just as we can teach children the rudiments of geometry by differentiating between the scales, dimensions and proportions of space, by measuring things with a length of string that can be knotted and stretched, the vector also provides us with a tool to access and survey the properties of screen space. In fact Deleuze likens the vector situation to a length of knotted rope, as indicated by the economics of directors Sam Peckinpah, Anthony Mann and Delmer Daves, whose western genre films depict a plurality of 'Wests', totalities that are composed of 'the broken stroke', 'genetic signs', 'heterogeneous critical instants' that create a totality that is 'like a knotted rope, twisting itself at each take, at each action, at each event' (C1: 168). The screen vector does perform this role of connecting 'both spaces and actions', as Bogue noted, and to this sense of thinking through connections Deleuze complicates the whole by asking us to consider the temporal mode (or style) of the film in question (Bogue 2003: 89–92). Creating a film that covers the dimensions of its world through the creation of a skeletal space often involves a fracturing of chronological time. We see this in Quentin Tarintino's *Kill Bill* films (2003–2004), or in Kenji Mizoguchi's *Zangiku Monogatari* (*The Story of the Late Chrysanthemums*, 1939), the latter's sequencing of different spaces referred to by Deleuze as creating a 'parallelism of vectors', giving rise to our comprehension of the function of the small form in the conception of space.

As Deleuze notes of the small form, 'it is "small" by its process, but its immensity derives from the connexion of the fragments which compose it, from the placing in parallel of different vectors (which retain their differences), from the homogeneity which is only formed progressively' (C1: 194). Both Mizoguchi and Tarantino employ extremely formal cinematic techniques to deploy their gradual construction of space to encompass the infinite range of cinema through small form.

Deleuze utilizes the mathematical sense of the vector to denote those instances on screen where there is a physical movement. These movements create links and variations in the screen situation. A vector will create a dynamic screen situation – through a particular screen action, sound or behaviour. This moment is not constituted through binary structures (say the difference between the calm air and the storm). Rather, the screen-vector is created through differences that are self-affecting in their constant variation and movement (see chapter 6 Affect). In *Nosferatu* the blood of the vampire is the vectorial point; it is regulatory of its own dimensions of being, *and* full of creative possibilities – like an egg. By increasing its community of vampires, Nosferatu's own status and power is altered. Such is the self-affecting nature of the screen, and any analysis of the medium must account for how much of that moving dimension has played itself out (such is the difficulty we experience in analysis of current events still in process). Event-based narratives all carry this potential for future affection. We see this in a diverse range of films that deal with the migration of viruses, as viralor blood-vectors, including the spread of HIV in *Kids* (dir. Larry Clark, 1995), or in the political allegory of *28 Days* (dir. Danny Boyle, 2003), where another 'blood' infection called Rage, decimates the British population. The vector appears in films that communicate other political paradigms, for example in *Shadows* (dir. John Cassavetes, 1959), where the politics of race-gender relations explode through a reaction to skin colour.

The vectorial point or space in Deleuze's cinema system describes specific screen situation's expressive movements. These movements are measured quantitatively and dynamically: the spatial change in a room at the point when the light is closed; when you hear a classical musical score, rhythmically accompanying a montage of death on screen; when you count the number of gunshots in a western; what you think of when you read the word *Hiroshima* on screen; the moment when you realize a character has now become a vampire. These are vectorial screen situations – movement (and as we shall describe in later chapters, temporal dynamics) effected by light, sound, narrative information and characterization. The vector is functional for thinking through and articulating the conditions that generate these situational points on screen. The vector is also useful for the recognition of constituent genre elements, the diversity of historical screen information, and for analysing screen sound, image, affects, actions and situations.

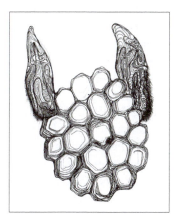

10

Time

Deleuze provides an extensive array of different types and forms of time-images that screen images produce and express. Deleuze's description of the time-image provides a philosophical and mathematical explanation for different aspects of the time-image, organizing them in philosophical terms, as 'commentaries on Bergson' (C2: contents). In Cinema 2 Deleuze devotes four core chapters to the topic, continuing with his ciné-thesis on Bergson from Cinema 1: Chapter 3, 'From recollection to dreams: third commentary on Bergson' (on recognition, the opsign and sonsign); Chapter 4, 'The crystals of time'; Chapter 5, 'Peaks of present and sheets of past: fourth commentary on Bergson' (on time and memory); and then the chapter which deals with the 'becoming as the third time-image', Chapter 6, 'The powers of the false'.

*Deleuze addresses how diverse and similar screen conditions produce
and destroy new time-based forms through processes of differentiation
(C2: 28–9; C2: 40; C2: 80–81).*

One of the promotional taglines for the 2001 film *Donnie Darko* (dir. Richard
Kelly) was the use of an eternal term: Dark. Just as light creates and destroys
forms, so does the dark.[1] Dark becomes darker, darkest and then darko, a
play with forms of 'reality' created by forms of 'knowledge', such that vision,
perception, imagination and intellect is impaired or modified in some way.
Donnie Darko's narrative follows the events of dissymmetrical pathways of
time and the moments when they split, thereby destroying certain trajectories and creating other forms by their detours and intersections. As if to
emphasize the interplay of light and dark, Donnie's psychiatrist (played by
actor Katharine Ross) tells his parents that Donnie (played by actor Jake
Gyllenhaal) is experiencing a 'daylight hallucination'. Donnie's 'hallucination'
is stylized on screen through the actors' bodies' reactions to extra light and
spaces in their world – light flares, connective and shimmering surfaces, vis-
cous mirrors. Meanwhile in the 'real world' darkness is indeed falling, with
strange dark clouds gathering and those once flickering surfaces now bruised,
decaying and darkened, until the end does indeed fall on the characters to the
soundtrack song of 'Mad World' by Andrews and Jules.

In *Donnie Darko* temporal stages of darkness affect the characters with
the darkening of the trajectory of time becoming the accepted way of being,
until 'the end' when the narrative realizes all stages of the 'darkness' as an
event wherein time-images are simultaneous and coextensive. A book titled
'the philosophy of time-travel' provides some narrative lucidity to draw the
storylines into its promised themes, but time as a state of becoming through
encounters and subsequent change provides one of the main story arcs, performed through various images in the film. The 'darkness' colours perception
by mapping that perception's movement through durational screen time that
in turn creates boundaries as it simultaneously rips open new places, creating
paths that allow you to see the 'channel into the future' (Darko).

Donnie Darko offers an example of Deleuzian direct and indirect time-images. We have a filmic whole made up of a range of temporal modes, examples that Deleuze has argued from the outset in the cinema books. Movement is a 'translation in space' (C1: 8), however, when we 'are confronted with a duration, or in a duration' – Deleuze writes, 'we may conclude that there exists somewhere a whole which is changing, and which is open somewhere' (C1: 9). As Deleuze describes it, the time-image occurs as an image 'beyond movement', recognizable through differential processes as 'duration-images, change-images, relation-images, volume-images' (C1: 11). These type of images are indirect time-images. Deleuze says the time-image 'cannot do without the movement-images which express it, and yet it goes beyond all relative movements forcing us to think an absolute of the movement of bodies, an infinity of the movement of light, a backgroundless [*sans fond*] of the movement of souls; the sublime' (C2: 238; for Deleuze's discussion of the sublime, see chapter 4 Montage and chapter 13 Thought).[2]

In time-images durational movement creates topological openings rather than translations of form – as we see with the various time-images in *Donnie Darko*.[3] Instead of having multiple selves within the different story arcs of the film, Donnie's character has a mutant reflection-image provided by multiple versions of Frank, a rabbit-headed character. The paradox of the hare and the tortoise, drawn from Zeno's story of Achilles's footrace with the tortoise, is played out with the rabbit-headed Frank and the often slow-registering Donnie, each character a mirror of the other with differences, on different trajectories; although bound through some dimensional cross-overs, each of their pathways remains distinctive. One of the Franks provides the pragmatic account of the design of a world, at one point noting: 'Twenty-eight days … six hours … forty-two minutes … twelve seconds. That … is when the world … will end' (*Donnie Darko*). American director Richard Kelly follows through time-signing of 'the end' – as a pathway offering both limitations and possibilities – created by temporal activities that *Donnie Darko* prophetically raised (made in 2001, the film is set in 1988, USA) and which Kelly's post-televisual film, *Southland Tales* (2007), continues. In *Southland Tales* the particular apocalyptic situation of *Donnie Darko* becomes more generalized through its repetition, with a narrator (Justin Timberlake) providing not just a narrative description but temporal method – directions for the development of the film. 'This is the way, the world ends,' he intones (in *Southland Tales*). The space and concept of 'film' is extended by Kelly with 'more temporal structures', as Deleuze predicted, wherein the cinematographic image 'has been able to grasp and reveal [those structures], and which can echo the teachings of science' (C2: xii; Kelly 2003; 2004).

As well as 'indirect' images of time, which Deleuze discusses in terms of the aesthetics of political ideas (C2: 243), Deleuze describes 'direct' images of time, including 'crystal' moments: 'seeds of time' where that 'beyond' 'without ground' is created through various functions of time such as memory, recollections, events (C2: 98). Through his discussion of the time-image, Deleuze engages this method of polar concepts of the indirect image of time. Taken in part from Nietzsche's use of a dyadic aesthetic, Deleuze's methodological approach to time draws up from the movement-image, an indirect image of time coming from affective fields of cognition, perception and events, to the direct image of time (cf. C2: 43). The direct image of time can be taken as a Deleuzian definition of the affective dimensions and topology of subjectivity. Deleuze describes his method of accounting for time by citing Federico Fellini: 'We are constructed in memory; we are *simultaneously* childhood, adolescence, old age and maturity' (C2: 99, original emphasis). In this approach we can see that the movement-image is an immanent embedded component of the time-image. Deleuze's Bergsonist mode of vitalist philosophy – wherein the past is present as a living force (habitual, mythical or becoming) – also figures largely in this polar methodology, just as the Nietzschian account of Apollonian destruction and Dionysian creation injects a certain philosophy of the new (C2: 239–240). With his account of the time-image, Deleuze's system describes the virtual nature (or ontology) of the cinema. Understanding this enables us to map the logic of the various structures at work within any given image.[4]

What is Time and the Deleuzian Time-image?

Deleuze approaches time in the terms he sets up through the movement-image, and then takes a 'detour' in order to reveal the 'essence' of time and cinema as a time-based medium (C2: 43). Deleuze will mark the appearance of time in the image not as past, present, future, but as direct and indirect time. The question that Fellini raised, as I discussed above, concerning subjectivity or being, is at the heart of Deleuze's proposal for a philosophy of difference rather than a philosophy of representation (C2: 99), where cinema is engaging a process of actualizing various conceptions of 'time'. Rather than oppose 'the real' and its illusory various cognitive states (perceptions or beliefs), Deleuze describes things in terms of the 'virtual' and 'actual' state of things (1994: 208). In discussing how film actualizes virtual states (such as thought and dreams), *Cinema 2* takes his earlier work on the philosophy of ideas (as an alternate proposition to the philosophy of representation) and extends his Bergsonian schema of creation through cinema's products and his discussion of cinema by thinkers like Artaud, and film makers including Welles, Resnais and Fellini. The actual or 'actualization' of things (for example, the actualization of Donnie's dreams or the theories of time from the pages of a textbook in *Donnie Darko*), in Deleuzian terms, is an act or process of 'genuine creation' (1994: 212).

Deleuze proposes Bergson's descriptions of the multi-planar dimensions of time as the method for discerning the various ways in which this actualization might occur, although he will describe how once certain 'crystalline images' or 'seeds of time' are created on screen, then the types of time-image enabled are in fact infinite (the theory behind this is Deleuze's Leibniz, see chapter 12 Topology). One of the key signaletic terms for the time-image, the crystalline image of time, is variously referred to in the cinema books as 'the time crystal', 'the crystal-image', 'seeds of time', 'mirrors of time' and the 'hyalosign', and appear where the expression of time coalesces, and the image both expresses and produces a composite (time-image) of different types of layers of time, and different signs of time, or crystalline circuits of time (see C2: Chapter 4, 'The Crystals of Time'). Each of these signs can then be discussed further in terms of the philosophical matter with which they are composed, and will create, and in terms of their relation with other sign-images. Deleuze also uses Bergson's tabulation of the different types of possible memory states: dreams, amnesia, déjà-vu, and conceptions of fantasy, hallucination and death; dream images (Deleuze calls these oniro-signs), memory-images (mnemosigns), thought-images (noosigns), order or relation-images (chronosigns), truth-images (genesigns), and sound-images (lectosigns). The *crystalline image of time* comes to describe its situation, as Deleuze explains the image is not one of a substitute sign (this sound-image standing in for that object), rather it has become the entire composition of time: 'Rosebud' (Welles 1941), or the ghost ship of *Les Trois couronnes du matelot* (*Three crowns of the sailor*; dir. Ruiz, 1982; cf. Goddard 2011) or the figure of Frank (Kelly 2001) (C2: 126). As such, the time-images will come to affect the values of the open-system of images, which Deleuze describes in terms of the 'powers of the false', in relation to description, narrative, and questions of 'truth' (see chapter 12 Topology and chapter 11 Politics). First, the terms of the Deleuzian time-image must be clarified.

Continuing the discussion of the movement-image, frame and shot, and montage of *Cinema 1*, Deleuze will discuss the way that montage can produce an 'image of time' through its activity of producing a whole (C2: 34–35). This is a stable form of time, where montage 'selects and co-ordinates' moments of time (images and sounds of events and icons that might be inserted into another image). Deleuze notes that this indirect image of time is contradicted when there appears to be no affective linkage of perception and action images; when there is a break in the 'sensory-motor schema' of the movement-image, and where time-images appear as direct images; 'pure optical and sound situations' (op-signs and son-signs) (C2: 40–41). These are instances of crystals of time appearing as an expression of a 'mutual image' (C2: 69): a crystal image, where an image enters into a relation with its own screen image (C2: 69). Through this exchange of actual and virtual images, the image becomes autonomous and independent of movement, and is a seed of time to be found in all types of environments and expressed in all kinds of screen conditions.

Through his discussion of the crystal-image, Deleuze references Bergson's diagrams for four different types of temporal schemas from *Matter and Memory* (each are reproduced in Deleuze's notes in *Cinema 2*):

1. The circuit (or the internal limit);
2. The inverse cone;
3. The dissymmetrical jets;
4. The event.

Each of these four diagrams influences the direction of Deleuze's discussion on particular aspects of the time-image (C2: 289, 294, 295, 297). In what follows I look at each of these in terms of Deleuze's methodological approach to the different aspects of the time-image.

The first diagram illustrates Bergson's first schema of time as the circuit of the internal limit (diagram illustration C2: 289). Deleuze discusses the 'circuit' of the actual and the virtual in terms of Bergsons's description of how 'memory [is] immediately consecutive to perception' (C2: 289). Deleuze variously describes this function on the time-image as a psychological issue of perception, or 'recognition' or 'reflection', a 'zone of recollections, dreams or thoughts', describing the doubling movement of 'creation and erasure', or creation and destruction of forms (C2: 44–46; C2: 126–147; Bogue 2003:112–133). This circuit describes a crystal of time (which Deleuze also refers to as hyalosigns); the beyond of the movement-image is created through op-signs and son-signs – these are points or vectors of direct-time. This is a circuit, such as Fellini describes, and which Donnie Darko experiences, where the past is present, but is in fact altered by its present state. The actualization of the past is the circuit. Deleuze discusses this, giving examples of various temporal/recollective states, including 'paramnesia' (the sense of *déja-vu*), memories and dreams (often technically constructed in film as 'flashbacks' or 'flash forwards', and outlines Bergson's 'major theses on time' as Kantian (C2: 79; 79–82; cf. Deleuze 1984). Deleuze gives three examples that express this circuit of 'being in time', of the 'internal' situation of time, of the definition of time as 'the affection of self by self': Dovzhenko's *Zvenigora* (1928, about life

in the Ukraine, part of a three part trilogy (see Liber 2002), Deleuze also mentions Dovzhenko's *Zemlya* (*Earth*, 1930)), Hitchcock's *Vertigo* (1958), and
Resnais's *Je t'aime, je t'aime* (1968) (C2: 82–3). Furthermore, different types
of interconnections are made on screen with opsigns and sonsigns through
other types of time-images, and thus are descriptive of Bergson's relational
circuit of 'constant creation or reconstruction' (Bergson 1994: 103; C2: 34;
cf. Bogue 2003: 108; cf. Colman 2005a). The circuit of 'exchange' between
actual image and virtual image creates new time-images and different types of
narrative strategies (C2: 68; 71). In *Donnie Darko* the image of Frank the rabbit functions to signal variations in time for Donnie. The instructions for the
ending of the world in *Southland Tales*, like the predictions given in *Donnie
Darko*, coalesce into the actual images of the film through an exchange of
temporal perception. This is made possible, says Deleuze, through a corre-
spondence between the 'two sides' of an image: 'actual and virtual' (C2: 68,
original emphasis). This is the crystal of time, as Deleuze describes it, or the
very being of cinema's time-process, its ontological process of the material
expression and the assemblage of ideas of time.

The second diagram is Bergson's inverted cone from *Matter and Memory*,
which Deleuze describes in *Difference and Repetition* as 'a gigantic memory'
(1994: 212; diagram illustration C2: 294). The cone illustrates what is created
through the circuit of the virtual image; between present and past through
recollection-images, this is the 'little crystalline seed' (C2: 81). Deleuze
performs a topological movement here, asking us to engage with the various circuits of the virtual actual and imagine them expanding outwards from
the seed. The cone illustrates the second aspect of the crystal-image, says
Deleuze, the first was the circuit, which defines its 'internal limit', the second,
the cone, illustrates its 'outer-most, variable and reshapable envelope [...] the
vast crystallisable universe' (81).

The third of Bergson's temporal schemas is the split into dissymmetrical
jets (diagram illustration C2: 295). This diagram illustrates the operations
of the time-image as a topology with two types of operational functions –
algebraic and quantum. The spilt, tearing or opening of time into new pathways, is one of the fundamental (and most commented upon aspects) of time

consistency. This is the moment where time splits 'at the same time as it sets itself out or unrolls itself', writes Deleuze; further, this split 'is time, that we *see in the crystal*' (C2: 81, original emphasis). How this fracture is depicted on screen provides much scope for film analysis.

The fourth diagram illustrates the event. This is Bergson's 'fourth schema of time', where the event is given value through a graphical method of memory intersecting with history. History is illustrated as longitudinal: something that 'passes along the event', intersecting with memory, as vertical region (diagram illustration C2: 297). Deleuze discusses this in his 'fourth commentary on Bergson', chapter 5 of *Cinema 2*, discussing Fellini's comment concerning a direct time-image, where the process of memory can be thought of in various ways – as a 'Being-memory' (for example Donnie Darko's character), or as a 'world-memory' (a character's composition through the larger world they inhabit and the relations and institutional laws that direct their disposition) (C2: 98). History is constituted through the organization of language and ideas, in which time has become the event. Deleuze explains this in terms of St Augustine's definition of time: a logic of a 'threefold present' that contains the present of present things, the present of past things, and the present of future things (C2: 99–10; St. Augustine 1962: 251–277). The time-image that contains this type of simultaneity 'gives narration a new value', says Deleuze, 'because it abstracts it from all successive action, as far as it replaces the movement-image with a genuine time-image' (C2: 101) (Deleuze gives the example of Robbe-Grillet's work, and engages a point of difference between Robbe-Grillet and Resnais (C2: 104), but we might equally consider Richard Kelly, David Lynch, Chantal Akerman or Sofia Coppola's respective films on this point). Thus, for Deleuzian film theory or for film philosophy to describe the temporal situation, analysis must first qualify its terms (or conditional regional values, correlations, etc.) as a specific point on the circuit. For an example of this specificity, consider Deleuze's taxonomic analysis of the variations of temporal repetition in Buñuel's work: a 'forgetfulness' in *Susana* (also known as *The Devil and the Flesh*, 1951), an 'exact repetition' in *El Ángel exterminador* (*The Exterminating Angel*, 1962), or a 'deepening' of the circuit in *Belle de Jour* (1967), and so on (C2: 102). On screen time can be organized

Patricia Pisters describes it, as a function of the brain that is shaped by film (2003: 39; 2011).

The time-image as a 'crystalline' image has also produced a number of interpretations. Rodowick sees it as 'multifaceted' (1997: 92). Rodowick will carefully qualify that, for Deleuze, the physical and mental description of something is mixed through the Bergsonian circuits of movement that the object and its mental image must go through (*ibid.*: 92–3). Bogue reminds us of the possibilities of surface facets of the crystal; as being both transparent and opaque simultaneously, and as an image that holds both the actual image (the thing) and its virtual (thought or non-physicality) (2003: 122–3). Deleuze provides a critical appraisal of two aspects of life as a virtual and mirrored existence (C2: 79), directing us to attend to the 'two orders of problems' that arise from consideration of this relationship of the exchange between 'mutual images' (C2: 69). This mutuality causes issues of the virtual and the actual or the real to be evoked in discussions of temporality, and the doubling of the image that occurs on screen.

To account for the range of new components of the image that this seeding opens up, Deleuze discusses the topological functions and modes of the image. The 'essential' point of the image is revealed not by a judgement of the 'true' or 'false' nature of the image (C2: 128). Rather the image can never be known, only expressed though a temporal 'fracture' or dislocation of space – points where narration becomes false movement (C2: 136).

11

Politics

Under the terms of a philosophy of difference, Deleuze's approach to film teaches us that every screen text is political. In the logic of this system, movement-images reveal the falsity of narrative 'truth' and time-images hold the 'potential' for different types of 'becoming' to happen. The Deleuzian ciné-system directs us to recognize the terms of perceptual activity that different activities of the screen enable as different choices, contingent upon and enabling political beliefs.

Politics is the practice and the theory of the organization and control of things. In the implementation of political authority, strategies and tactics will vary according to activity and beliefs. While many filmmakers, theorists and philosophers will deny that their work is 'political', the fact remains that a work – screen work or philosophy – is composed through a particular aesthetic territory and situated by a specific political culture that marks the production of even the most abstracted of ideas. As an entity funded through a variety of different sources, the types of political persuasions that influence the outcomes of philosophy and screen-based media production are as many as the work itself is able to generate.

What Deleuze's theory of the cinema shows us is that image-based media are able to actualize things through their relational circuit of images and produce new autonomous things by this circuit. It is not a matter of the 'representation' of time as 'real' or 'imaginary' or 'virtual' or 'psychological' in film that concerns Deleuze's discussion of time on screen (C2: 109). Instead, Deleuze continues his philosophical exegesis of the actualization of worlds created and events of belief and of bodies charted in cinema. Deleuze extends his Bergsonian approach to the movement of time with Nietzschian perspective on the components of the topologies of time that cinema is able to produce, as the 'actual present' (C2: 109). As Patricia Pisters contends, the time-image is thus fundamentally an image of a political cinema where a 'change in the relation between image and life' means that 'the time-image can no longer be judged in opposition to life' (Pisters 2003: 77). Hence, the potential of this medium lies in its ability to provide, facilitate and develop political expression. It is what philosopher Jean-Luc Nancy referred to in relation to Iranian director Abbas Kiarostami's work as 'the affirmation of cinema by cinema' (Nancy 2001: 10; cf. Kiarostami 2002). But in Deleuzian terms, the cinematic extends beyond an affirmation to create a doubled production that mutates and creates and causes specific differences to affected images and objects. In discussing his open-system as one where 'appearances' are clearly demonstrated to be linked to systems of judgement (C2: 138), where the 'conditions' of the image need to be accounted for not in terms of the aesthetics of 'the real and the imaginary' or in the political terms of 'the true and the false' (C2: 274), but in terms of thought and events (C2: 272), then it is clear that Deleuze's project with cinema has all along been to engage it as *the* political media of the twentieth century. Deleuze's argument is one that is developed extensively in the work of diverse authors: for example, Steven Shaviro with attention to the types of cinematic bodies that cinema produces (Shaviro 1993); Kara Keeling with regard to black women on screen (Keeling 2007); Alison Butler in relation to 'women's cinema' and the 'minor' (Butler 2002); and Jonathon Beller with regard to the modes of production that the different type of organizations that film taps into is able to mediate (Beller 2006).

What is Political Cinema?

Exactly what constitutes a 'political' cinema will vary according to cultural specificity. For example, the implicit type of workers and health and safety jokes of the Disney Pixar production of *Ratatouille* (dirs. Brad Bird and Jan Pikava, 2007) will not translate to audiences whose notion of the cultural politics of cooking are not invested in a Disneyfied French culture. Other films with scenes of the dimensions of the preparation of food engage entirely different sets of cultural economies. Compare the breadth of political differences between films such as *Tampopo* (dir. Juzo Itami, 1985), *Babettes gæstebud* (*Babette's feast*; dir. Gabriel Axel, 1987); *Politiki Kouzina* (*Political kitchen*; dir. Tassos Boulmetis, 2003) and *Bakjwi* (*Thirst*; dir. Chan-wook Park, 2009). The theme of sustenance, while a universal human activity, does not convey a universal political condition.

Different industry expectations and culturally specific values impact upon forms of cinema. The terms of nationally specific censorship laws and the markets of global distribution impose further limitations on screen products. Genre films may mask national controls, for example, as in the neo-western *Fah talai jone* (*Tears of the black tiger*; dir. Wisit Sasanatieng, 2000: the first film from Thailand to be selected for competition at the Cannes Film Festival). *Fah talai jone*'s style demonstrates the colonial tensions and break-up between peoples using a non-explicit aesthetic. In *Sud Sanaeha* (Blissfully yours; dir. Apichatpong Weerasethakul, 2002), the tensions between Thailand and its ex-colonial neighbour, The Republic of the Union of Myanmar (Burma), are carefully wrapped in the humidity of the landscape and characters, and the political activity of medical care of another. Films like these tacitly engage

Goya does in 'The Disasters of War' (1810 and 1820). The chiaroscuro line is part of how Deleuze thinks through his notion of vector forms, linking points of heterogeneous elements in what he calls the skeleton-space, theoretically developed through a combination of French art historian François Cheng's theory of empty and full space in Chinese landscape painting (1979) and French philosopher Henri Maldiney's notions of affect and space (1973).

Throughout his discussion of the time-image Deleuze frequently makes topological allusions, continuing his discussion of Plato's theory of Forms (cf. Cooper 1997; Fine 1995). These include references to the common idea of 'space', but include more nuanced and complex accounts of spatial forms. Deleuze develops the notion of 'strata', previously discussed in *A Thousand Plateaus,* as a geological allusion to the philosophical ground upon which he draws in order to construct his philosophy of difference (cf. Protevi and Bonta 2004). Further, there are two parts to this hidden ground that Deleuze develops through topological thinking: (1) 'presents which pass', and (2) 'pasts which are preserved' (C2: 98). These are the terms of memory and the terms of recollection. Deleuze divides these two into further categories. Memory has a number of different states (as we previously discussed with the time-image) in terms of the topology of time. Deleuze is interested to qualify the chronosign, or the ordering and relation-image of time. He defines two types of chronosigns topologically:

1. *'aspects'* (regions and layers of time);
2. *'accents'* (points of view) (C2: 101).

This topology of time sets up two divergent paths for Deleuze. On the one hand he discusses the 'stubborn geometry' of the visual image in reference to the life-long work of Cézanne who created an exhaustive series of paintings and drawings of Mont Sainte-Victoire in Aix-en-Provence, France. On the counter side, to further investigate topological aspects and accents, Deleuze gives even more figures of thinking stemming from the action-image and the time-image: the dialectic of respiration and the crystal seed. Russian cinema gives this form: 'With Dovzhenko, the large form – SAS'– receives from the dialectic a "respiration", an oneiric and symphonic power overflowing the boundaries of the organic' (C1: 180).

The topology of movement appears in the montage image where Deleuze notes that a development of different types of perception occurred – at the molecular and the molar levels (C1: 80). Deleuze describes 'liquid' and 'solid' perception (*ibid.*). As Tom Conley has explained, the molecular is what 'enables Deleuze to move from a philosophy of relation (or difference and repetition) to chemistries of being, and then on to delicate issues of perception in cinema, music, literature and painting' (Conley 2005: 173–174). Similarly, the molar is a conception of the elemental and chemical constitution of things. In Deleuze and Guattari's conception the molar provides the eternal dimensions (as in Whitehead's conception of eternal objects) of things and aesthetics – at both an organic and at a machinic level (cf. Guattari 1995; Robinson 2008). In his cinema books Deleuze will engage the natural and manufactured elemental range of earth, fire, air and water as paradigmatic provisos of material and virtual values for articulating eternal aspects of aesthetic and political cinemas. Again, as Conley points out, the important effect of this unique methodological approach to cinema 'tends to jettison the psychological inflections' for an elemental approach to demonstrating and discussing the cinematographic (Conley 2005: 171–172). The appearance of molar elements in the cinema books can be realized as a signal for the switching of poles, and the registration of micro or macro events. The event is the screen event itself, but also the events of the screen itself – actioning agency for new or mutated forms and meanings to be consolidated or actualized.

Topologies are formed, says Deleuze, by the redistributed, coexistent, transformed and fragmented forms (C2: 119–120). Cinematic conditions continually produce topologies through these shifts and constant layers of images. The various forms of action-image, for example, open out multiple modes for the trans-morphological situation of an action to a new or mutated form (as both molar and molecular forms). Consideration of the topological dimensions of this built image enable Deleuze to consider the dynamic qualities and potential capacity of the screen (C1: 13). This enables Deleuze to argue how the functional 'reality' of objects and settings that appear in an action-image film are determined by their situations. This multiplicity is substantive, which may be contradictory, limiting or even 'impossible' – such as the temporal domains inferred in films like *Un Chien Andalou* (dirs. Luis Buñuel and Salvador Dali, 1928) or *Ritual in Transfigured Time* (dir. Maya Deren, 1946), *La Jetée* (dir. Chris Marker, 1962), *Dark City* (dir. Alex Proyas, 1998), *Donnie Darko, The Hours* (dir. Stephen Daldry, 2002), *Dolls* (dir. Takeshi Kitano, 2002), whose spaces Deleuze explains, after Leibniz, as the 'incompossible worlds' of complex narratives (C2: 131: 303 n5).[6] Or we might consider the layered images of histories and memories which Deleuze will discuss in terms of 'de-actualized peaks of the present' and 'virtual sheets of the past' (C2: 130). For example, consider the topological forms created through the inferences and images of the present and past in films such as *Yeogo goedam* (*Whispering corridors*; dir. Park Ki-hyung, 1998), a ghost story that is embedded with various histories of Korea, or *Marie Antoinette* (dir. Coppola, 2006), where the siting of a historical narrative is mutated and multiplied through the various sound-images that re-situate the story (converse sneakers and 'Hong Kong Garden' (Siouxsie and the Banshees, 1978) in Versaille, France).

What such images do, says Deleuze, is create the 'incompossible' worlds that Leibniz describes, but also create a 'new co-ordinate of the image', namely the power to 'falsify' (C2: 132). The 'form of the true' is something that Deleuze has addressed throughout the cinema volumes, used as a test against 'false movement', and he marks a philosophical shift in thinking about the differences between these two powers (as staged, variously, by figures such as Leibniz, Nietzsche, Melville, Borges) to the cinematographic power that replaced the false and the true with the 'powers of life' (C2: 133–135).

Deleuze also conceptualizes cinematic changes through the 'topological and cartological limits' that historical shifts and types of images and their corresponding signs create (C2: 118). The 'break' is something that 'reveals' what exists 'before or after speech, before or after man' – this is the 'strata' of the visual-image, which Deleuze says is now (after 'the break') '*archaeological, stratigraphic, tectonic*' (C2: 243, original emphasis). The break in the Deleuzian, neo-Platonic sense as created by screen-based forms shows itself to be the space that Blanchot identified: where a 'vertigo of spacing' generates not only new places (in both horrific and awesome forms) but also engages the circuit of subjectivity (C2: 180; cf. Blanchot 1992). This is the image of thought that is created through a body acting as a 'topological, cerebral space' (C2: 147). There are five physical laws Deleuze associates with the large form – including different types of narrational strategies useful for genre analysis and description – 'nested' structures, gaps and passages between action, and other structural devices. Deleuze addresses the large form through classical cinema genres – the western, noir and classical documentary film. It is also useful to think of large form in terms of the screen genres it engages, of war on screen, science-fiction screen forms, and serial formats, such as dramas and comedies. Conceptually the large form describes collectives, which are at the opposite spectrum of screen situations to vectors (the small forms described in *Vector*). A collective structure is readily explored through a community – and what better place to see a community in inter/action than in a western (cf. Colman 2009a; dir. Jarmusch 1995).

The 'crystalline seed' is the process Deleuze describes as introducing potential time sites with which to bring about a whole crystal of time. The crystalline seed is 'a component element' of the 'infinite' state of a time crystal. This seeding is different to creating vectorial moments in the cinema, although similar in terms of the spatial creation of a screen field, the crystalline seed has 'a capacity for indefinite growth' and the vector situates a specific point in space (C2: 89). Deleuze gives the example of Resnais's filmmaking, where the vectorial point, 'the centre or fixed point', disappears from the film altogether (C2: 116). The vector is replaced with the seed and the difference is neuronic – the seed will make us think, will invoke memory conditions, introduce other topologies of time, and is not concerned with narrative continuity or creating breaks that would later be filled.

Deleuze further breaks down this organization of space on screen by the crystal into main types (C2: 82–90):

1. ritornello (sound territory (C2: 92));
2. memory (multiple and simultaneous (C2: 99));

3. historical and social (the 'too-late' of history (C2: 92));
4. archaeological (entropic (C2: 93));
5. kinaesthetic (where Deleuze points to the mirror crystal, not movement).

Deleuze describes a number of different situations where these different types of crystal-image occur. The ritornello is a concept defined through thinking about sound territories such as a bird that sings at sunrise, marking the new day (cf. Deleuze and Guattari 1987: 299, 308). A ritornello is Guattari's Italian word for the refrain, a recognizable song (C2: 92, 296 n34). On screen sound is used as a sign for images as well as being a stand-alone image. Deleuze describes how sound in cinema is able to create a 'passage' from 'one world to another' and this power holds a profoundly political as well as stylistic topological agency (C2: 63). Characters in narrative film, for example, engage the refrain/ritornello as a way of marking out as well as testing territorial boundaries: for example, see the actions of Tony Manero (actor John Travolta) in *Saturday Night Fever* (dir. John Badham, 1977), or the (nameless) man (actor Kang-sheng Lee) and the woman (actor Kun-huei Lin) in *Dong* (*The Hole*; dir. Tsai Ming-liang, 1998), or Tracy Turnblad (actor Nicki Blonsky) in *Hairspray* (dir. Adam Shankman, 2007). Territorial affects are also created through sound topologies, as in *Jaws* (dir. Steven Spielberg, 1975) or *Dead Man* (dir. Jarmusch, 1995). Deleuze also comments on how musicals can create topologies through their 'dreamlike power', how 'reality' is restaged by the musical's staging of passages between worlds, 'breaking in and exploring' (C2: 61–67). Deleuze describes the affective behaviour of comic figures Stan Laurel and Oliver Hardy, Buster Keaton, and Jerry Lewis, and gives examples from classic Hollywood genre films, including director Stanley Donen's films *Singin' in the Rain* (1952) and *The Pyjama Game* (1957), Vincente Minnelli's films *An American in Paris* (1951), *The Band Wagon* (1953), *Brigadoon* (1954) and Jacques Tati's films *Les Vacances de Monsieur Hulot* (*Monsieur Hulot's Holiday*, 1953), *Play Time* (1967), *Trafic* (1971), noting that with Lewis and Tati, the 'set' replaces the 'situation' of the image (C2: 67).

Another key example Deleuze discusses is how the event of war produces 'the crystal-image' as a direct presentation of time, an event of the here and now, even if it is one of an 'hallucinatory' landscape (C2: 128–9). Deleuze will discuss how Fellini develops his method of accessing different modes of time through the figure of the 'crystal' and the 'crystalline seed', which he describes in topological terms. Rather like the vector, the crystal in Fellini's work, says Deleuze, is an 'entrance', infinite and multiple (C2: 88–89). 'The crystal image was not time, but we see time in the crystal' (C2: 81). In addition to post-war film styles Deleuze marks other points of change with various events in the cinema books – the 'new wave' of cinemas (he mentions examples from French, Italian, Japanese, German but these occur globally at different times), other activities of militarism, or surveillance society, national incidents, stylistic shifts, and the philosophical epistemic break caused by the cinematographic depiction of time putting 'the notion of truth into crisis' (C2: 130).

Deleuze also notes that change does not always imply quantitative movement. Rather change can occur in-place, that is to say, in specific sites and bodies such as in memory or consciousness and in what we term the temporal dimension. Change can also be qualitative, enabling perception in the sometimes dark, complex places created by virtual and actual data that coagulate as quantum energies. These become vectorial points for further movement or provide reference points: signs and indices. The images in *Struktura kryształu* (Zanussi), *4* (Khzhanovsky), *M* (Lang), *Donnie Darko* (Kelly), or *The Virgin Suicides* (Coppola, 1999), *Stranger than Fiction* (dir. Marc Forster, 2006), or *Angus, Thongs and Perfect Snogging* (dir. Gurinder Chadha, 2008) provide cinematographic consciousness of this data-change, creating forms of time-images that measure, organize and express the course of perception, duration, thought, becoming, time. Movement becomes stilled as different types of time-images – what Deleuze describes as the 'crystal-image' acts as vectors, forms and layers of time (C2: 68). Deleuze's approach shows that even within a singular there is an 'open list of logical conjunctions ("or", "therefore", "if", "because", "actually", "although …")', plus *'and'* itself (C2: 23; 214). Such conjunctions may be added to indicate a result, however, as we can see within any vectorial field of the screen an infinite array of the different types and modes of cinema arise. When a 'break' occurs,

What is Thought/the Thought-image?

How, when you watch and listen to films, do they make you think? Is there time within the filmic construction to allow you to reflect upon what is unfolding, or drawing you in, or making you emotively react? Or is the screen work so tightly constructed that there are no gaps outside of its world, or is it edited together so fast that there are no pauses for your thoughts to enter the sound-images that your brain is processing, and it is not until afterwards that the ideas of the image start to take form?

Thought is a process that cinema equally stimulates and stifles. Thought is something that is produced or directed by images. Critical consideration of thought in and as produced by the screen is still in its infancy, as developments in realms of new forms of media and new understanding of the neurological and physiological processes of the human body continue to expand our understanding of the capacity of the thinking being (cf. Ione 2005; Frampton 2006; Pisters 2011). Deleuze argues that a new image of attitudes of the body eventualize: 'The body is sound as well as visible, all the components of the image come together on the body' (C2: 193).

Deleuze begins his chapter on 'Thought and Cinema' with a series of propositions about cinema as a very specific art form and the cerebral medium of thought (C2: 156). The points he makes in the opening pages of this chapter revisit and develop the opening pages of his first 'Thesis on movement' on 'movement and instant' in *Cinema 1* (C1: 1–3). Deleuze begins by reminding us that the technical nature of producing the cinematographic image means that images automatically have movement. In that, they differ from static art forms or performative forms already attached to a moving body. Most images in the cinema are of an intellectual kind which we recognize through cognitive processes. Deleuze contends that when movement 'becomes automatic' then the 'artistic essence' of an image is realized and the image changes (C2: 156). If cognition is disturbed, shocked or interrupted, then our intellectual thoughts move from an automatic intellectual movement to a state of 'spiritual' automatism (*ibid.*). The terms Deleuze uses to describe these different types of thought-images are 'automatic movement' (from art historian Eli

Faure) and 'spiritual automaton' (from Spinoza) (C2: 308 n1, n3; C2: 310 n 19; Bogue 2003: 165–166). In his notes Deleuze cites Faure who argues that between materialist and spiritual images 'there is a constant reversibility between technical and affective nature' (C2: 308 n1). Deleuze engages this reversibility through his method of duelling and various movement-image forms, asking if images can instigate a kind of cerebral massage, a vibration to the nervous system, that 'shocks' the viewer into thinking, or if images merely reinforce already determined worlds and patterns of thought (C2: 156–157; cf. Massumi 2002b).

As Deleuze calls it, the utopic promise of cinema as an art form that would alter the thoughts of men was never realized: 'this pretension of the cinema, at least among the greatest pioneers, raises a smile today' (C2: 157). Deleuze is of course referring to the *sublime* ideas of early cinema, such as the 'mathematical' of Gance, the 'dynamic' of F.W. Murnau, and the 'dialectical' of Eisenstein (C2: 157). Instead, as Deleuze notes of Virilio's thesis, 'the system of war mobilizes perception' to the extent that 'the whole of civil life' 'passes into the mode of the mise-en-scène' (C2: 309 n16). In his two books on the cinema and in *Nietzsche and Philosophy* and *Difference and Repetition*, Deleuze reminds us of the nature of the *technologically expanded relationship* between image and thought that is at once immanent and productive of a range of spiritual automaton. 'Cinema is dying, then, from its quantitive mediocrity', he writes in the second part of 'Cinema and thought' (C2: 164). In *Difference and Repetition* Deleuze also explored the question of thinking, noting that 'Artaud said that the problem (for him) was not to orient his thought, or to perfect the expression of what he thought, or to acquire application and method or to perfect his poems, but simply to manage to think something' (1994: 147). Deleuze opens his chapter on 'Thought and Cinema' with a comparative consideration of thinking itself, citing German philosopher Martin Heidegger: 'Man can think in the sense that he posses the possibility to do so. This possibility alone, however, is no guarantee to us that we are capable of thinking' (C2: 156). Heidegger's question of the as-yet untapped capacity for humans to think provides a catalytic point for Deleuze's focus on 'Thought and Cinema' (C2: 156). Heidegger also viewed the product of creative work as holding some form of spiritual resonance, and his work thus provides an interesting comparative juncture for thinking Deleuze and cinematographic consciousness (cf. Bolt 2004: 100). Like Heidegger's historical investigation of the question of 'being', Deleuze sketches out a historicization of the question of thinking as it is determined by the nature of cinema (cf. Lampert 2006). In this framework Bergson's thesis of cinematographic consciousness still holds true, and Deleuze refocuses his taxonomy of thought-images on the site of that consciousness – the body.

The states of the body must be considered in terms of their everydayness and their theatricalization. Plato's cave of political prisoners and masters provides a useful model here (cf. Sinnerbrink 2009: 29). The Spinozist affective topology Deleuze discusses in the affection-image and in the creation of a political cinema leads him to reverse the 'philosophical formula' of body before thought; instead Deleuze places the 'unthinking body' first (C2: 189). 'Life will no longer be made to appear before the categories of thought; thought will be thrown into the categories of life' (*ibid.*). Instead, Spinoza's request 'give me a body then', he writes, 'is to first mount the camera on an everyday body' (C2: 189). It is by doing this, or the conceptualization of this, that the 'everyday body' can become the 'ceremonial body', thereby freeing the individualized body from its rigid series of meaning, and opening up the potential of becoming something else, of joining another temporal pathway or finding another 'attitude of the body' (C2: 190–191).

How Deleuze Uses Thought

Deleuze credits director Hitchcock for making obvious the mental relations cinema produces as the thought-image. 'Hitchcock's premonition will come true,' he writes at the start of *Cinema 2*: 'a camera-consciousness which would no longer be defined by the movements it is able to follow or make, but by the mental connections it is able to enter into' (C2: 23). It is Hitchcock, Deleuze confirms at the end of *Cinema 2*, who 'introduces the mental image into the cinema' (C2: 203). The cinema is able to create new kinds of spaces through the 'architecture of vision', but more specifically, as Deleuze points out, through the architectural relations created by bodies in space. The 'attitudes and postures of the body', create a 'scenery' (C2: 193; cf. Hitchcock 1945; 1954). Hitchcock's is an intellectual cinema, a cinema that offers obvious cognitive functionality, as he had first included the viewer in the film, notes Deleuze, and then inverts this identification so that 'the character has become some kind of viewer' (C2: 3; cf. Hitchcock's films *Rope*, 1948; *Rear Window*, 1954; *Vertigo*, 1958).

Deleuze argues that mental reflection, the thought-image, is 'a cinema of bodies which mobilizes the whole of thought' (C2: 206). He arrives at this point by making a series of thematic conjunctions charting the evolution of cinematic forms of the movement and time-images of the twentieth century. He distinguishes two forms of cinema – intellectual and physical – giving the example of Antonioni as being a director whose style encompasses both camps (C2: 204). The themes of the everyday – such as we see in Akerman, Warhol (*Empire*, 1964, *Eat*, 1963, *Kiss*, 1963), or Abbas Kiarostami (*Ten*, 2002; *Ta'm e guilass* (*A Taste of Cherry*), 2005) – develop under the lens to extremes of stylization and exaggeration of themes, acting, narratives and abstract associations. In this way the screen turns the 'physics of the body' into the 'everyday or the ceremonial', or the 'formal and informal "eidetics" of the spirit' – a division that roughly follows the technical and affective nature that Faure sketched out (C2: 204).

If we look at the first division Deleuze makes here, we can see the physics of the body determining screen forms. For example, the vernacular burlesque of Charlie Chaplin *The Immigrant* (1917) informs the standing characters of everyday life. This interest begins to realize itself through cinema that focuses increasingly upon actors' gestures and bodies in ordinary situations, such as we see in *Jeanne Dielman* or the encounter with a young girl's pregnant belly in *Umberto D* (C2: 1–2) (De Sica 1952), or in scenes of the 'volcanic island of poor fisherman' (C2: 20) in Visconti's *La Terra Trema* (*The earth trembles*, 1948) – but there is a shift in the perceptual ability of the types of characters on screen and in the viewer's perceptual ability. Deleuze argues this comes about through the actions of neorealist cinema, where the 'eye takes up a clairvoyant function' (Deleuze recalling the clairvoyant of *Ladri di biciclette* (*Bicycle Thief*; dir. De Sica, 1948) (C2: 22). Deleuze charts this perceptual shift through twentieth-century cinematic styles, from the Italian neorealist era, addressing specific scenes, characters and themes from films by Rossellini (1945; 1946; 1948; 1952), De Sica (1948; 1952), Visconti (1948; 1960) to the Italian New Wave era of Antonioni (1960) and Fellini, and French New Wave of Godard (C2: 170). Artaud's writing on the cinema provides much of the impetus for Deleuze's understanding that the 'new cinema' (of neo-realism, of new waves of the 1960s, and other new waves) functions *organically*, as op-posed to the movement of sensorially oriented action-images. Artaud's 1933 essay, 'The Premature Old Age of the Cinema', provides some catalyzing and clarifying points for Deleuze's orientation in his own chapter on thought. Here Artaud lays out a foundation for thinking about the 'organic functioning' of the 'study' of the cinema (Artaud 1976: 311).[1]

The second division – Deleuze constantly searches and expresses the linguistic constraints of expressing the *eidetic function* of the sound-image through both cinema volumes. That is, the cinematic mode of production of sound-images is a medium that is exceptionally vivid in its perception of the world: a form that gives shape to the affective movement of thought. This is the cinema of the brain which 'reveals the creativity of the world' (C2: 205; Deleuze discusses Kubrick's films; *2001: A Space Odyssey*, 1968; *A Clockwork Orange*, 1971; *The Shining*, 1980; and Resnais's *Van Gogh*, 1948; *Je t'aime, je t'aime*, 1968; *Mon oncle d'Amérique* (*My American Uncle*), 1980). The cin-ematic image works by 'affective composition' where, as Deleuze argues, even the different types of the use of metaphor can be seen not as a 'technique' but as a 'fusion' (C2: 160–161). For example, psychological memory can be expressed in film as a flashback (often signalled by a visual or sound motif) to create what Deleuze described as 'dream-images' (C2: 273). 'Even when the European cinema restricts itself to dream, fantasy, or day-dreaming, its ambition is to bring the *unconscious mechanisms of thought* to conscious-ness' (C2 160, emphasis in original). Deleuze notes that dream-images 'affect the whole', as they 'project the sensory-motor situation to infinity, sometimes by ensuring the constant metamorphosis of the situation, sometimes by replacing the action of the characters with a movement of the world' (C2: 273). We see these images in a range of films, *La coquille et la clergyman* (dir. Germain Dulac, 1928); *I Was a Teenage Werewolf* (dir. Gene Fowler Jr, 1957); Hitchcock's *Spellbound*; *Harry Potter and the Prisoner of Azkaban* (dir. Cuarón, 2004). Resnais provides a focal point for much of Deleuze's address of the thought-image. 'Resnais conceives of cinema not as an instrument for representing reality but as the best way of approaching the way the mind functions.' (C2: 121).

Deleuze provides three points for orienting his address of the new cinema of the body and the brain:

1. the point-cut;
2. relinkage;
3. the black or white screen.

The point-cut is the quality of something (as Deleuze discusses with the affection-image). 'The brain has lost its Euclidean co-ordinates, and now emits other signs' (C2: 278). Relinkage is the image of thought – the noosign 'an image which goes beyond itself towards something which can only be thought' (C2 Glossary). Relinkage is the concept of the intellectual or elastic mind in its serial mutation. The black and white screen is the 'inpower of thought' that Blanchot describes as what 'forces us to think' (C2: 168): the space for thinking – Jarmusch's black screen, Derek Jarman's blue screen or the Straub's political cinema, or the camera-less cinema of Len Lye (C2: 215; cf. dir. Jarman's *Blue*, 1993; Macarow 2003; dir. Lye 1958–1979).

Deleuze rejects previous philosophical positions on the metaphysics of concepts of 'the self', 'God' and 'world'. Instead he offers a method of how virtual relations create new conditions for life through an infinite passage of 'becoming' in which previously framed questions of 'true and false', 'belief' and 'reality', are replaced by questions of ethics and the forms of political topology. Becoming is a central concept in his final work, *Pure Immanence: Essays on a Life* (Deleuze 2001b). Developed through work on Nietzsche (1983), the cinema, with Guattari in *A Thousand Plateaus* (1987: 232–309), and finally in *Pure Immanence,* 'becoming' as a different/ciated passage critiques and dismantles previous conceptions of objective and finite positions (Deleuze 1994: 168ff; see chapter 13 Thought). As determined though the political framework of screen-based topologies (media forms of all kinds), *becoming* within the type of rhetorical cultures of perceptual militarization and infantalization that screen-based media configure is a concept that Deleuze explores and the mediatized movement of becoming is a question that his peers Foucault, Guattari and Virilio were also asking in their respective works (Guattari 1995; Virilio 1989; Deleuze 309 n16).

The Function of Thought

As Deleuze constructs them, *thought-images* operate through rhizomic means – as multiple networks that coalesce at points to form plateaus, planes of immanence, platforms of communication and new concepts (cf. Deleuze and Guattari 1987: 10). The cinema books lead us closer to identifying the types and modalities of thought that are produced by a particular film. This has political and ethical implications; Deleuze describes film as a method that makes us slaves bound to the chain of images. Philosophers will recognize the famous allusion here – it is the story that Plato told to describe cognition of the practice of institutional epistemology that makes people believe in their own slavery as the reality of the world (C2: 209).

Above all, thought has a political function for Deleuze – this is where the cinema screen has overtaken philosophy proper as the producer of thought. Deleuze gives many examples of this process through both cinema books. To take just one theme here, the nationalist structure of films concerning wars is addressed by Deleuze in terms of a Foucauldian biopolitics that performs its mutable genre of political differentiation (see chapter 11 Politics). The films that do this best, under the Deleuzian aesthetic criteria of exactly that 'operation' (C2: 179), are the films that perform 'the psychomechanics' of their cinematic perception. In this Deleuze cites Pasolini's 'insight about modern cinema' – the freedom to be gained through 'a free indirect discourse'

(C2: 183) where there is a 'demonstration' of the thought of the self-affecting 'cinema-form' (C2: 178). Godard's 'reflexive genres' are exemplars, argues Deleuze, of a series of genre *movements* where the 'determination of thought [and] choice' of this cinema-form is to be found in the intersticial. This is what Deleuze describes as the old associative agit-prop one might find in the dialectic sublimes of Eisenstein's montages (e.g., in *Oktyabr* (*October*), 1928, of monumental and the vernacular icons of a city, of objects of worship and fetish) – variously described by Deleuze as 'the point-cut' (C2: 213/215); 'a slip [lapsus]' (C2: 212); 'the relinkage of independent images' (C2 214; 215); and the screen itself as 'abstract or eidetic', 'black or white' (C2: 215) – each process creating an image where a sign or an axis of thought can occur. It is at these junctures, intensive moments, interstices and vectors, Deleuze says, where the 'cerebral process' occurs: 'A flickering brain, which relinks or creates loops – this is cinema' (C2: 215).

As we have already noted, the 'image' in the Deleuzian system is an element of the set (as in ensemble) of movement-images, of which the *perception-image* is a part. This set (comprised of movement-images of all types – including noise, soundtrack, dialogue and images) contributes to the *immanent nature of the image*, where any perceptual consciousness is 'in' something (rather than being as observed 'of' something). In Deleuze's philosophy *immanence* is the opposite of the type of transcendent position that phenomenology proposes (as a privileged mode of 'experience' of something, whether an economic, spiritual or gendered state). Deleuze takes Spinoza's position on immanence, regarding experience as being something created within a particular state or situation (Deleuze 1992: 169–172). Thus immanent states, such as perception, are to be understood in the Deleuzian sense as expressions created within the conditions of the image, not against or outside of them; they are an 'image of thought' (cf. Deleuze and Guattari 1994: 37; Lawlor 2003: 81). 'With the cinema, it is the world which becomes its own image', Deleuze argues, 'and not an image which becomes world' (C1: 57). We see this thesis produced by the disparate worlds of the skater in *Dogtown and Z Boys* (dir. Stacy Peralta 2001), the school children in Van Sant's *Elephant*, and in the communities in *Encounters at the End of the World* (dir. Herzog 2007).

Concerned with the technical at the level of the methods by which one can elaborate upon the material that the cinema provides, Deleuze will come up with his own technical language to express the cinematographic consciousness that the screen creates. How can we articulate the cinema's incredible ability to capture the sense of a moment in time, an impression of something or someone, a texture, a taste, a rendering of temporal modes such as memory and thought itself! Beyond the wonder of the technological feats of the cinematic lies the wonder of the neurological and sensorial affects of the image. How is it that we can watch something on screen and imagine a state of a future that could affect our conception of a past and how we then might interact with other things that we engage with in this world, with this virtual knowledge? In the spirit of thinking through the dimensions of the *reciprocity* required for the world to function humanely, Deleuze's ciné-philosophy engages these terms. 'When one relates movement to any-moment-whatevers, one must be capable of thinking the production of the new, that is, of the remarkable and the singular, at any one of these moments: this is the complete conversion of philosophy' (C1: 7).

The function of thought is political. *With our thoughts we make the world!*

14

Conclusion: Cinematographic Ethics

Classifying signs is an endless business, not least because there are an endless number of different classifications. What interests me is a rather special discipline, taxonomy, a classification of classifications, which, unlike linguistics, can't do without the notion of a sign.

Deleuze, *Negotiations: 1972–1990*

The breadth of the Deleuzian ciné-system enables Deleuze to consider the smallest of gestures that we might see on film in relation to the largest thing we can imagine. As Deleuze reminds us, it is the remarked upon smell from a bag of oranges from southern Italy that is able to present a sound-image that instantly sums up the dynamic temporal histories at play in Visconti's 1960 film *Rocco e i suoi fratelli* (*Rocco and His Brothers*) (C2: 4, 95). Deleuze is drawn to Visconti's work, as he charts in films like *Rocco* the 'inventory' of its setting, while in *Ludwig* (dir. Visconti 1973) 'little history is seen', but history

1. Deleuze's ciné-system determines the components of the moving sound image;
2. the system generates a language with which to express the nature of these cinematic elements;
3. it charts a ciné-philosophy that provides a new theory of forms and concepts, based on cinematographic consciousness.

As I demonstrate in this book, Deleuze's taxonomic approach is productive of many different methods for screen analysis, and these are not limited to pre-existing categories of analysis for screen-based works. For reasons of economy there are many components of the sound-image that Deleuze describes that I could not touch upon here. However, the reader should see that understood in the terms that I outline above, Deleuze's system offers a pragmatic taxonomy of cinema and a model of a dynamic film-philosophy, not a meta-philosophy. It composes and applies the discipline of taxonomy against the cinema's organic (movement-images) and crystalline (time-images) systems. The function of that taxonomy of the cinema is the production of a new philosophy from the cinematographic and this offers all kinds of extensions for and from film work (C2: 280; see also Mullarky's summation of Deleuze's cinema work in Mullarky 2009; and for examples in extensions of the Deleuzian film thinking, see Alliez 1996; 2004; Powell 2005; 2007; Zepke 2005; Keeling 2007; del Rio 2008; Rodowick 2010).

What are Cinematographic Ethics?

The philosophical significance of the cinema volumes is that they make explicit key aspects of the advent of Deleuze's mature philosophical thinking. They provide a conceptual bridge from the ancient theory of Forms through to an engagement with his peers Virilio, Foucault and Guattari's respective works on the politics of aesthetics and media forms, through to the writing of *Immanence, A Life* (Deleuze 2001b). In this way, these volumes register and provide a new theory of forms and concepts, based on cinematographic consciousness.

In the Deleuzian sense ethics have nothing to do with the sense of 'morality' that is associated with making a judgement on whether or not something is 'right' or 'wrong'.

Through his work Deleuze engages Spinoza's conception of ethics. This is a non-hierarchical method of considering the movement of bodies, which Deleuze develops in the context of the forms of movement-images produced and recorded by screen media and film. But with his discussion of the time-image Deleuze engages more of a Nietzschian approach to addressing the 'problem of judgement' that philosophers have always set for themselves. This problem, and its naming raised in relation to film, enables Deleuze to take a fresh look at a problem as addressed by *the* medium of the twentieth century. As I have discussed through this book, one of the fundamental themes running through both cinema books is Deleuze's continual address of the questions of 'the false and the true' and the 'question of truth'. In cinema Deleuze finds some technical stresses and perspectives embodied and engaged. 'Truth' may be what some directors (and their critics or theorists) articulate as 'style', but this is not what Deleuze is after in his cinema books. It becomes clear that he is continuing his work in *Difference and Repetition*, in which he insisted that for philosophy to continue as a relevant discipline then it must learn the art of dramatization, of narrativization, and the practice and craft involved in the telling of stories (in the same way that we see cinema as a practice) (Deleuze 1994: 206–213). What Deleuze engages in the cinema books, then, is not an account about the different types of filmic genres that 'tell stories', but how the conditions created by screen time enable a range of modes of narrativisation, evidenced in movement-images and time-images which create different forms of what he describes as 'functionalism' (C2: 121).

In many ways in the cinema books Deleuze finesses and simplifies many of the concepts he raised in *Difference and Repetition*. The core issues for both books are the same: the philosophical episteme of the true and false, and how the very act of the posing of a 'problem' has the effect of determining what kind of 'solution' will be arrived at. Instead of this approach Deleuze advocates the process of differentiation as a way of understanding notions of the variable event as a way to consider the complexities of life (Deleuze

Chapter 2: Movement: the *Movement-image*

1. The term striation is from the word 'stria', a term referencing grooves or tracks left through geomorphic changes, such as glacial movements, erosion, grooves cut by mechanical methods, phonograph grooves, etc. Deleuze and Guattari compare striation with 'smooth' spaces, following the mathematician Bernhard Riemann (cf. Deleuze and Guattari 1987: 474–485; see chapter 12 Topology).
2. It is significant that Deleuze references Aristotle's observer pedagogy here. Aristotle divided the world into either sublunar or trans-lunar forms. Aristotle's sub-lunar world was made up of four elements in varying states of generation or decay, composed of the elements of earth, air, fire and water. The minerals, plants, animals and humans of the earth comprise the form and matter of the sub-lunar. The trans-lunar world was made up of 'ether' – the 'fifth element' - an unchanging substance. The heavens and celestial bodies were formed of ether and were thus incorruptible whereas man was formed from an infinitely corruptible body (cf. Aristotle *Physics*).
3. For a summary of auterist theory, see Bazin 2008; Fournier Lanzoni 2002: 17; Hayward 2000: 30–33.
4. I use 'event' in the Deleuzian sense here, see his chapter 'What is an Event?' (Deleuze 2001: 76–82).
5. The infinite is different to a philosophy of transcendence (Deleuze and Guattari 1994: 47; see chapter 5 Perception).

Chapter 3: Frame, Shot and Cut

1. Drawing from Proust's *A Recherche du Temps Perdu* (*In Search of Lost Time*) Deleuze explores how Proust is able to make meaning through his fragmentary narrative style.
2. Multiplicity is a major theme in Deleuze's work, where he engages with the philosophy of Husserl and Bergson, see chapter 10 Time. Deleuze uses the word multiplicity in a number of ways in the cinema books to investigate the properties of space and duration, extending his discussion of the multiple from *Difference and Repetition* and his investigation of the continuous production of ideas through multiplicity (Deleuze 1994: 182–186). For critical appraisal of this work see Hughes 2009 and Williams 2003.

3. See also Jacques Rancière discussion of the terms of Deleuze's engagement with Bresson (Rancière: 2006: 120).

4. Virginia Woolf's character of *Mrs Dalloway* (1925) provides an important reference for understanding Deleuze and Guattari's notion of 'becoming' through rhizomatic actions (see Deleuze and Guattari 1987: 276–280).

5. For further discussion of the critical aspect of the perspective presented in a Deleuzian sense of the frame, see Pascal Bonitzer's essay 'Décadrages' (Deframings) (*Cahiers du Cinéma* 284, January 1978) – Bonitzer refers to the 'Deleuzian terms' in the 'art of deframing' (reproduced in Wilson 2000: 197–203; 200).

Chapter 4: Montage

1. These are the terms of aesthetics that film makers, producers, directors, writers, cinematographers, and critics, audiences, theorists and philosophers choose (cf. Rancière 2006; Levitin *et al.* 2003; Godard 2004).

2. Deleuze references some formative twentieth-century texts on screen montage throughout his cinema books, notably many of Eisenstein's essays from *Film Form*, including 'Methods of Montage' (Eisenstein 1949; C1: 44; 223, n17) Narboni, Sylie Pierre and Rivette's 1969 essay on 'Montage' from *Cahiers du Cinema* (Deleuze references this twice: C1: 28, 222 n29 and C2: 41, 288 n22), and Russian director Andrei Tarkovsky's essay discussing the shot and montage, ' On the cinematographic figure', which Deleuze notes has 'important implications' for examining the 'pressure of time in the shot' (C2: 42).

Chapter 5: Perception

1. Alekan was also the cinematographer on *La Belle et la Bête* (*Beauty and the Beast*) dir. Jean Cocteau, 1946), *Roman Holiday* (dir. William Wyler 1953), and *Topkapi* (dir. Jules Dassin 1964).

2. Although we could easily substitute any other number of scenes for this discussion – the lighthouse scene in *Happy Together* 1997; the point of view of the dual characters of Nikki Grace and Susan Blue (played by Laura Dern) in *Inland Empire* (dir. Lynch, 2006); the dream sequence in *Persepolis* (dirs. Paronnaud and Satrapi

2007), the paths of Lola in *Lola rennt* (*Run Lola Run*; (dir.) Tykwer, 1998) or the lawlessness of *Dogville* (dir. Von Trier, 2003). David Martin-Jones provides a good discussion of the perception-image and its movement into the recollection-image, playing out in a scene in Hitchcock's 1958 film *Vertigo* (Martin-Jones 2006: 55–57).

3. For example see *Meshes of the Afternoon* (dir. Deren and Hammid 1943), *Window Water Baby Moving* (dir. Brakhage 1962); *Je tu il elle* (dir. Akerman, 1974), *Just Another Girl on the IRT* (dir. Harris, 1992); *Cliffhanger* (dir. Harlin, 1993), *Lola Rennt* (*Run Lola run*); dir. Twyker, 1998); *Romance* (dir. Breillat, 1999); *Le scaphandre et le papillon* ((*The diving bell and the butterfly*); dir. Schnabel, 2007); *Fantastic Mr Fox* (dir. Anderson, 2009).

4. The reference to a '*Mitsein*' (English translation of the German is 'being-with') by Deleuze follows Mitry, who has argued within the pages Deleuze cites that the ambiguities presented by the perception of a film may be summarized by Heidegger's phrase 'the experience of unity in diffusion' (Mitry 2000: 55). *Mitsein* is Heidegger's thesis on the 'being-with' shared cultural and historical worlds that we inhabit (cf. Inwood 1999: 31; Carel 2006: 148).

5. Garin Dowd has described the significance of the maritime space for post-war thinkers such as Serge Daney, Paul Virilio and Deleuze (Dowd 2009: 130–131).

6. There has been some significant work done around this concept of the brain, affect, and as William Connolly terms it, neuropolitics (cf. essays in Flaxman 2000; Connolly 2002 and Pisters 2011).

7. Deleuze discusses these issues concerning image perception, in the historical context of the work of Bergson, Husserl, Sartre and Merleau-Ponty. Deleuze notes that Husserl does not mention cinema in his work (C1: 56; in particular we might note Husserl's work on transcendental phenomenology in the early twentieth century, which explores different perceptual situations including hallucination but ignores the moving-image cf. Husserl 1970). Deleuze further notes that Sartre's *The Imaginary* ([1940] 2004 incorrectly translated in the English cinema books as 'The Imagination') 'does not cite the cinematographic image' (C1: 57) – even though Sartre critiques Husserl's thesis of phenomenological intentionality and describes perception in terms of images in the world, a phrasing that Deleuze will qualify in his own terms throughout the cinema books.

8. Phenomenology is a method of study of the experiences of the structures of consciousness, as determined through the first-person perspective or point of view. Phenomenology engages degrees of 'intentionality', in that they direct their study toward a thing or an experience which in Deleuzian terms has the effect of

constructing the reality of that thing or experience. Deleuze rejects the phenomenological position of Merleau-Ponty because it entails drawing from a pre-existing framework of clichéd opinions, experiences and knowledge, precisely the type of deterministic methodology Deleuze opposes in his ciné-philosophy (Deleuze and Guattari 1994: 149–150); see also Helen A. Fielding's discussion of Merleau-Ponty, film and perception (Fielding 2009: 81–90).

Chapter 7: Action

1. Some of the terminology and ideas behind the action-image can be further engaged by looking at Deleuze's other work on the philosophical problems he discusses in *Difference and Repetition*, where the philosophical debate on Plato and forms that underpins most of the cinema books is made more explicit. Deleuze also discusses Platonism as a 'selective doctrine' where transcendence (Plato's theory of ideas/ Forms) is situated within immanence, which is productive of different temporal modes – Chronos and Aion (cf. Deleuze 1994: 164–168; 1997: 136–137).

Chapter 8: Transsemiotics

1. Stones sequence recorded at Olympic Sound Studios, Barnet, West London (studios closed in 2009) in June 1968. For background and review of *One Plus One/ Sympathy for the Devil* see Glynn (2007).
2. Godard's work has a significant influence on Deleuze's thinking about the image and the situations it produces (cf. Deleuze and Guattari 1987: 98; Deleuze [1976] 1995: 37–45; C1: 213–214; C2: 194–196). It is beyond the remit of this chapter, but Godard's work may have easily been replaced in this discussion with any of the films of, for example, Abbas Kiarostami, Claire Denis, Julie Dash, Marlene Gorris, Quentin Tarantino, Zhang Yimou, each of whom, we may observe, engages types of images that may readily be interpreted as signs for certain types of cultural attitudes, but which may also be interpreted as abstractions from their everyday situations. See Deleuze's comments on the 'judgement' of 'codes' (C2: 285 n4).
3. See Godard's notes for 'My Approach in Four Movements' – for his film *Deux ou trois choses que je sais d'elle* (*Two or three things that I know about her*, 1967) – but

which also apply here (Godard 1986: 241–242); Deleuze also describes Godard's technique of *and*, which he describes in terms of a pedagogy of thought (Deleuze 1995: 37–45; C2: 22–23).

4. This is a key topic of the era that enabled major shifts in epistemological practices (cf. Jameson 1984; Wollen 1993; Braidotti 1994: 173–190). Deleuze's cinema books come at the cumulation of many of the critical debates, providing him with an advantageous position. For example, see Jacques Derrida *Of Grammatology* (1967), Michel Foucault *The Archaeology of Knowledge* ([1969] 1972) and *Discipline and Punish* (1975), Pierre Bourdieu *Distinction: A Social Critique of the Judgement of Taste* ([1979] 1984) and Gilles Deleuze and Félix Guattari *A Thousand Plateaus: Capitalism and Schizophrenia* (1980). For an overview of Godard's film philosophy see Baross (2009) and on Godard's semiotics, see Rancière (2006: 143–153).

5. It almost goes without saying, but following Deleuze and Guattari's method, this approach is not advocating another master narrative; rather a 'transsemiotic' is an approach that engages an open rhizomic method in order to debate and articulate a specific expression (1987: 136). The 'trans' for Deleuzian thinking should accommodate Guattari's notion of 'transversality', as Janell Watson has argued, 'transversality' is a term that engages the notions of 'transference and language, the "twin pillars" of psychoanalytic treatment' (Watson 2009: 23), and thus offers a critique for semiotic structuring activity (see also Genosko 2009b: 48–68). For screen applications, cf. Marciniak *et al.* (2007). For a discussion of the issues of the 'master narrative' in relation to film theory, and a good overview of what 'theorization' attempts to achieve, see Nichols (2000), Mohanty (2003). For a definition of the rhizomic in Deleuze's work, see Colman (2005c: 231–233).

6. In *A Thousand Plateaus* Deleuze and Guattari invoke a number of film makers/films to support their thesis, in the context of signification, notably: Godard (1987: 98); Pasolini (2005: 106), Herzog (1987: 110). There is insufficient space to extend this discussion here, but Deleuze and Guattari are not alone in this position – for example, see the arguments of Butler 2002; Collins and Davis 2004; Derrida and Stiegler 2002; Pines and Willemen 1989; Porton 1999; Rancière 2004; Shapiro 2008.

7. In this sense, Deleuze is engaging a philosophical dialogue with Aristotle in terms of categorization of the world into recognizable things, ultimately productive of modes of realism (cf. Ackrill 1963; Aristotle 1953; 1963), and Kant on the question of the possible judgement of categories of things (Kant 1958). Kant comes to figure in terms of the category of the sublime (C1: 53) and how immaterial qualities come to figure within sign-images (C1: 182).

Chapter 9: Signs (Vector)

1. The term 'living relation' is Merleau-Ponty's, who in his book *Phenomenology of Perception* discusses the creation of perceptual conditions for the anchoring of a subject through certain spatial settings (C1: 57; see chapter 5 Perception).
2. Cf. Sergei Eisenstein, 'The Montage of Film Attractions' (1924) (Eisenstein 1998: 35–52).
3. In its etymological sense the vector is constructed from the Latin meaning 'carrier' (OED).
4. Deleuze develops his concept of small form (skeleton-space) and large form (respiration-space) from François Cheng's discussion of Chinese painting as 'philosophy in action' and the 'empty and full' spaces of Chinese painting (cf. Cheng 1994; chapter 12 Topology; C1: 168, 186–187, 239).

Chapter 10: Time

1. In *Cinema 1*, Deleuze discusses light in the pre-war French school through filmmakers like Grémillon and Rivette as an 'alternation' from the darkness in German Expressionist film forms (C1: 45, 49–50).
2. Indirect time-images are also created by some sound-images, for example listen to the opening scene of Donnie Darko with the soundtrack overlaid with the postpunk pop song, 'The Killing Moon' (Echo and the Bunnymen, 1984), producing a transformative temporal space.
3. Ronald Bogue provides a detailed discussion of the different parts of Bergson's *Creative Evolution* and *Matter and Memory* that Deleuze draws on for the distinction between 'translation' in movement and 'transformation'; through duration (Bogue 2003: 22).
4. I do not have the space in this chapter to develop this discussion on the content in Kelly's films, but Deleuze's purpose with making the time-image stand as an explicitly political empirical marker are developed in the chapter on 'political cinema'. Deleuze chooses the films of Resnais, for example *Hiroshima Mon Amour* (Resnais 1959) and *Nuit et brouillard* (Resnais 1955) to discuss the time-image, both films charting the political events of their respective eras. Anna Powell provides a further Deleuzian theoretical reading of *Donnie Darko* (Powell 2007: 156; 160–161).

becoming	movement over duration
chronosign	an image where time appears for itself (refer to topology), and not as a subordinate product of movement. Deleuze refers to chronosigns as points (vectors) and as sheets that may be folded (topologies, large form).
cinematographic	image created from the camera
cinematographic consciousness	the image set
cinematography	the image in camera and post-production
ciné-system	open set
classical cinema	logical film space formed through sensory-motor schema
classical Hollywood	studio-controlled film making system in Hollywood from sound era to late 1940s
close-up shot	an object is framed by the camera in such a way that it alters the scale of the object, making it appear larger, for example a close-up shot of a human head which fills the screen
continuity editing	a technique of classical cinema to edit together sequences that unfold in logical order according to the narrative
crane shot	shot constructed when camera is mounted on a crane
cut	break in scene
crosscutting	editing together of two or more shots that may occur in different places simultaneously
crystal	temporal figure that seeds the exchange between virtual and actual
decoupage	construction of the total shot pre- and post-production

depth of field	comparative measurement of distance between things in shot to determine focus and focal points
diegesis/diegetic	everything contained within the screen world. Extra diegetic – things that the screen world refers to but are not overtly included within that world, for example, the use of an actor, prop, or sound whose body has appeared in other screen/ non-screen worlds bring an extra-diegetic reference to the situation.
difference	the internal (not comparative) particularity of things
differentiation	the actualization of the virtual
digital	data technology for recording uses non-continuous data harvesting of sequences and coded languages (as opposed to continuous storage of analogue types of film)
dir.	director
dissolve	fade of one shot into another
dop.	director of photography/main cinematographer/camera person
duration	consciousness of changes in lived states
edit	selection of shots
ellipsis	missing duration where parts are cut
figure	sign which can be reflect, invert or be discursive of its own or related object
fixed camera	non-moving cinematic camera
form	the components of the ciné-system
frame	an image set
icon	Peircean sign that refers to a set of design-ated characteristics for an object. Deleuze

	uses to designate the affect expressed by a facial image (face or equivalent)
image	an infinite set
incompossible	divergent series that depend on singularities
iris	a moving circular masking of the image that opens or closes to provide focal points
hodological	space determined by sensory-motor schema
large form	situation (S), an action (A), then a modified situation (S') = SAS'
line of the universe	vector; a line that is marked by moments of intensity and singular points
long-exposure	holding the camera aperture open for an extended period of time, usually with a still camera, *pose* (C1, 5)
milieu or mileux	a French word etymologically inferring a 'middle place', and in the context that Deleuze uses the term in the cinema books, it infers the environment, either social environment, cultural climate, or generally a place from which meanings change and are influenced
mise-en-scène	the design and style of a shot – everything you can see and hear within a shot, including the mode of performance and the action
modern cinema	determined by non sensory-motor schemas; fragmentation; the production of the intolerable
money	order of time
montage	a process of shot editing using Eisenstein's rule that the relation between two shots

	produces a third meaning, exterior to the *mise-en-scène*. Meanings of the montaged shots are also controlled by the rhythm and the duration of the intercut shots.
movement-image	set of variable elements that act on and react to each other
narration	spoken guide either within or outside of the *mise-en-scène*
narrative	story
opsign	visual sign
pace	rhythm of a film
pan	movement of camera from left to right or right to left around an imaginary vertical axis of which the camera is the centre. Panning is different to a tracking shot.
perception-image	subtractive image composed from a set
plan	French for (camera) shot
plan-américain	a shot framing of a body (animate or inanimate) that alters the scale of the object. Also known as a medium long shot when a human figure is not in scene. With a human figure the shot is generally from the shins to the head of the body.
plan-séquence	a long take; a single-shot scene
plot	how the story is told
point-of-view shot (pov.)	a shot which shows the scene from the point of view of a character, thing, or object, for example, compare the pov of the shark in *Jaws* with a character looking at that shark
pull-back shot	a zoom or tracking shot that moves back from its initial subjects to reveal the larger context of a scene

qualitative	inherent, distinguishing properties
quantitative	measurable properties
ritornello	a territory defined by noise, sound or music
rhythm	pace shots are edited together, productive of graphic relations
set (ensemble)	the components of the image
small form	action (A), a situation (S), then a modified action (A') = (ASA')
shot	pure movement/descriptive geometry/*plan*
shot reverse shot	two or more shots edited together in alternating sequence whose rhythm contributes to the final set
sign	a type of image either bipolar or genetic
story	the content produced by the arrangement of the componenets of the image and the sequencing of events
time-image	process of differentiation
transsemiotic	the rhizomic or multiple ways that signs (including those produced by sound images) produce a 'mixed semiotics' comprised of four components: generative, transformational, diagrammatic and machinic
topology	the transformation and or coexistence of different times in the one screen space, and the relational space between things. Also known as the Boulanger transformation.
topological	space determined by non-sensory-motor schemas
track/tracking shot	a smooth continuous shot where the camera is fixed on a form of tracking (like railway lines)

trans-morphological forms	deformations, transformations or transmutations
vector	sign of minute intensive perceptions
virtual	recollection-image which may or may not be actualized into form

Bibliography

For film references see Films Listed by Director and the Filmography.

Ackrill, J. L. 1963. *Aristotle's Categories and De Interpretatione* (translation with notes). Oxford: Clarendon Press.

Alliez, E. [1991] 1996. *Capital Times*. Minneapolis: University of Minnesota Press.

Alliez, E. [1993] 2004. *The Signature of the World*. London: Continuum.

Anderson, L. and Krathwohl, D. 2001. *A Taxonomy for Learning, Teaching and Assessing: A Revision of Bloom's Taxonomy of Educational Objectives*. New York: Longman.

Andrew, D. 1976. *The Major Film Theories*. New York and Oxford: Oxford University Press.

Andrew, D. 1984. *Concepts in Film Theory*. Oxford: Oxford University Press.

Andrew, D. 2006. 'An Atlas of World Cinema'. In S.Dennison and S.H.Lim (eds), *Remapping World Cinema: Identity, Culture and Politics in Film*. London & New York: Wallflower Press, pp. 19–29.

Andrew, G. and Jarmusch, J. 1999. 'Jim Jarmusch interviewed by Geoff Andrew', *Guardian Unlimited*, November 15, accessed January 2007 from http://film.guardian.co.uk/Guardian_NFT/interview/0,,110607,0.html#b

Aristotle 350 BC. *Physics*. Translated by R. P. Hardie and R. K. Gaye. Online: http://classics.mit.edu/Aristotle/physics.html

Aristotle. 1953. *Metaphysics*. Tranlated by W. D. Ross. Oxford: Clarendon Press.

Aristotle. 1963. *Categories*. Translated by J. L. Ackrill. Oxford: Clarendon Press.

Artaud, A. [1933] 1976. 'The Premature Old Age of the Cinema'. Translated by H.Weaver. In S. Sontag (ed.), *Artaud: Selected Writings*. Berkeley: University of California Press, pp. 311–314.

Augé, M. 2002. *In the Metro*. Translated by T. Conley. Minneapolis: University of Minnesota Press.

Aumont, J. 1987. *Montage Eisenstein*. London: BFI.

Bachelard, G. [1938] 2002. *The Formation of the Scientific Mind: A Contribution to a Psychoanalysis of Objective Knowledge*. Translated by M. McAllester Jones. Manchester: Clinamen.

Barthes, R. [1964] 1968. *Elements of Semiology*. Translated by A. Lavers and C. Smith. New York: Hill and Wang.

Barthes, R. 1972. *Mythologies*. Translated by A. Lavers. New York: Hill & Wang.

Barthes, R. 1974. *S/Z*. Translated by R. Miller. New York: Hill & Wang.

Barthes, R. 1977. *Image-Music-Text*. Translated by S. Heath. New York: Hill and Wang.

Baross, Z. 2009. 'Jean-Luc Godard'. In F. Colman (ed.), *Film, Theory and Philosophy: The Key Thinkers*. Durham: Acumen, pp. 134–144.

Bazin, A. [1958–59] 1967. *What is Cinema?* Vol. 1, Essays selected by H. Gray. Berkeley, CA: University of California.

Bazin, A. [1961–62] 1971. *What is Cinema?* Vol. 2, Essays selected by H. Gray. Berkeley, CA: University of California.

Bazin, A., [1971] 1992. *Jean Renoir*. Translated by W.W.Halsey II and W.H.Simon. New York: DeCapo Press.

Bazin, A. [1957] 2008. 'De la Politique des Auteurs'. In B.K.Grant (ed.), *Auteurs and Authorship: A Film Reader*. Oxford: Blackwell, pp. 19–28.

Beller, J. 2006. *The Cinematic Mode of Production: Attention Economy and the Society of the Spectacle*. Hanover, New Hampshire: Dartmouth College Press by University Press of New England.

Bellour, R. 2000. *The Analysis of Film*. C. Penley (ed.), Bloomington: Indiana University Press.

Belsey, C. [1980] 2002. *Critical Practice*. London: Routledge.

Bergson, H. [1889] 1910. *Time and Free Will: An Essay on the Immediate Data of Consciousness*. Translated by F.L. Pogson. London: George Allen and Unwin.

Bergson, H. [1922] 1965. *Duration and Simultaneity, with Reference to Einstein's Theory*. Translated by L. Jacobson. Indianapolis: Bobbs-Merrill.

Bergson, H. [1896] 1994. *Matter and Memory*. Translated by N.M. Paul and W.S. Palmer. New York: Zone Books.

Bergson, H. [1907] 1983. *Creative Evolution*. Translated by A. Mitchell. Boston: University Press of America.

Bergson, H. 2007. *Mind-Energy*. Translated by H.W. Carr. K. Ansell Pearson and M. Kolkman (eds), London: Palgrave-Macmillan.

Blanchot, M. [1969] 1992. *The Infinite Conversation*. Translated by S. Hanson. Minneapolis: University of Minnesota Press.

Bloom, B.S. and Krathwohl, D.R. 1956. *Taxonomy of Educational Objectives: The Classification of Educational Goals, by a Committee of College and University Examiners*. Handbook I: *Cognitive Domain*. New York: Longman Green.

Bobo, J. 1995. *Black Women as Cultural Readers*. New York: Columbia University Press.

Bogue, R. 1989. *Deleuze and Guattari*. London and New York: Routledge.

Bogue, R. 2003. *Deleuze on Cinema*. London and New York: Routledge.

Bogue, R. 2006. 'Fabulation, Narration, and the People to Come'. In C. Boundas (ed.), *Deleuze and Philosophy*. Edinburgh: Edinburgh University Press, pp. 202–223.

Bolt, B. 2004. *Art beyond Representation: The Performative Power of the Image*. London: I.B. Tauris.

Bonta, M. and Protevi, J. 2004. *Deleuze and Geophilosophy: A Guide and Glossary*. Edinburgh: Edinburgh University Press.

Bordwell, D. 1985. *Narration in the Fiction Film*. Madison: University of Wisconsin Press.

Bordwell, D., Staiger, J. and Thompson, K. 1985. *The Classical Hollywood Cinema: Film Style and Mode of Production to 1960*. London: Routledge and Kegan Paul; New York: Columbia University Press.

Bordwell, D. and Thompson, K. 2003. *Film Art: An Introduction* (7th edition). Boston and London: McGraw-Hill.

Boundas, C.V. (ed.) 2004. *Deleuze and Philosophy*. Edinburgh: Edinburgh University Press.

Bourdieu, P. [1979] 1984. *Distinction: A Social Critique of the Judgement of Taste*. Translated by R. Nice. London: Routledge.

Boyer, C.B. 1949. *The History of the Calculus and Its Conceptual Development*. New York: Dover.

Braidotti, R. 1994. *Nomadic Subjects: Embodiment and Sexual Difference in Contemporary Feminist Theory*. New York: Columbia University Press.

Braidotti, R. 2006. *Transpositions: On Nomadic Ethics*. Cambridge: Polity.

Brentano, F. [1894] 1995. *Psychology from an Empirical Standpoint*. Translated by A. C. Rancurello, D. B. Terrell and L. L. McAlister. London and New York: Routledge.

Bresson, R. [1975] 1977. *Notes on Cinematography*. Translated by Jonathon Griffin. Los Angeles: Green Integer.

Bresson, R. 1986. *Notes on the Cinematographer*. Translated by J.M.G. Le Clézio. London: Quartet Encounters.

Browne, N. (ed.) 1990. *Cahiers du cinéma*. Vol.3, *1969–1972: The Politics of Representation: An Anthology from 'Cahiers du cinéma', nos. 210–239, March 1969–June 1972*. London: Routledge and British Film Institute.

Bruno, G. 1991. 'Heresies: The Body of Pasolini's Semiotics'. *Cinema Journal* 30: 3 Spring: 29–42.

Bruno, G. 2002. *Atlas of Emotion: Journeys in Art, Architecture, and Film*. London: Verso.

Buchanan, I. 2008. *Deleuze and Guattari's Anti-Oedipus*. London and New York: Continuum.

Buchanan, I. and Colebrook, C. (eds) 2000. *Deleuze and Feminist Theory*. Edinburgh: Edinburgh University Press.

Buchanan, I. and Lambert, G. (eds) 2005. *Deleuze and Space*. Edinburgh: University of Edinburgh Press.

Buchanan, I. and MacCormack, P. (eds) 2008. *Deleuze and the Schizoanalysis of Cinema*. London: Continuum.

Buckland, W. 2000. *Film Theory and Contemporary Hollywood Movies*. New York and London: Routledge.

Burch, N. [1969] 1973. *Theory of Film Practice*. Translated by H. R. Lane. New York: Praeger.

Burch, N. 1980. 'Foreword'. In *Theory of Film Practice*. Translated by H. R. Lane. New York: Praeger, pp. v–x.

Burchill, L. 2010. 'Becoming-Woman. A Metamorphosis in the Present Relegating Repetition of Gendered Time to the Past'. *Time and Society* 19.1: 81–97.

Busbea, L. 2007. *Topologies: The Urban Utopia in France, 1960–1970*. Cambridge, Mass.; London: MIT.

Butler, J. [1990] 1999. *Gender Trouble: Feminism and the Subversion of Identity*. New York and London: Routledge.

Butler, A. 2002. *Women's Cinema: The Contested Screen*. London and New York: Wallflower.

Carel, H. 2006. *Life and Death in Freud and Heidegger*. Amsterdam and New York: Rodopi.

Carroll, N. 1981. 'The Future of Allusion: Hollywood in the Seventies and Beyond'. In *October* 34 Summer: 51–81.

Cheng, F. [1979] 1994. *Empty and Full: The Language of Chinese Painting.* Translated by Michael H. Kohn. Boston and London: Shambala.

Chion, M. 2003. *Film: A Sound Art.* Translated by C. Gorbman. New York: Columbia University Press.

Codell, J.F. (ed.) 2007. *Genre, Gender, Race, and World Cinema.* Malden and Oxford : Blackwell.

Colebrook, C. 2001. *Gilles Deleuze.* New York: Routledge.

Collins, F. and Davis, T. 2004. *Australian Cinema after Mabo.* Cambridge: Cambridge University Press.

Colman, F. 2005a. 'Deleuze's Kiss: The Sensory Pause of Screen Affect'. *Pli: The Warwick Journal of Philosophy* 16: 101–113.

Colman, F. 2005b. 'Feminism'. In A. Parr (ed.), *The Deleuze Dictionary.* Edinburgh: Edinburgh University Press, pp. 100–102.

Colman, F. 2005c. 'Rhizome'. In A.Parr (ed.), *The Deleuze Dictionary.* Edinburgh: Edinburgh University Press, pp. 231–233.

Colman, F.J. 2009a. 'Affective Sounds for Social Orders'. In Graeme Harper (ed.), *The Continuum Companion to Sound in Film and the Visual Media.* London: Continuum, pp. 194–207.

Colman, F.J. 2009b. 'Affective Imagery: Screen Militarism'. In E.W. Holland,

D.W. Smith and C.J. Stivale (eds), *Gilles Deleuze: Image and Text.* London: Continuum, pp. 143–159.

Colman, F.J. 2009c. 'Introduction: What is Film-philosophy?' In F. Colman (ed.), *Film, Theory and Philosophy.* Durham: Acumen Publishing, pp. 1–15.

Colman, F. 2010. 'Affective Self: Feminist Thinking and Feminist actions'. In *Contemporary French and Francophone Studies: Sites* 14. 5: 543–552.

Conley, T. 2005. 'Molecular'. In A.Parr (ed.), *The Deleuze Dictionary.* Edinburgh: Edinburgh University Press, pp. 172–174.

Conley, T. [1991] 2006. *Film Hieroglyphs: Ruptures in Classical Cinema.* Minneapolis: University of Minnesota Press.

Connolly, W.E. 2002. *Neuropolitics: Thinking, Culture, Speed.* Minneapolis: University of Minnesota Press.

Cooper, J. M. (ed.) 1997. *Plato: Complete Works.* Indianapolis: Hackett.

Cubitt, S. 1991. *Timeshift: On Video Culture.* London and New York: Routledge.

Cubitt, S. 2004. *The Cinema Effect.* Cambridge, MA: MIT.

Daly, F. and Dowd, G. 2003. *Leos Carax.* Manchester: Manchester University Press.

Chicago: University of Chicago Press.

Derrida, J. and Stiegler, B. [1996] 2002. *Echographies of Television: Filmed Interviews*. Translated by J. Bajorek. London: Polity Press.

Dosse, F. (2007] 2010. *Gilles Deleuze and Félix Guattari: Intersecting Lives*. Translated by D.Glassman. New York: Columbia University Press.

Dowd, G. 2009. 'Serge Daney'. In F.Colman (ed.), *Film, Theory and Philosophy*. Durham: Acumen, pp. 122–133.

Drummond, P. (ed.) 1979. *Film as Film: Formal Experiment in Film, 1910–1975* Exh. Cat. London: Arts Council of Great Britain.

Duffy, S. (ed.) 2006a. *The Logic of Expression: Quality, Quantity, and Intensity in Spinoza, Hegel and Deleuze*. Hampshire, UK and Burlington, USA: Ashgate.

Duffy, S. (ed.) 2006b. *Virtual Mathematics: The Logic of Difference*. Bolton: Clinamen Press.

Duffy, S. 2006c. 'The Mathematics of Deleuze's Differential Logic and Meta-physics'. In S. Duffy (ed.), *Virtual Mathematics: The Logic of Difference*. Bolton: Clinamen, pp. 118–144.

Eagleton, T. 1990. *The Ideology of the Aesthetic*. Oxford: Blackwell.

Eisenstein, S. 1949. *Film Form. Essays in Film Theory*. Translated by J.Leyda. New York: Harcourt Brace Jovanovich.

Eisenstein, S. [1929] 1998. *The Eisenstein Reader*. Edited by R.Taylor. Translated by R. Taylor and W. Powell. London: British Film Institute.

Eisner, L. H. 1964. *Murnau*. Berkeley: University of California Press.

Eisner, L.H. [1953] 1973. *The Haunted Screen: Expressionism in the German Cinema and the Influence of Max Reinhardt*. London: Secker & Warburg.

Ehrat, J. 2005. *Cinema and Semiotic: Piece and Film Aesthetics, Narration, and Representation*. Toronto: University of Toronto Press.

Fielding, H.A. 2009. 'Maurice Merleau-Ponty'. In F. Colman (ed.), *Film, Theory and Philosophy*. Durham: Acumen, pp. 81–90.

Fine, G. 1995. *On Ideas: Aristotle's Criticism of Plato's Theory of Forms*. Oxford: Oxford University Press.

Flaxman, G. (ed.) 2000. *The Brain is the Screen: Deleuze and the Philosophy of Cinema*. Minneapolis: University of Minnesota Press.

Foucault, M. 1970. 'Theatrum Philosophicum'. Translated by D. F. Bouchard and S. Simon. In *Language, Counter-Memory, Practice*. Ithaca: Cornell University Press, pp. 165–196.

Foucault, M [1969] 1972. *The Archaeology of Knowledge*. Translated by A. Sheridan. London: Tavistock.

Foucault, M. [1966] 1977. *The Order of Things*. Translated by A. Sheridan. London: Tavistock.

Foucault, M. [1975] 1977. *Discipline and Punish: The Birth of the Prison*. Translated by A. Sheridan. London: Allen Lane.

Foucault [1967] 1984. 'Of Other Spaces'. Translated by J. Miskowiec. *Architecture/Mouvement/Continuité* (October) Online: http://foucault.info/documents/heteroTopia/foucault.heteroTopia.en.html

Foucault, M. [1974] 1989. 'Film and Popular Memory'. Translated by M. Jordin. In S. Lotringer (ed.), *Foucault Live – Interviews 1966–84*. New York: Semiotexte, pp. 89–106. (Originally published in *Cahiers du cinéma* 251/252.)

Foucault, M. 2006. *History of Madness*. Translated by J. Murphy and J. Khalfa. London: Routledge.

Fournier Lanzoni, R. 2002. *French Cinema: From its Beginnings to the Present*. London: Continuum.

Frampton, D. 2006. *Filmosophy: A Manifesto for a Radically New Way of Understanding Cinema*. London & New York: Wallflower.

Gardner, C. 2004. *Joseph Losey*. Manchester and New York: Manchester University Press.

Gatens, M. and Lloyd, M. 1999. *Collective Imaginings: Spinoza, Past and Present*. London: Routledge.

Genosko, G. 2009a. 'Félix Guattari'. In F.Colman (ed.), *Film, Theory and Philosophy*. Durham: Acumen, pp. 243–252.

Genosko, G. 2009b. *Félix Guattari: A Critical Introduction*. London: Pluto.

Gidal, P. 1989. *Materialist Film*. London: Routledge.

Gledhill, C. and Williams, L. (eds) 2000. *Reinventing Film Studies*. London: Arnold & New York: Oxford University Press.

Glynn, S. 2007. 'Sympathy For The Devil' (film review). In *Scope* Issue 7 (February) n.p. Online: http://www.scope.nottingham.ac.uk/filmreview.php?issue=7&id=196

Godard, J.-L. 1986. *Godard on Godard*. Edited and translated by T. Milne. New York: De Cap Press.

Godard, J.-L. and Ishaghpour, Y. [2000] 2005. *Cinema: The Archaeology of Film and the Memory of a Century*. Translated by J.Howe. Oxford & New York: Berg.

Goddard, M. 2011. *The Cinema of Raúl Ruiz: Impossible Cartographies*. London: Wallflower.

Goethe, J. W. von. [1795–1796] 1917. *Wilhelm Meister's Apprenticeship*. Vol. XIV. New York: P.F. Collier & Son.

Guattari [1977 and 1980] 1984. *Molecular Revolution: Psychiatry and Politics*. Translated by R. Sheed (a selection of essays from *Psychanalyse et tranversalité* and the two French versions (each different) of *La revolution moleculaire*). New York: Penguin.

Guattari, F. [1992] 1995. *Chaosmosis*. Translated by P. Bains and J. Pefanis. Bloomington: Indiana University Press.

Gunning, T. 1995. 'An Aesthetic of Astonishment'. In L. Williams (ed.), *Viewing Positions: Ways of Seeing Film*. New Jersey: Rutgers University Press, pp. 114–33.

Hammett, D. [1930] 2005. *The Maltese Falcon*. London: Orion.

Harding, S. 1991. *Whose Science, Whose Knowledge?* Buckingham: Open University Press.

Hawks, T. 1977. *Structuralism and Semiotics*. London: Routledge.

Hayward, S. 2000. *Cinema Studies: The Key Concepts*. London: Routledge.

Hegel, G.W.F. 1975. *Hegel's Aesthetics: Lectures on Fine Art*. Oxford: Oxford University Press.

Heidegger, M. 1971. *Poetry, Language, Thought*. Translated by A. Hofstadter. New York: Harper and Row.

Heidegger, M. [1927] 1982. *The Basic Problems of Phenomenology*. Translated by A. Hofstadter. Bloomington: Indiana University Press.

Heidegger, M. 1996. *Being and Time*. Translated by J. Stambaugh. Albany: State University of New York Press.

Hendricks, C. and Oliver, K. 1999. *Language and Liberation: Feminism, Philosophy, and Language*. New York: State University of New York Press.

Hickey-Moody, A. and Malins, P. (eds) 2007. *Deleuzian Encounters: Studies in Contemporary Social Issues*. Hampshire and New York: Palgrave Macmillan.

Hillier, J. (ed.) 1985. *Cahiers du cinéma*. Vol.1, *1950s: Neo-realism, Hollywood, New Wave*. London: Routledge & Kegan Paul and the British Film Institute.

Hillier, J. (ed.) 1986. *Cahiers du cinéma*. Vol.2, *1960–1968: New Wave, New Cinema, Reevaluating Hollywood*. Cambridge, MA: Harvard University Press.

Hjelmslev, L. [1943] 1961. *Prolegomena to a Theory of Language*. 2nd edition, revised. Translated by F. J. Whitfield. Madison: University of Wisconsin Press.

hooks, b.1990. *Yearning: Race, Gender, and Cultural Politics*. Toronto: Between the Lines.

hooks, b. 1996. 'The Oppositional Gaze: Black Female Spectators'. In b. hooks *Reel to Reel. Race, Sex, and Class at the Movies*. London and New York: Routledge, pp. 197–213.

Hughes, J. 2009. *Deleuze's Difference and Repetition*. London and New York: Continuum.

Husserl, E. [1936/54] 1970. *The Crisis of European Sciences and Transcendental Phenomenology*. Translated by D. Carr. Evanston: Northwestern University Press.

Husserl, E. [1900–1901] 2001. *Logical Investigations*. Vols. 1 and 2. Translated by J.N. Findlay and revised translation and edited by D. Moron. London and New York: Routledge Kegan Paul.

Inwood, M.J. 1999. *A Heidegger Dictionary*. Oxford: Wiley-Blackwell.

Ione, A. 2005. *Innovation and Visualization: Trajectories, Strategies and Myths*. Amsterdam, New York: Rodopi.

Irigaray, L. [1978] 1985. 'Women on the Market'. In Irigaray, *This Sex Which is Not One*. Translated by C. Porter. Ithaca and New York: Cornell University Press, pp. 170–191.

Jameson, F. 1984. 'Periodizing the 60s'. In S. Sayres (ed.), *The 60s without Apology*. Minneapolis: University of Minnesota Press in cooperation with Social Text, pp. 178–209.

Jenkins, H. 2000. 'Reception theory and audience reseach: The mystery of the vampire's kiss'. In Gledhill, C. and Williams, L. (eds), *Reinventing Film Studies*. London : Arnold, pp. 165–182.

Johnston, C. [1973] 1977. 'Myths of Women in the Cinema'. In K.Kay and G.Perry (eds), *Women and the Cinema*. New York: Dutton, pp. 407–411.

Kant, Immanuel [1781] 1958. *Critique of Pure Reason*. Translated by N. Kemp. London: Macmillan.

Keeling, K. 2007. *The Witch's Flight: The Cinematic, the Black Femme, and the Image of Common Sense*. Durham and London: Duke University Press.

Kelly, R. 2003. *The Donnie Darko Book*. London: Faber & Faber.

Kennedy, B. 2000. *Deleuze and Cinema: The Aesthetics of Sensation*. Edinburgh: Edinburgh University Press.

Körner, S. 1955. *Kant*. Harmondsworth: Penguin.

Körner, S. 1970. *Categorial Frameworks*. Oxford: Blackwell.

Krathwohl, D. R., Bloom, B.S. and Masia, B.S. 1964. *Taxonomy of Educational Objectives: The Classification of Educational Goals. Handbook II: Affective Domain*. New York: David McKay Co., Inc.

Kristeva, J. [1969] 1980. *Desire in Language: A Semiotic Approach to Literature and Art*. Translated by T.Gora, A. Jardine and L.S.Roudiez. Oxford: Blackwell.

Kristeva, J. [1988] 1991. *Strangers to Ourselves*. Translated by L. S. Roudiez. New York: Columbia University Press.

Lacan, J. 1977. *Écrits: A Selection.* Translated by A. Sheridan. New York: W.W. Norton.

Lambert, J. 2006. *Deleuze and Guattari's Philosophy of History.* London & New York: Continuum International.

Lecercle, J.-J. 2002. *Deleuze and Language.* Basingstoke, Hampshire & New York: Palgrave Macmillan.

Lambert, G. 2004. *The Return of the Baroque in Modern Culture.* New York and London: Continuum Books.

Lampert, J. 2006. *Deleuze and Guattari's Philosophy of History.* New York & London: Continuum.

Levitin, J., Plessis, J. and Raoul, V. (eds) 2003. *Women Filmmakers: Refocusing.* New York and London: Routledge.

Landy, M. 2003. ' "The Dream of the Gesture": The Body of/in Todd Haynes's Films'. *boundary 2* 30.3: 123–140.

Lawlor, L. 2002. *Derrida and Husserl: The Basic Problem of Phenomenology.* Bloomington: Indiana University Press.

Lawlor, L. 2003. *Thinking through French Philosophy: The Being of the Question.* Bloomington: Indiana University Press.

Legge, E. 2009. *Michael Snow: Wavelength.* London: Afterall, Central Saint Martins College of Art and Design, distributed by The MIT Press.

Liber, G.O. 2002. *Alexander Dovzhenko: A Life in Soviet Film.* London: BFI.

Lipovetsky, M. 2005, 'Of Clones and Crones: Review of Ilya Khrzhanovski, 4 (Chetyre) 2004'. *KinoKultura* 9/10/05, np.

Lotman, Y. M. 1976. *Semiotics of Cinema.* Translated by M. E. Suino. Michigan Slavic contributions no.5. Ann Arbor: University of Michigan.

Macarow, K. 2003. 'I am a Heterodemon' (on Derek Jarman). *Refractory: Journal of Entertainment Media.* 'Special Issue on The Sounds of Vision: Spectatorship and Aural Perception'. Vol. 4 edited by F.Colman n.p:

Online: http://blogs.arts.unimelb.edu.au/refractory/2003/08/27/i-am-a-heterodemon-keely-macarow/

MacCormack, P. 2008. *Cinesexuality.* Hampshire and Burlington: Ashgate.

McMahon, M. 2005. 'Difference, Repetition'. In C.J. Stivale (ed.), *Giles Deleuze: Key Concepts.* Chesham: Acumen, pp. 42–52.

Malabou, C. 2004. *The Future of Hegel: Plasticity, Temporality and Dialectic.* London: Routledge.

Maldiney, H. 1973. *Regard, Parole, Espace.* Lausanne: L'Âge d'Homme.

Marciniak, K, Imre, A., and O'Healy, Á. (eds) 2007. *Transnational Feminism in Film and Media.* London: Palgrave Macmillan.

Marks, J. 1998. *Gilles Deleuze. Vitalism and Multiplicity*. London and Sterling: Pluto Press.

Margulies, I. 1996. *Nothing Happens. Chantal Akerman's Hyperrealist Everyday*, Durham and London: Duke University Press.

Martin, A. and Rosenbaum, J. 2003. *Movie Mutations: The Changing Face of World Cinephilia*. London : British Film Institute.

Martin-Jones, D. 2006. *Deleuze, Cinema and National Identity*. Edinburgh: Edinburgh University Press.

Massumi, B. 2002a. *Parables for the Virtual: Movement, Affect, Sensation*. Durham and London: Duke University Press.

Massumi, B. (ed.) 2002b. *A Shock to Thought: Expressions after Deleuze and Guattari*. London and New York: Routledge.

Mattelart, M. [1986] 2000. 'Everyday Life'. In C. Gledhill and L. Williams (eds), *Reinventing Film Studies*. London: Arnold, pp. 23–35.

Merleau-Ponty, M. 1964. 'The Film and the New Psychology'. Translated by H. Dreyfus and P. A. Dreyfus. In *Sense and Non-Sense*. Evanston: Northwestern University Press, pp. 48–59.

Merleau-Ponty, M. [1961] 1968. *The Visible and The Invisible*. Translated by A. Lingis. Evanston: Northwestern University Press.

Merleau-Ponty, M. [1945] 1996. *Phenomenology of Perception*. Translated by C. Smith. London: Routledge & Kegan Paul.

Merleau-Ponty, M. 2003. *Merleau-Ponty, Nature: Course Notes from the Collège de France*. Translated by R. Vallier. Evanston: Northwestern University Press.

Metz, C. 1974a. *Film Language: A Semiotics of the Cinema*. Translated by M. Taylor. New York: Oxford University Press.

Metz, C. 1974b. *Language and Cinema*. The Hague: Mouton.

Metz, C. 1979. 'The Cinematic Apparatus as a Social Institution: An Interview with Christian Metz'. *Discourse: Journal for Theoretical Studies in Media and Culture* 3: 7–38.

Metz, C. [1977] 1982. *Psychoanalysis and Cinema: The Imaginary Signifier*. Translated by C. Britton *et al.* London: Macmillan.

Metz, C. 1985. 'Photography and Fetish'. *October* 34: 81–90.

Milne, T. 1969. *Rouben Mamoulian*. London: Thames & Hudson.

Minh-ha, Trinh T.1989. *Woman, Native, Other: Writing Postcoloniality and Feminism*. Bloomington: Indiana University Press.

Mitry, J. [1963] 2000. *The Aesthetics and Psychology of the Cinema.* Translated by C. King. Bloomington and Indianapolis: Indiana University Press.

Mohanty, C.T. 2003. *Feminism without Borders: Decolonising Theory, Practicing Solidarity.* Durham, NC: Duke University Press.

Monaco, J. 1977. *How to Read a Film.* New York: Oxford University Press.

Morin, E. [1956/1978] 2005. *The Cinema, or, The Imaginary Man.* Translated by L. Mortimer. Minneapolis: University of Minnesota Press.

Mullarkey, J. 2009a 'Gilles Deleuze'. In F. Colman (ed.), *Film, Theory and Philosophy.* Acumen Publishing: Durham, pp. 179–189.

Mullarkey, J. 2009b. *Refractions of Reality: Philosophy and the Moving Image.* Basingstoke : Palgrave Macmillan.

Naficy, H. 2001. *An Accented Cinema: Exilic and Diasporic Filmmaking.* Princeton and Oxford: Princeton University Press.

Nancy, J.-L. 2001. *The Evidence of Film: Abbas Kiarostami.* Translated by C. Irizarry and V. A. Conley. Brussels: Yves Gevaert.

Ndalianis, A. 2005. *Neo-Baroque Aesthetics and Contemporary Entertainment.* Cambridge, MA: MIT Press.

Negri, A. 1991. *Savage Anomaly: Power of Spinoza's Metaphysics and Politics.* Minneapolis and Oxford: University of Minnesota Press.

Nichols, B. 2000. 'Film theory and the Revolt against Master Narratives'. In C. Gledhill and L. Williams (eds), *Reinventing Film Studies.* London: Arnold & New York: Oxford University Press, pp. 34–52.

Olkowski, D. 1999. *Gilles Deleuze and the Ruin of Representation.* Berkeley: University of California Press.

Olkowski, D. 2009. 'Henri Bergson'. In F. Colman (ed.), *Film, Theory and Philosophy*, Durham: Acumen, pp. 71–80.

O'Sullivan, S. and Zepke, S. (eds) 2008. *Producing the New: Deleuze, Guattari and Contemporary Art.* London & New York: Continuum.

Parr, A. (ed.) 2005. *The Deleuze Dictionary.* Edinburgh: Edinburgh University Press.

Pasolini, P.P. [1972] 2005. *Heretical Empiricism.* Translated by B.Lawton and L.K.Barnett. 2nd edition. Washington, D.C.: New Academia Press.

Patton, P. (ed.) 1996. *Deleuze: A Critical Reader.* Oxford: Blackwell.

Pearce, L. 1997. *Feminism and the Politics of Reading.* London: Hodder Arnold.

Pearce, L. 2003. *The Rhetorics of Feminism: Readings in Contemporary Cultural Theory and the Popular Press*. New York: Routledge.

Péguy, C. 1958. *Temporal and Eternal*. Translated by A. Dru. London: Harvill Press.

Phillips, J. 2008. 'Glauber Rocha: Hunger and Garbage'. In J. Phillips (ed.), *Cinematic Thinking: Philosophical Approaches to the New Cinema*. Stanford: Stanford University Press, pp. 90–108.

Pines, J. and Willemen, P. (eds) 1989. *Questions of Third Cinema*. London: BFI.

Pisters, P. (ed.) 2002. *Micropolitics of Media Culture: Reading the Rhizomes of Deleuze and Guattari*. Amsterdam: Amsterdam University Press.

Pisters, P. 2003. *The Matrix of Visual Culture: Working with Deleuze in Film Theory*. Stanford: Stanford University Press.

Pisters, P. 2011. *The Neuro-Image: A Deleuzian Filmphilosophy of Digital Screen Culture*. Stanford: Stanford University Press.

Plotnitsky, A. 2006, 'Manifolds: On the Concept of Space in Riemann and Deleuze'. In S. Duffy (ed.), *Virtual Mathematics: The Logic of Difference*. Bolton: Clinamen Press, pp. 187–208.

Porton, R. 1999. *Film and the Anarchist Imagination*. New York: Verso.

Powell, A. 2005. *Deleuze and Horror Film*. Edinburgh: Edinburgh University Press.

Powell, A. 2007. *Deleuze, Altered States and Film*. Edinburgh: Edinburgh University Press.

Powrie, P. 1997. *French Cinema in the 1980's: Nostalgia and the Crisis of Masculinity*. Oxford: Oxford University Press.

Prager, B. 2007. *The Cinema of Werner Herzog: Aesthetic Ecstasy and Truth*. London and New York: Wallflower Press.

Protevi, J. 2009. *Political Affect: Connecting the Social and the Somatic*. Minneapolis and London: University of Minnesota Press.

Rajchman, J. 2000. *The Deleuze Connections*. Cambridge, MA and London: MIT

Rancière, J. 2004. *The Politics of Aesthetics: The Distribution of the Sensible*. Translated by G. Rockhill. London & New York: Continuum.

Rancière, J. 2006. *Film Fables*. Translated by E. Battista. Oxford, New York: Berg.

Reynaud, B. 2000. 'Introduction: *Cahiers du Cinéma* 1973–1978'. In D. Wilson (ed.), *Cahiers du Cinéma* Volume Four: *1973–1978: History, Ideology, Cultural Struggle*. London and New York: Routledge, pp. 1–44.

Stivale, C.J. 2008. *Gilles Deleuze's ABCs: The Folds of Friendship*. Baltimore: Johns Hopkins University Press.

Surin, K. 2005. 'Force'. In C.J. Stivale (ed.), *Gilles Deleuze: Key Concepts*. Chesham: Acumen, pp. 19–30.

Tan, E. 1995. *Emotion and the Structure of Narrative Film: Film as an Emotion Machine*. London: Routledge.

Taylor, P. 2002. *Oulipo*. Online: http://www.nous.org.uk/oulipo.html

ThatGameCompany. 2008. *Flower*. (PS3) http://thatgamecompany.com/games/flower/.

Tsiolkas, C. 2003 '11'09"01– September 11: The Rest Is Silence', *Senses of Cinema* No. 24, Jan-Feb. Online. http://www.sensesofcinema.com/contents/03/24/sept_11.html

Tuan, Y.-F. 1974. *Topophilia: A Study of Environmental Perception, Attitudes, and Values*. Englewood Cliffs, NJ: Prentice-Hall.

Vaughan, H. 2009. 'André Bazin'. In F. Colman (ed.), *Film, Theory and Philosophy: The Key Thinkers*. Durham: Acumen, pp. 100–108.

Virilio, P. [1984] 1989. *War and Cinema: The Logistics of Perception*. Translated by P. Camiller. London: Verso.

Voloshinov, V.N. [1929] 1973. *Marxism and the Philosophy of Language*. Translated by L. Matejka and I.R. Titunik. New York: Seminar Press.

Wartenberg, T.E. and Curran, A. (eds) 2005. *The Philosophy of Film: Introductory Texts and Readings*. Oxford: Blackwell.

Watson, J. 2009. *Guattari's Diagramatic Thought*. New York and London: Continuum.

Wenders, W. [1986] 1989. *Emotion Pictures: Reflections on the Cinema*. Translated by S. Whiteside. London: Faber and Faber.

Wenders, W. 2001. *On Film: Essays and Conversations*. Translated by M. Hoffmann. London: Faber and Faber.

Williams, J. 2003. *Gilles Deleuze's 'Difference and Repetition': A Critical Introduction and Guide*. Edinburgh: Edinburgh University Press.

Williams, J. 2005. 'Immanence'. In A. Parr (ed.), *Deleuze Dictionary*. Edinburgh: Edinburgh University Press, pp. 125–127.

Williams, L. [1991] 2007. 'Film Bodies: Gender, Genre, and Excess'. In J. Codell (ed.), *Genre, Gender Race, and World Cinema*. Oxford: Blackwell, pp. 23–37.

Williams, L. 2008. *Screening Sex*. Durham and London: Duke University Press.

Wilson, D. (ed.) 2000. *Cahiers du Cinéma*. Vol.4: *1973–1978: History, Ideology, Cultural Struggle*. London and New York: Routledge.

Wölfflin, H. 1932. *Principles of Art History: The Problem of the*

Development of Style in Later Art. Translated by M.D. Hottinger. London: G. Bell and Sons.

Wollen, P. 1993. *Raiding the Icebox: Reflections on Twentieth-Century Culture*. Bloomington: Indiana University Press.

Woolf, V. [1925] 1950. *Mrs Dalloway*. London: Chatto & Windus in association with Hogarth Press.

Zepke, S. 2005. *Art as Abstract Machine: Ontology and Aesthetics in Deleuze and Guattari*. New York: Routledge.

Films Listed by Director

Akerman, C. 1974. *Je tu il elle* (*I you he she*).

Akerman, C. 1975. *Jeanne Dielman, 23 Quai du Commerce, 1080 Bruxelles*.

Akerman, C. 1984. *J'ai faim, j'ai froid* (*episode in Paris vu par ... 20 ans après*).

Altman, R. 1970. *MASH*.

Altman, R. 1993. *Short Cuts*.

Altman, R. 2001. *Gosford Park*.

Anderson, P.T. 2007. *There Will be Blood*.

Anderson, W. 2009. *Fantastic Mr Fox*.

Andersson, R. 2000. *Sånger från andra våningen* (*Songs from the second floor*).

Anger, K. 1964. *Scorpio Rising*.

Anger, K. 1965. *Kustom Kar Kommandos*. Puck Film Productions.

Antonioni, M. 1950. *Cronaca di un amore* (*Chronicle of a love*).

Antonioni, M. 1953. *La signora senza camelie* (*The Lady without Camelias*).

Antonioni, M. 1957. *Il Grido* (*The cry*).

Antonioni, M. 1960. *L'Avventura* (*The adventure*).

Antonioni, M. 1961. *La notte* (*The Night*).

Antonioni, M. 1962. *L'Eclisse* (*The eclipse*).

Antonioni, M. 1975. *Professione: reporter* (*The passenger*).

Axel, G. 1987. *Babettes gæstebud* (*Babette's feast*).

Badham, J. 1977. *Saturday Night Fever*.

Bigelow, K. 1991 *Point Break*.

Bigelow, K. 2008. *The Hurt Locker*.

Bird, B. and Pikava, J. 2007. *Ratatouille*.

Blystone, J. G. and Keaton, B. 1923. *Our Hospitality*.

Bong, J.-H. 2006. *Gwoemul* (*The Host*).

Boulmetis, T. 2003. *Politiki kouzina* (*Political kitchen*, also known as *A Touch of Spice*).

Boyle, D. 2002. *28 Days Later.*

Brakhage, S. 1962. *Window Water Baby Moving.*

Brakhage, S. 1971. *The Act of Seeing with One's Own Eyes.*

Breillat, C. 1999. *Romance.*

Breillat, C. 2001. *À ma soeur!* (*For my sister*, also known as *Fat Girl*).

Breillat, C. 2002. *Sex is Comedy.*

Bridges, J. 1979. *The China Syndrome.*

Brigand, A. 2002. *11'09"01– September 11.*

Browning, T. 1932. *Freaks.*

Buñuel, L. 1930. *L'Âge d'or* (*The golden age*).

Buñuel, L. 1951. *Susana* (also known as *The Devil and the Flesh*).

Buñuel, L. 1962. *El Ángel exterminador* (*The Exterminating Angel*).

Buñuel, L. 1967. *Belle du Jour.*

Buñuel, L. and Dali, S. 1929. *Un Chien Andalou.*

Cameron, J. 1984. *The Terminator.*

Campion, J. 1996. *The Portrait of a Lady.*

Carax, L. 1991. *Les Amants du Pont-Neuf* (*Lovers on the ninth bridge*).

Carax, L. 1999. *Pola X.*

Cassavetes, J. 1959. *Shadows.*

Chadha, G. 2008. *Angus, Thongs and Perfect Snogging.*

Chaplin, C. 1917. *The Immigrant.*

Chaplin, T. 2007. *Turning on the Mind: French Philosophers on Television.*

Chong, G.-J. and Shin, S.-O. 1985. *Pulgasari* (also known as *Bulgasari*).

Clark, L. 1995. *Kids.*

Clarke, A. 1989. *Elephant.*

Cocteau, J. 1946. *La Belle et la Bête* (*Beauty and the Beast*).

Coen, J. and Coen, E. 1991. *Barton Fink.*

Cooper, M.C. and Schoedsack, E.B. 1933. *King Kong.*

Coppola, S. 1999. *The Virgin Suicides.*

Coppola, S. 2006. *Marie Antoinette.*

Crisp, D. and Keaton, B. 1924. *The Navigator.*

Csupo, G. 2007. *Bridge to Terabitha.*

Cuarón, A. 2004. *Harry Potter and the Prisoner of Azkaban.*

Cuarón, A. 2006. *Children of Men.*

Daldry, S. 2002. *The Hours.*

Dash, J. 1991. *Daughters of the Dust.*

Dassin, J. 1964. *Topkapi.*

Davies, T. 1988. *Distant Voices, Still Lives.*

Debord, G. 1973. *La Société du Spectacle* (*Society of the Spectacle*).

De Bont, J. 1996. *Twister.*

De Heer, R. and Djigirr, P. 2006. *Ten Canoes.*

Del Toro, G. 2006. *El laberinto del fauno* (*Pan's labyrinth*).

Deren, M. 1946. *Ritual in Transfigured Time.*

Deren, M. and Hammid, A. 1943. *Meshes of the Afternoon.*

De Sica, V. 1948. *Ladri di biciclette (Bicycle Thief)*.

De Sica, V. 1952. *Umberto D.*

Donen, S. 1952. *Singin' in the Rain.*

Donen, S. 1957. *The Pyjama Game.*

Dovzhenko, A. 1928. *Zvenigora.*

Dovzhenko, A. 1929. *Arsenal (January Uprising in Kiev in 1918).*

Dovzhenko, A. 1930. *Zemlya (Earth).*

Dreyer, C. 1928. *La passion de Jeanne d'Arc (The Passion of Joan of Arc).*

Dulac, G. 1928. *La coquille et la clergyman (The Seashell and the Clergyman).*

Duras, M. 1975. *India Song.*

Duras, M. 1977. *Le Camion (The lorry).*

Duras, M. 1981. *L'homme atlantique.*

Duras, M. 1981. *Agatha et les lectures illimitées.*

Edwards, B. 1961. *Breakfast at Tiffany's.*

Eggeling, V. 1924. *Symphonie diagonale (Diagonal symphony).*

Eisenstein, S. 1925. *Bronenosets Potyomkin (Battleship Potemkin).*

Eisenstein, S. 1928. *Oktyabr (October).*

Emmerich, R. 2004. *The Day After Tomorrow.*

Epstein, J. 1923. *Cœur fidèle (Faithful Heart).*

Favreau, J. 2008. *Iron Man.*

Favreau, J. 2010. *Iron Man 2.*

Fellini, F. 1963. *8 1/2.*

Fellini, F. 1969. *Satyricon.*

Fellini, F. 1965. *Giulietta degli spiriti (Juliet of the Spirits).*

Fellini, F. 1970. *I clowns (The clowns).*

Fellini, F. 1972. *Fellini's Roma.*

Fellini, F. 1980. *La città delle donne (City of Women).*

Flaherty, R. 1922. *Nanook of the North.*

Fleming, V. 1939. *The Wizard of Oz.*

Ford, J. 1940. *The Grapes of Wrath.*

Forster, M. 2006. *Stranger than Fiction.*

Fowler, G.1957. *I Was a Teenage Werewolf.*

Fuller, S. 1963. *Shock Corridor.*

Gance, A. 1927. *Napoléon.*

Godard, J.-L. 1960. *À bout de souffle (Breathless).*

Godard, J.-L. 1963. *Le mépris (Contempt).*

Godard, J.-L. 1963. *Les Carabiniers (The soldiers).*

Godard, J.-L. 1964. *Bande à part (Band of outsiders).*

Godard, J.-L. 1965. *Pierrot le fou.*

Godard, J.-L. 1967. *La Chinoise.*

Godard, J.-L. 1967. *Deux ou trois choses que je sais d'elle (Two or three things that I know about her).*

Godard, J.-L. 1967. *Week End.*

Godard, J.-L. 1968. *One Plus One/ Sympathy for the Devil.*

Godard, J.-L. 1990. *Nouvelle Vague.*

Godard, J.-L . 1991. *Allemagne Neuf Zéro (Germany Year 90 Nine Zero).*

Godard, J.-L. 2004. *Notre Musique (Our Music).*

Godard, J.-L. 2007. *Histoire(s) du cinema.*

Gorris, M. 1997. *Mrs Dalloway.*

Grémillon, J. 1941. *Remorques (Stormy Waters).*

Griffith, D.W. 1915. *Birth of a Nation.*

Griffith, D.W. 1916. *Intolerance.*

Haneke, M. 2005. *Caché (Hidden).*

Hardy, R. 1973. *The Wicker Man.*

Harlin, R. 1993. *Cliffhanger.*

Harris, L. 1992. *Just Another Girl on the I.R.T.*

Hawks, H. 1932. *Scarface.*

Hawks, H. 1946. *The Big Sleep.*

Hawks, H. 1953. *Gentlemen Prefer Blondes.*

Haynes, T. 1987. *Superstar: The Karen Carpenter Story.*

Haynes, T. 1991. *Poison.*

Haynes, T. 1995. *SAFE.*

Haynes, T. 1998. *Velvet Goldmine.*

Haynes, T. 2002. *Far From Heaven.*

Haynes, T. 2006. *I'm not there.*

Heckerling, A. 1995. *Clueless.*

Herzog, W. 1972. *Aguirre, der Zorn Gottes (Aguirre, wrath of God).*

Herzog, W. 1979. *Nosferatu the Vampyre.*

Herzog, W. 1997. *Little Dieter Needs to Fly.*

Herzog, W. 2005. *Grizzly Man.*

Herzog, W. 2007. *Encounters at the End of the World.*

Hitchcock, A. 1938. *The Lady Vanishes.*

Hitchcock, A. 1941. *Mr & Mrs Smith.*

Hitchcock, A. 1945. *Spellbound.*

Hitchcock, A. 1946. *Notorious.*

Hitchcock, A. 1948. *Rope.*

Hitchcock, A. 1954. *Rear Window.*

Hitchcock, A. 1958. *Vertigo.*

Hitchcock, A. 1960. *Psycho.*

Hitchcock, A. 1963. *The Birds.*

Honda, I. 1954. *Gojira (Godzilla).*

Hopper, D. 1969. *Easy Rider.*

Hou, H.-H. 2001. *Qian xi man po (Millenium mambo).*

Huston, J. 1941. *The Maltese Falcon.*

Itami, J. 1986. *Tampopo.*

Jackson, P. 2005. *King Kong.*

Jarman, D. 1978. *Jubilee.*

Jarman, D. 1993. *Blue.*

Jarmusch, J. 1984. *Stranger than Paradise.*

Jarmusch, J. 1989. *Mystery Train.*

Jarmusch, J. 2003. *Coffee and Cigarettes.*

Jarmusch, J. 1995. *Dead Man.*

Jarmusch, J. 1991. *Night on Earth.*

Jarmusch, J. 1999. *Ghost Dog: Way of the Samurai.*

Jarmusch, J. 2005. *Broken Flowers.*

Johnston, J. 1999. *October Sky.*

Jonze, S. 2002. *Adaptation.*

Kalatozov, M. 1964. *Soy Cuba (I am Cuba).*

Kassovitz, M. 1995. *La Haine (The hate).*

Kelly, R. 2001. *Donnie Darko.*

Kelly, R. 2004. *Donnie Darko: The Director's Cut.*

Kelly, R. 2007. *Southland Tales.*

Khzhanovsky, I. 2005. *4.*

Kiarostami, A. 1997. *Ta'm e guilass (A Taste of Cherry).*

Kiarostami, A. 2002. *Ten*.

Kieslowski, K. 1993. *Trois couleurs: Bleu (Three Colours: Blue)*.

Kim, J.-W. 2003a. *Janghwa, Hongryeon (A tale of two sisters)*.

Kim, K.-D. 2003b. *Bom yeoreum gaeul gyeoul geurigo bom (Spring, Summer, Autumn, Winter... and Spring)*.

King, J. 2006. *Black Sheep*.

Kitano, T. 2002. *Dolls*.

Konopka, B. 2009. *Królik po berlinsku (Rabbit à la Berlin)*.

Koreeda, H. 1998. *Wandâfuru raifu (After Life)*.

Kubrick, S. 1968. *2001: A Space Odyssey*.

Kubrick, S. 1971. *A Clockwork Orange*.

Kubrick, S. 1980. *The Shining*.

Kurosawa, A. 1954. *Shichinin no samurai (Seven Samurai)*.

Kustirica, E. 1995. *Underground*.

LaBruce, B. and Castro, R. 1996. *Hustler White*.

LaBruce, B. 2004. *The Raspberry Reich*.

Land, O. (Landow, G.) 1967. *Bardo Follies*.

Lang, F. 1931. *M*.

Laughton, C. 1955. *The Night of the Hunter*.

Lee, A. 2005. *Brokeback Mountain*.

Lehmann, M. 1989. *Heathers*.

Losey, J. 1948. *The Boy with Green Hair*.

Lumière, A. and Lumière, L. 1896. *L'Arrivée d'un train à La Ciotat (Arrival of a Train at La Ciotat)*.

Lye, L. 1958–1979. *Free Radicals*.

Lynch, D. 2001. *Mulholland Dr*.

Lynch, D. 2006. *Inland Empire*.

Lyne, A. 1997. *Lolita*.

Makavejev, D. 1974. *Sweet Movie*.

Makhmalbaf, S. 2002. *God, Construction and Destruction* – part of *11'9"01 September 11*.

Malik, T. 1998. *The Thin Red Line*.

Malle, L. 1992. *Vayna on 42nd Street*.

Malle, L. 1987. *Au Revoir, les Enfants (Goodbye, children)*.

Mamoulian, R. 1931. *Dr Jekyll and Mr Hyde*.

Mankiewicz, J. 1950. *All About Eve*.

Marker, C. 1962. *La Jetée*.

Maybury, J. 1998. *Love is the Devil: Study for a Portrait of Francis Bacon*.

Maysles, A and Maysles, D. 1970. *Gimme Shelter*.

McLaren, N. 1948. *Workshop Experiment in Animated Sound*.

McLaren, N. 1949. *Begone Dull Care*.

McLaren, N. 1955. *Blinkity Blank*.

Meadows, S. 2006. *This is England*.

Meirelles, F. 2005. *The Constant Gardener*.

Miller, F. and Rodriguez, R. 2005. *Frank Miller's Sin City*.

Miller, G. 1979. *Mad Max*.

Minnelli, V. 1951. *An American in Paris*.

Minnelli, V. 1953. *The Band Wagon*.

Minnelli, V. 1954. *Brigadoon*.

Mizoguchi, K. 1939. *Zangiku Monogatari (The Story of the Late Chrysanthemums)*.

Mungiu, C. 2007. *4 luni, 3 saptamâni si 2 zile (4 Months, 3 Weeks and 2 Days)*.

Murnau, F.W. 1922. *Nosferatu, eine Symphonie des Grauens (Nosferatu, A Symphony of Horror)*.

Murnau, F.W. 1924. *Der Letzte Mann (The Last Laugh)*.

Murnau, F.W. 1927. *Sunrise: A Song of Two Humans*.

Ngulesco, J. 1953. *How to Marry a Millionaire*.

Ozu, Y. 1952. *Ochazuke no aji (The Flavour of Green Tea over Rice)*.

Ozu, Y. 1960. *Akibiyori (Late Autumn)*.

Pakula, A.J. 1976. *All the President's Men*.

Park, C.-W. 2003. *Oldboy*.

Park, C.-W. 2006. *Saibogujiman kwenchana (I'm a cyborg, but that's OK)*.

Park, C.-W. 2009. *Bakjwi (Thirst)*.

Park, K.-H. 1998. *Yeogo goedam (Whispering corridors)*.

Parker, A. 1987. *Angel Heart*.

Paronnaud, V. and Satrapi, M. 2007. *Persepolis*.

Pasolini, P.P. 1962. *Mama Roma*.

Pasolini, P.P. 1975. *Salò o le 120 giornate di Sodoma (Salò, or the 120 Days of Sodom)*. Peck, R. 2005. *Sometimes in April*.

Penn, S. 2007. *Into the Wild*.

Peralta, S. 2001. *Dogtown and Z Boys*.

Perrault, P. 1970. *Un pays sans bon sens! (A country with no common sense!)*

Perrault, P. 1980. *Le pays de la terre sans arbre ou Le mouchouânipi (Land Without Trees, or The Mouchouânipi)*.

Pontocorvo, G. 1966. *La Bataille D'Alger (The Battle of Algiers)*.

Proyas, A. 1998. *Dark City*.

Pudovkin, V. 1926. *Mat (Mother)*.

Renoir, J. 1935. *La Règle du jeu (The rules of the game)*.

Renoir, J. 1936. *Le Crime de Monsieur Lange*.

Resnais, A. 1948. *Van Gogh*.

Resnais, A. 1950. *Guernica*.

Resnais, A. 1955. *Nuit et brouillard (Night and fog)*.

Resnais, A. 1959. *Hiroshima Mon Amour (Hiroshima, my love)*.

Resnais, A. 1966. *La Guerre est finie (The war is over)*.

Resnais, A. 1968. *Je t'aime, je t'aime*.

Resnais, A. 1980. *Mon oncle d'Amérique (My American Uncle)*.

Rocha, G. 1964. *Deus e o diabo na terra do sol (Black god, white devil)*.

Rocha, G. 1967. *Terra em transe (Land in Anguish* also known as *Entranced Earth)*.

Roeg, N. 1976. *The Man Who Fell to Earth.*

Roeg, N. 1980. *Bad Timing.*

Romm, M. 1962. *9 dney odnogo goda (Nine Days of One Year).*

Rossellini, R. 1945. *Roma, città aperta (Rome, Open City).*

Rossellini, R. 1946. *Paisà.*

Rossellini, R. 1948. *Germania anno zero (Germany Year Zero).*

Rossellini, R. 1952. *Europa '51.*

Rouch, J. 1955. *Les Maîtres fous (The Mad Masters).*

Rouch, J. 1958. *Moi un noir (I, a Negro).*

Ruiz, R. 1982. *Les Trois couronnes du matelot (Three crowns of the sailor).*

Sasanatieng, W. 2000. *Fah talai jone (Tears of the Black Tiger).*

Schnabel, J. 2007. *Le scaphandre et le papillon (The Diving Bell and the Butterfly).*

Schneider, A. 1964. *Film.*

Scorsese, M. 1976. *Taxi Driver.*

Seidi, U. 2007. *Import/Export.*

Sembene, O. 1977. *Ceddo (Outsiders).*

Shankman, A. 2007. *Hairspray.*

Sherman, C. 1997. *Office Killer.*

Sjöström, V. 1928. *The Wind.*

Smithson, R. 1970. *Spiral Jetty.*

Snow, M. 1967. *Wavelength.*

Snow, M. 1971. *La Région Centrale.*

Sono, S. 2001. *Jisatsu sâkuru (Suicide Club).*

Spielberg, S. 1975. *Jaws.*

Syberberg, H.-J. 1978. *Hitler: ein Film aus Deutschland (Our Hitler).*

Tarantino, Q. 1997. *Jackie Brown.*

Tarantino, Q. 2003. *Kill Bill: Vol 1.*

Tarantino, Q. 2004. *Kill Bill: Vol 2.*

Tarantino, Q. 2009. *Inglourious Basterds.*

Tarkovsky, A. 1972. *Solyaris (Solaris).*

Tarr, B. 1989. *Kárhozat (Damnation).*

Tati, J. 1953. *Les vacances de Monsieur Hulot (Monsieur Hulot's Holiday).*

Tati, J. 1967. *Play Time.*

Tati, J. 1971. *Trafic.*

Thornton, W. 2009. *Samson and Delilah.*

Tsai, M.-L. 1997. *He liu (The River).*

Tsai, M.-L. 1998. *Dong (The Hole).*

Tsukamoto, S. 1989. *Tetsuo.*

Tykwer, T. 1998. *Lola rennt (Run Lola Run).*

Van Sant, G. 1989. *Drugstore Cowboy.*

Van Sant, G. 2003. *Elephant.*

Van Sant, G. 2005. *Last Days.*

Varda, A. 1962. *Cleo de 5 à 7 (Cleo from 5 to 7).*

Varda, A. 1985. *Sans toit ni loi. (Without roof nor rule* also known as *Vagabond).*

Varda, A. 2000. *Les glaneurs et la glaneuse (The Gleaners and I).*

Vertov, D. 1929. *Chelovek s kino-apparatom (Man with a Movie Camera).*

Vidor, K. 1928. *The Crowd.*

Vidor, K. 1931. *A Street Scene.*

Vidor, K. 1934. *Our Daily Bread.*

Vidor, K. 1944. *An American Romance.*

Vigo, J. 1934. *L'Atalante*.

Visconti, L. 1948. *La Terra Trema:
Episodio del mare* (*The earth
trembles*).

Visconti, L. 1960. *Rocco e I suoi fratelli*
(*Rocco and His Brothers*).

von Trier, L. 1991. *Zentropa* (also
known as *Europa*).

von Trier, L. 2000. *Dancer in the Dark*.

von Trier, L. 2003. *Dogville*.

Von Trotta, M. 1981. *Die Bleierne Zeit*
(*The leaden time* also known as *The
German Sisters*).

Warhol, A. 1963. *Eat*.

Warhol, A. 1963. *Kiss*.

Warhol, A. 1964. *Empire*.

Waters, M. 2004 *Mean Girls*.

Wenders, W. 1974. *Alice in den Städten*
(*Alice in the Cities*).

Wenders, W. 1975. *Falsche Bewegung*
(*False movement* also known as
Wrong Move).

Wenders, W. 1976. *Im Lauf der Zeit* (*In
the course of Time*, commonly known
as *Kings of the Road*).

Wenders, W. 1982. *Der Stand der Dinge*
(*The State of Things*).

Wenders, W. 1985. *Tokyo-Ga*.

Wenders, W. 1987. *Der Himmel über
Berlin* (*Wings of Desire*).

Weerasethakul, A. 2002. *Sud Sanaeha*
(*Blissfully yours*).

Weerasethakul, A. 2004. *Sud pralad*
(*Tropical Malady*).

Weerasethakul, A. 2006. *Sang sattawat*
(*Syndromes and a Century*).

Welles, O. 1941. *Citizen Kane*. Mercury
Productions/RKO Radio Pictures.

Welles, O. and Cortez, S. 1942. *The
Magnificent Ambersons*.

Wiene, R. 1920. *Das Cabinet des
Dr. Caligari* (*The Cabinet of Dr.
Caligari*).

Wilder, B. 1950. *Sunset Boulevard*.

Winterbottom, M. 2003. *Code 46*.

Wong K.-W. 1997. *Chunguag Zhaxie*
(*Happy Together*).

Wong K.-W. 2004. *2046*.

Wright, E. 2010. *Scott Pilgrim vs. The
World*.

Wyler, W. 1953. *Roman Holiday*.

Wyler, W. 1959. *Ben-Hur*.

Zanussi, K. 1969 *Struktura krysztalu*
(*The Structure of Crystals*).

Zhang, K.-J. 2008. *24 City*.

Zwick, E. 2006. *Blood Diamond*.

Filmography

4. I. Khzhanovsky (dir.) (Filmocom/ Hubert Bals Fund, 2005).

4 luni, 3 saptamâni si 2 zile (4 Months, 3 Weeks and 2 Days). C. Mungiu (dir.) (Mobra Films/CNC/Mindshare Media/Televiziunea Romana/*et al.*, 2007).

8 1/2. F. Fellini (dir.) (Cineriz/Francinex, 1963).

24 City. K.-J. Zhang (dir.) (Bandai Visual Company/Bitters End/China Resources/Office Kitano/Shanghai Film Group/Xstream Pictures, 2008).

28 Days Later. D. Boyle (dir.) (DNA Films/British Film Council, 2002).

2001: A Space Odyssey. S. Kubrick (dir.) (MGM/Polaris/Stanley Kubrick Productions, 1968).

2046. K.-W. Wong (dir.) (Arte/Block 2 Pictures/China Film Co-Production Corporation/Classic/Columbia Pictures/Fortissimo Films/Franc 3 Cinéma/Jet Tone Production, 2004).

À bout de souffle (Breathless). J.-L. Godard (dir.) (Les Productions Georges de Beauregard/Société Nouvelle de Cinématographie (SNC), 1960).

À ma soeur! (For my sister, also known as *Fat Girl)*. C. Breillat (dir.) (CB Films/Canal+/Centre National de la Cinématographie/Flach Film/ Immagine e Cinema/Urania Pictures/ arte France Cinéma, 2001).

Act of Seeing with One's Own Eyes, The. S. Brakhage (dir.) (Stan Brakhage, 1971).

Adaptation. S. Jonze (dir.) (Beverly Detroit/Clinica Estico/Good Machine/ Intermedia/Magnet Productions/ Propaganda Films, 2002).

Agatha et les lectures illimitées. M. Duras (dir.) (Institut National de

l'Audiovisuel/Les Productions
Berthemont, 1981).

Âge d'or, L' (*The golden age*). L. Buñuel
(dir.) (Vicomte de Noailles, 1930).

Aguirre, der Zorn Gottes (*Aguirre,
wrath of God*). W. Herzog (dir.)
(Werner Herzog Filmproduktion/
Hessischer Rundfunk, 1972).

Akibiyori (*Late Autumn*). Y. Ozu (dir.)
(Shôchiku Eiga, 1960).

Alice in den Städten (*Alice in the
Cities*). W. Wenders (dir.) (Filmverlag
der Autoren/Westdeutscher
Rundfunk/Wim Wenders Produktion,
1974).

Allemagne Neuf Zéro (*Germany Year
90 Nine Zero*). J.-L. Godard (dir.)
(Antenne-2/Production Brainstorm/
Gaumont/Périphéria, 1991).

All the President's Men. A.J. Pakula (dir.)
(Warner Bros. Pictures/Wildwood,
1976).

Amants du Pont-Neuf, Les (*Lovers on
the ninth bridge*). L. Carax (dir.)
(Films A2/Gaumont International/Les
Films Christian Fechner, 1991).

An American Romance. K. Vidor (dir.)
(MGM/Loew's, 1944).

An American in Paris. V. Minnelli (dir.)
(Loew's, 1951).

Angel Heart. A. Parker (dir.) (Carolco
International N.V./Winkast Film
Productions/Union, 1987).

Ángel exterminador, El (*The
Exterminating Angel*). L. Buñuel

(dir.) (Producciones Gustavo
Alatriste, 1962)

Angus, Thongs and Perfect Snogging.
G. Chadha (dir.) (Goldcrest Pictures/
Internationale Filmproduktion
Stella-del-Süd/Nickelodeon Movies/
Paramount Pictures, 2008).

Arrivée d'un train à La Ciotat, L'
(*Arrival of a Train at La Ciotat*).
A. Lumière and L. Lumière (dirs)
(Lumière, 1896).

Arsenal (*January Uprising in Kiev in
1918*). A. Dovzhenko (dir.) (VUFKU,
1929).

Atalante, L'. J. Vigo (dir.) (Gaumont,
1934).

Avventura, L' (*The adventure*). M.
Antonioni (dir.) (Cino del Duca/
Produzioni Cinematografiche
Europee/Societé Cinématographique
Lyre, 1960).

Au Revoir, les Enfants (*Goodbye,
children*). L. Malle (dir.) (Nouvelles
Éditions de Films/MK2 Productions/
Stella Film/N.E.F. Filmproduktion
und Vertriebs/Centre National
de la Cinématograaphie/Soficas
Investimages/Images Investissements/
Sofica Créations/Rai Uno
Radiotelevisione, 1987).

Babettes gæstebud (*Babette's feast*).
G. Axel (dir.) (Panorama Film
A/S/Det Danske Filminstitute/
Nordisk Film/Rungstedlundfonden,
1987).

Bad Timing. N. Roeg (dir). (Recorded Picture Company/The Rank Organisation 1980).

Bakjwi (*Thirst*). C.-W. Park (dir.) (CJ Entertainment/Focus Features International/Moho Films, 2009).

Band Wagon, The. V. Minnelli (dir.) (MGM/Loew's, 1953).

Bande à part (*Band of outsiders*). J.-L. Godard (dir.) (Columbia Films/Anouchka Films/Orsay Films, 1964).

Bardo Follies. Land, O. (Landow, G.). (dir.) (George Landow, 1967).

Barton Fink. J. Coen and E. Coen (dirs) (Circle Films/Working Title Films, 1991).

Bataille D'Alger, La (*The Battle of Algiers*). G. Pontocorvo (dir.) (Igor Film/Casbah Film, 1966).

Begone Dull Care. N. McLaren (dir.) (Ottawa: National Film Board of Canada, 1949).

Belle du Jour. L. Buñuel (dir.) (Robert et Raymond Hakim/Paris Film Productions/Five Film, 1967).

Belle et la Bête, La (*Beauty and the Beast*). J. Cocteau (dir.) (DisCina, 1946).

Ben-Hur. W. Wyler (dir.) (MGM/Loews, 1959).

Big Sleep, The. H. Hawks (dir.) (Warner Bros. Pictures, 1946).

Birds, The. A. Hitchcock (dir.) (Universal Pictures/Alfred J. Hitchcock Productions, 1963).

Birth of a Nation. D.W.Griffith (dir.) (David W. Griffith Corp./Epoch Producing Corporation, 1915).

Black Sheep. J. King (dir.) (New Zealand Film Commission/New Zealand On Air/The Daesung Group/Escapade Pictures/Live Stock Films/Singlet Films, 2006).

Bleierne Zeit, Die (*The leaden time* also known as *The German Sisters*). M. Von Trotta (dir.) (Bioskop Film/SFB, 1981).

Blinkity Blank. N. McLaren (dir.) (Ottawa: National Film Board of. Canada, 1955).

Blood Diamond. E. Zwick (dir.) (Warner Bros. Pictures/Virtual Studios/Spring Creek Productions/Bedford Falls Productions/Initial Entertainment Group (IEG)/Lonely Film Productions GmbH & Co. KG, 2006).

Blue. D. Jarman (dir.) (Basilisk Communications/Uplink Co./Arts Council of Great Britain/Channel Four Films/BBC Radio/Opal, 1993).

Bom yeoreum gaeul gyeoul geurigo bom (*Spring, Summer, Autumn, Winter... and Spring*). K.-D. Kim (dir.) Korea Pictures/LJ Film/Pandora Filmproduktion/Cineclick Asia, 2003).

Boy with Green Hair, The. J. Losey (dir.) (RKO Pictures, 1948).

Breakfast at Tiffany's. B. Edwards (dir.) (Jurow-Shepherd, 1961).

Bridge to Terabitha. G. Csupo (dir). (Hal Lieberman Company/Lauren Levine Productions/Walden Media, 2007).

Brigadoon. V. Minnelli (dir.) (MGM, 1954).

Broken Flowers. J. Jarmusch (dir.) (Focus Films/Five Roses/Bac Films, 2005).

Brokeback Mountain. A. Lee (dir.) (Alberta Film Entertainment/Foucs Features/Good Machine/Paramount Pictures/River Road Entertainment, 2005).

Bronenosets Potyomkin (*Battleship Potemkin*). S. Eisenstein (dir.) (Goskino, 1925).

Cabinet des Dr. Caligari, Das (*The Cabinet of Dr. Caligari*). R. Wiene (dir.) (Decla-Bioscop AG, 1920).

Caché (*Hidden*). M. Haneke (dir.) (Les Films du Losange/Wega Film/Bavaria Film/BIM Distribuzione/Uphill Pictures, 2005).

Camion, Le (The lorry). M. Duras (dir.) (Auditel/Cinéma 9, 1977).

Carabiniers, Les (*The soldiers*). J.-L. Godard (dir.) (Concinor/Les Films Marceau/Rome Paris Films/Leatitia Films, 1963).

Ceddo (*Outsiders*). Sembene, O. (dir.) (Films Domireew/Sembene, 1977).

Chelovek s kino-apparatom (*Man with a Movie Camera*). D. Vertov (dir.) VUFKU, 1929).

Chien Andalou, Un. L. Buñuel and S. Dali (dirs) (Luis Buñuel, 1929).

Children of Men. A. Cuarón (dir.) (Universal Pictures/Strike Entertainment/Hit and Run Productions, 2006).

China Syndrome, The. J. Bridges (dir.) (IPC Films, 1979).

Chinoise, La. J.-L. Godard (dir.) (Anouchka Films/Les Productions de la Guéville/Athos Films/Parc Film/Simar Films, 1967).

Chunguag Zhaxie (*Happy Together*). K.-W. Wong (dir.) (Block 2 Pictures/Jet Tone Production/Prénom H Co Ltd/Seowoo Film company, 1997).

Città delle donne, La (*City of Women*). F. Fellini (dir.) (Gaumont/Opera Film Produzione, 1980).

Citizen Kane. O. Welles (dir.) (Mercury Productions/RKO Radio Pictures, 1941).

Cleo de 5 à 7 (*Cleo from 5 to 7*). A. Varda (dir) (Ciné Tamaris/Rome Paris Films, 1962).

Cliffhanger. R. Harlin (dir.) (Carolco Pictures/Canal+ (as Le Studio Canal+)/Pioneer/RCS Video (in association with)/Cliffhanger Productions, 1993).

Clockwork Orange, A. S. Kubrick (dir.) (Warner Bros./Hawk Films, 1971).

Clowns, I (*The clowns*). F. Fellini (dir.) (Radiotelevisione Italiana/Compagnia Leone Cinematografica/Office de Radiodiffusion Télévision Française/Bavaria Film, 1970).

Clueless. A. Heckerling (dir.) (Paramount Pictures, 1995).

Cronaca di un amore (*Chronicle of a love*). M. Antonioni (dir.) (Viliani Film, 1950).

Code 46. M. Winterbottom (dir.) (BBC/Revolution Films, 2003).

Cœur fidèle (*Faithful Heart*). J. Epstein (dir.) (Pathé Consortium Cinéma, 1923).

Coffee and Cigarettes. J. Jarmusch (dir.) (Asmik Ace Entertainment/BIM/Smokescreen Inc., 2003).

Constant Gardener, The. F. Meirelles. (dir.) (Potboiler Productions/Epsilon Motion Pictures/Scion Films/UK Film Council/Vierte Babelsberg Film, 2005).

Coquille et la clergyman, La (*The Seashell and the Clergyman*). G. Dulac (dir.) (Délia Film, 1928).

Crime de Monsieur Lange, Le. J. Renoir (dir.) (Films Obéron, 1936).

Crowd, The. K. Vidor (dir.) (MGM, 1928).

Dancer in the Dark. L. von Trier (dir.) (Zentropa Entertainments [...], 2000).

Daughters of the Dust. J. Dash, J. (dir.) (American Playhouse/Geechee Girls/WMG Film, 1991).

Dead Man. J. Jarmusch (dir.) (Pandora Filmproduktion/JVC Entertainment Networks/Newmarket Capital Group/12 Gauge Productions, 1995).

Deus e o diabo na terra do sol (*Black god, white devil*). G. Rocha (dir.) (Banco Nacional de Minas Gerais/Copacabana Films/Luiz Augusto Mendes Produções Cinematográficas, 1964).

Deux ou trois choses que je sais d'elle (*Two or three things that I know about her*). J.-L. Godard (dir.) (Argos Films/Anouchka Films/Les Films du Carrosse/Parc Film, 1967).

Distant Voices, Still Lives. T. Davies (dir.) (British Film Institute (BFI)/Channel Four Films, 1988).

Dogtown and Z Boys. S. Peralta (dir.) (Agi Orsi Productions/Vans off the Wall, 2001).

Dogville. L. von Trier (dir.) (Zentropa Entertainments [...] 2003).

Dolls. T. Kitano (dir.) (Bandai Visual Company/Office Kitano/TV Tokyo/Tokyo FM Broadcasting Co., 2002).

Dong (*The Hole*). M.-L. Tsai (dir.) (Arc Light Films/Central Motion Pictures Corporation/China Television/Haut et Court/La Sept-Arte, 1998).

Donnie Darko. R. Kelly (dir.) (Pandora Cinema/Flower Films/Adam Fields Productions/Gaylord Films, 2001).

Donnie Darko: The Director's Cut. R. Kelly (dir.) (Pandora Cinema/Flower Films/Adam Fields Productions/Gaylord Films, 2004).

Dr Jekyll and Mr Hyde. R. Mamoulian (dir.) (Paramount Pictures, 1931).

Drugstore Cowboy. G. Van Sant (dir.) (Avenue Picture Productions, 1989).

Easy Rider. D. Hopper (dir.) (Columbia Pictures Corporation/Pando Company Inc./Raybert Productions, 1969).

Eat. A. Warhol (dir.) (Andy Warhol, 1963).

Eclisse, L' (The eclipse). M. Antonioni (dir.) (Cineiz/Interopa film/Paris film, 1962).

Elephant. A. Clarke (dir.) (BBC Northern Ireland, 1989).

Elephant. G. Van Sant (dir.) (HBO Films/ Fine Line Features/Meno Films/ Blue Relief Productions/Fearmaker Studios, 2003).

Empire. A. Warhol (dir.) (Andy Warhol, 1964).

Encounters at the End of the World. W. Herzog (dir.) (Discovery Films, 2007).

Europa '51. R. Rossellini (dir.) (Ponti-De Laurentiis Cinematografica, 1952).

Fah talai jone (Tears of the Black Tiger). W. Sasanatieng (dir.) (Aichi Arts Center/Film Bangkok/Five Star Production Co. Ltd, 2000).

Falsche Bewegung (False movement also known as *Wrong Move).* W. Wenders (dir.) (Albatros Produktion/ Solaris Film/Westdeutscher Rundfunk/Wim Wenders Produktion, 1975).

Fantastic Mr Fox. W. Anderson (dir.) (Twentieth Century Fox Film Corporation/Indian Paintbrush/ Regency Enterprises/American Empirical Pictures, 2009).

Far From Heaven. T. Haynes (dir.) (Focus Features/Vulcan Productions/ iller Films/John Wells Productions/

Section Eight/Clear Blue Sky Productions/USA Films, 2002).

Fellini's Roma. F. Fellini (dir.) (Ultra Film/Les Productions Artists Associés, 1972).

Film. A. Schneider (dir.) (Evergreen, 1964).

Frank Miller's Sin City. F. Miller and R. Rodriguez (dirs) (Dimension Films/ Troublemaker Studios, 2005).

Freaks. T. Browning (dir.) (MGM, 1932).

Free Radicals. L. Lye (dir.) (Len Lye, 1958–1979).

Gentlemen Prefer Blondes. H. Hawks (dir.) (Twentieth Century-Fox Film Corporation, 1953).

Ghost Dog: Way of the Samurai. J. Jarmusch (dir.) (Pandora Filmproduktion/ARD/Degeto Film/ Plywood Productions/Bac Films/ Canel+/JVC Entertainment Networks, 1999).

Giulietta degli spiriti (Juliet of the Spirits). F. Fellini (dir.) (Rizzoli Film/ Francoriz Production, 1965).

Gimme Shelter. A. Maysles and D. Maysles (dirs) (Maysles Films/ Penforta, 1970).

Glaneurs et la glaneuse, Les. (The Gleaners and I). A. Varda (dir.) (Ciné Tamaris, 2000).

God, Construction and Destruction – part of *11'9''01 September 11.* S. Makhmalbaf (dir.) (CIH shorts *et al.,* 2002).

Gojira (Godzilla). I. Honda (dir.) (Toho Film, 1954).

Gosford Park. R. Altman (dir.) (USA Films/Capitol Films/Film Council/Sandcastle 5 Productions/Chicagofilms/Medusa Produzione, 2001).

Grapes of Wrath, The. J. Ford (dir.) (Twentieth Century Fox Film Corporation. 1940).

Grido, Il (The cry). M.Antonioni (dir.) (SpA Cinematografica/Robert Alexander Productions, 1957).

Grizzly Man. W. Herzog (dir.) (Lions Gate Film/Discovery Docs./Real Big Production, 2005).

Gwoemul (The Host). J.-H. Bong (dir.) (Chungeorahm Film/Showbox/Mediaplex/Happinet Corporation, 2006).

Guerre est finie, Le (The war is over). A. Resnais (dir.) (Europa Film/Sofracima, 1966).

Guernica. A. Resnais (dir.) (Pathéon Productions, 1950).

Hairspray. A. Shankman (dir.) (New Line Cinema/Ingenious Film Partners/Zadan/Meron Productions/Offspring Entertainment/Legion Entertainment/Storyline Entertainment, 2007).

Haine, La (The hate). M. Kassovitz (dir.) (Canal+/Cofinergie 6/Egg Pictures/Kasso Inc. Productions/La Sept Cinéma/Les Productions Lazennec/Polygram Filmed Entertainment/Studio Image, 1995).

Harry Potter and the Prisoner of Azkaban. A. Cuarón (dir.) (Warner Bros. Pictures/1492 Pictures/Heyday Films/P of A Productions Ltd, 2004).

Heathers. M. Lehmann (dir.) (New World Pictures/Cinemarque Entertainment, 1989).

He liu (The River). M.-L. Tsai (dir.) (Tsai, 1997).

Himmel über Berlin, Der (Wings of Desire). W. Wenders (dir.) (Road Movies Filmproduktion/Argos Films/Westdeutscher Rundfunk (WDR), 1987).

Hiroshima Mon Amour (Hiroshima, my love). A. Resnais (dir.) Argos Films/Como Films/Daiei Studios/Pathé Entertainment, 1959).

Histoire(s) du cinema. J.-L. Godard (dir.) (DVD version, Gaumont, 2007).

Hitler: ein Film aus Deutschland (Our Hitler). H.-J. Syberberg (dir.) (TMS Film GmbH/Solaris Film/Westdeutscher Rundfunk/Institute National de l'Audiovisuel/BBC, 1978.)

Homme atlantique, L'. M. Duras (dir.) (Des Femmes Filment/Institut National de l'Audiovisuel/Les Productions Berthemont, 1981).

Hours, The. S. Daldry (dir.) (Paramount Pictures/Miramax Films/Scott Rudin Productions, 2002).

How to Marry a Millionaire. J. Ngulesco (dir.) (Twentieth Century Fox Film Corporation, 1953)

Hurt Locker, The. K. Bigelow (dir.) (Voltage Pictures/Grosvenor Park Media/Film Capital Europe Funds/ First Light Production/Kingsgate Films/Summit Entertainment, 2008).

Hustler White. B. LaBruce and R. Castro (dirs) (Dangerous to Know Swell Co./ Hustler White Productions, 1996).

Im Lauf der Zeit (In the course of Time, commonly known as *Kings of the Road).* W. Wenders (dir.) (Wim Wenders Produktion. Westdeutscher Rundfunk/Wim Wenders Produktion, 1976).

Immigrant, The. C. Chaplin (dir.) (Lone Star Corporation, 1917.)

I'm not there. T. Haynes (dir.) (Killer Films/John Welles Productions/John Goldwyn Productions/Endgame Entertainment/Film & Entertainment VIP Medienfonds 4 GmbH & Co. KG/ Grey Water Park Productions/Rising Star/Wells Productions, 2006).

Import/Export. U. Seidi (dir) (Ulrich Seidl Film Produktion/ Société Parisienne de Production/ Zweites Deutsches Fernsehen/ Österreichischer Rundfunk.

India Song. M. Duras (dir.) (Les Films Armorial/Sunchild Productions, 1975).

Inglourious Basterds. Q. Tarantino (dir.) (Universal Pictures/Weinstein Company/A Band Apart/Zehte Babelsberg/Visiona Romantica, 2009).

Inland Empire. D. Lynch (dir.) (Studio Canal/Fundacja Kultury/Camerimage Festival/Absurda/Asymmetrical Productions/Inland Empire Productions, 2006).

Intolerance. D.W.Griffith (dir.) (Triangle Film Corporation/Wark Productions, 1916).

Into the Wild. S. Penn (dir.) (Paramount Vantage/Art Linson Productions/Into the Wild/River Road Entertainment, 2007).

Iron Man. J. Favreau (dir.) (Paramount Pictures/Marvel Enterprises/Marvel Studios/Fairview Entertainment/Dark Blades Films, 2008).

Iron Man 2. J. Favreau (dir.) (Paramount Pictures/Marvel Enterprises/Marvel Studios/Fairview Entertainment, 2010).

I Was a Teenage Werewolf . G. Fowler (dir.) (Sunsett Productions, 1957).

Jackie Brown. Q. Tarantino (dir.) (Miramax/A Band Apart/Lawrence Bender Productions, 1997).

J'ai faim, j'ai froid (episode in Paris vu par … 20 ans après). C. Akerman (dir.) (Film A2/J.M.Productions, 1984).

Janghwa, Hongryeon (A tale of two sisters). J.-W. Kim (dir.) (B.O.M. Film Productions Company/Masulpiri Films, 2003).

Jaws. S. Spielberg (dir.) (Zanuck/Brown Productions for Universal Pictures, 1975).

Jeanne Dielman, 23 Quai du Commerce, 1080 Bruxelles. C. Akerman (dir.) (Ministère de la Culture Française de Belgique/Paradise Films/Unité Trois, 1975).

Je t'aime, je t'aime. A. Resnais (dir.) (Les Productions Fox Europa/Parc Film, 1968).

Jetée, La. C. Marker (dir.) (Argos Films, 1962).

Je tu il elle (*I you he she*). C. Akerman (dir.) (French Ministry of Foreign Affairs/Paradise Films, 1974).

Jisatsu sâkuru (*Suicide Club*). S. Sono (dir.) (Omega Project/Biggubito/For Peace Co. Ltd/Fyûzo, 2001).

Jubilee. D. Jarman (dir.) (Megalovision/Whaley-Malin Productions, 1978).

Just Another Girl on the I.R.T. L. Harris (dir.) (Miramax Films/Truth 24 F.P.S, 1992).

Kárhozat (*Damnation*). B. Tarr (dir.) (Hungarian Film Institute/Hungarian Television/Mokép, 1989).

Kids. L. Clark (dir.) (Guys Upstairs/Independent Pictures/Kids NY Ld/Miramax Films/Shining Excalibur Films, 1995).

Kill Bill: Vol 1. Q. Tarantino (dir.) (Miramax/A Band Apart/Super Cool ManChu, 2003).

Kill Bill: Vol 2. Q. Tarantino (dir.) (Miramax/A Band Apart/Super Cool ManChu, 2004).

King Kong. M.C. Cooper and E.B. Schoedsack (dirs) (RKO Radio Pictures, 1933).

King Kong. P. Jackson (dir.) (Bif Primate Pictures/Universal Pictures/WingNut Films/MFPV Film, 2005).

Kiss. A. Warhol (dir.) (Andy Warhol, 1963).

Królik po berlinsku (Rabbit à la Berlin). B. Konopka (dir.) (MS Films/Ma.Ja. De Filmproduktion/Telewizja Polska/Mitteldeutscher Rundfunk (MDR)/Lichtpunt/Vrijzinnig Protestantse Radio Omroep (VPRO)/Polish Film Institute/Media/Andrzej Wajda Master School of Film Directing, 2009).

Kustom Kar Kommandos. K. Anger (dir.) (Puck Film Productions, 1965)

Laberinto del fauno, El (Pan's labyrinth). G. Del Toro (dir.) (Estudios Picasso/Tequila Gang/Esperanto Filmoj/Sententia Entertainment/Telecino/OMM, 2006).

Ladri di biciclette (*Bicycle Thief*). V. De Sica (dir.) (Produzioni De Sica, 1948).

Lady Vanishes, The. A. Hitchcock (dir.) (Gainsborough Pictures, 1938).

Last Days. G. Van Sant (dir.) (HBO Films/Meno Film Company/Picturehouse entertainment/Pie Films Inc, 2005).

Letzte Mann, Der (*The Last Laugh*). F.W. Murnau (dir.) (UFA, 1924).

Little Dieter Needs to Fly. W. Herzog (dir.) (Werner Herzog

Filmproduktion/Zweites Deutsches Fernsehen/ZDF Enterprises/BBC/Arte/ Media Ventures, 1997).

Lola rennt (Run Lola Run). T. Tykwer (dir.) (X-Filme Creative/Pool/ Westdeutscher Rundfunk (WDR)/ Arte, 1998).

Lolita. A. Lyne (dir.) (Guild/Lolita Productions/Pathé, 1997).

Love is the Devil: Study for a Portrait of Francis Bacon. J. Maybury (dir). (BBC, 1998).

M. F. Lang (dir.) (Nero-Film AG, 1931).

Mad Max. G. Miller (dir.) (Kennedy Miller Productions/Crossroads/Mad Max Films, 1979).

Magnificent Ambersons, The. O. Welles and S. Cortez (dirs) (Mercury Productions/RKO Radio, 1942).

Maîtres fous, Les (The Mad Masters). J. Rouch (dir.) (Les Films de la Pléiade, 1955).

Maltese Falcon, The. J. Huston (dir.) (Warner Bros. Pictures, 1941).

Mama Roma. P.P. Pasolini (dir.) (Arco Film, 1962).

Man Who Fell to Earth, The. N. Roeg (dir). (British Lion Film Corporation/ Cinema 5, 1976).

MASH. R. Altman (dir.) (Aspen Productions/Ingo Preminger Productions/Twentieth Century Fox Film Corporation, 1970).

Marie Antoinette. S. Coppola (dir.) (Columbia Pictures/American

Zoetrope/I Want Candy/Price!/ Tohokushinsha Film, 2006).

Mean Girls. M. Waters (dir.) (Paramount/ M.G.Films/Broadway Video, 2004).

Mépris, Le (Contempt). J.-L. Godard (dir.) (Les Films Concordia/ Rome Paris Films/Compagnia Cinematographica Champion, 1963).

Meshes of the Afternoon. M. Deren and A. Hammid (dirs) (Maya Deren, 1943).

Moi un noir (I, a Negro). J. Rouch (dir.) (Les Films de la Pléiade, 1958).

Mon oncle d'Amérique (My American Uncle). A. Resnais (dir.) (Philippe Dussart/Andrea Films/TF1, 1980).

Mr & Mrs Smith. A. Hitchcock (dir.) (RKO Radio Pictures, 1941).

Mrs Dalloway. M. Gorris (dir.) (First Look International/Bayly/Pare Productions/Bergen Film & TV/ Newmarket Capital Group/BBC Films/European Co-production Fund/Nederlandse Programma Stichting/Dutch Co-Production Fund/ Nederlands Fonds voor de Film, 1997).

Mulholland Dr. D. Lynch (dir.) (Les Films Alain Sarde/Assymetrical Productions/Babbo Inc./Canal +/The Picture Factory, 2001).

Mystery Train. J. Jarmusch (dir.) (JVC Entertainment Networks/Mystery Train, 1989).

Nanook of the North. R. Flaherty (dir.) (Les Freres Revillon/Pathé Exchange, 1922).

Napoléon. A. Gance (dir.) (Abel Gance/ Société génerale des films, 1927).

Navigator, The. Crisp, D. and Keaton, B. (dirs) (Buster Keaton Productions, 1924).

Night of the Hunter, The. C. Laughton (dir.) (Paul Gregory Productions, 1955).

Night on Earth. J. Jarmusch (dir.) (Victor Company of Japan/Victor Musical Industries/Pyramide Productions/Canal+/Pandora Cinema/ Pandora Filmproduktion/Channel Four Films/JVC Entertainment Networks/Locus Solus Entertainment, 1991).

North by Northwest. A. Hitchcock (dir.) (MGM, 1959).

Nosferatu, eine Symphonie des Grauens (*Nosferatu, A Symphony of Horror*). F.W. Murnau (dir.) (Jofa-Atelier Berlin-Johannisthal/Prana-Film GmbH, 1922).

Notorious. A. Hitchcock (dir.) (Vanguard Films/RKO Radio Pictures, 1946).

Notre Musique (*Our Music*). J.-L. Godard (dir.) (Avventura Films/Les Films Alain Sarde/Périphéria/France 3 Cinéma/ Canal+/Télévision Suisse-Romande (TSR)/Vega Film, 2004).

Notte, La. M. Antonioni (dir.) (Nepi Film/ Silver Films/Sofitedip, 1961).

Nouvelle Vague. J.-L. Godard (dir.) (Sara Films/Peripheria/Canal+/Vega Film/Télévision Suisse-Romande (TSR)/Antenne-2/Centre National de la Cinématographia/Soficas Investimages, 1990).

Nuit et brouillard (*Night and fog*). A. Resnais (dir.) (Argos films, 1955).

Ochazuke no aji (*The Flavour of Green Tea over Rice*). Y. Ozu (dir.) (Shôchiku Eiga, 1952).

October Sky. J. Johnston (dir.) Universal Pictures, 1999).

Oktyabr (*October*). S. Eisenstein (dir.) (Sovkino, 1928).

Oldboy. C.-w. Park (dir.) (Egg Films/ Show East, 2003).

One Plus One/Sympathy for the Devil. J.-L. Godard (dir.) (Cupid Productions, 1968).

Our Daily Bread. K. Vidor (dir.) (King W. Vidor Productions, 1934).

Our Hospitality. J.G. Blystone and B. Keaton (dirs) (Joseph M. Schenck Productions, 1923).

Passion de Jeanne d'Arc, La (*The Passion of Joan of Arc*). C. Dreyer (dir.) (Société generale des films, 1928).

Pays de la terre sans arbre ou Le mouchouânipi, Le (*Land Without Trees, or The Mouchouânipi*). P. Perrault (dir.) (National Film Board of Canada, 1980).

Pays sans bon sens!, Un. (*A country with no common sense!*) P. Perrault

Shining, The. S. Kubrick (dir.) (Warner Bros. Pictures/Hawk Film/Peregrine/ Producers Circle, 1980).

Shock Corridor. S. Fuller (dir.) (Leon Fromkess-Sam Firks Productions, 1963).

Short Cuts. R. Altman (dir.) (Fine Line Features/Spelling Films International/ Avenue Picture Productions, 1993).

Signora senza camelie, La (*The Lady Without Camelias*) M. Antonioni (dir.) (Produzioni Domenico Forges Davanzati/Ente Nazionale Industrie Cineatographafiche, 1953).

Singin' in the Rain. S. Donen (dir.) (Loew's, 1952).

Société du Spectacle, La (*Society of the Spectacle*). G. Debord (dir.) (Simar Films, 1973).

Solyaris (Solaris). A. Tarkovsky (dir.) (Creative Unit of Writers & Cinema Workers/Mosfilm/Unit Four, 1972).

Sometimes in April. R. Peck (dir.) (CINEFACTO/HBO Films/Velvet Film/ thinkfilm, 2005).

Southland Tales. R. Kelly (dir.) (Universal Pictures/Cherry Road Films/Darko Entertainment/ MHF Zweite Academy Film/ Eden Roc Productions/Persistent Entertainment/Academy Film/ Destination Films/Inferno Distribution/Wild Bunch, 2007).

Soy Cuba (*I am Cuba*). M. Kalatozov (dir.) (ICAIC/Mosfilm, 1964).

Spellbound. A. Hitchcock (dir.) (Vanguard Films/Selznick International Pictures, 1945). *Spiral Jetty*. R Smithson (dir.) (Robert Smithson 1970).

Stand der Dinge, Der (*The State of Things*). W. Wenders (dir.) (Gray City/Pro-ject Filmproduktion/Road Movies Filmproduktion/V.O.Filmes/ Wim Wenders Produktion/Zweites Deutsches Fernsehen, 1982).

Stranger than Fiction. M. Forster (dir.) (Columbia Pictures/Mandate Pictures/ Three Strange Angels/Crick Pictures/ Ebeling Group, 2006).

Stranger Than Paradise. J. Jarmusch (dir.) (Cinesthesia Productions/ Grokenberger Film Produktion/ Zweites Deutsches Fernsehen, 1984).

Street Scene, A. K. Vidor (dir.) (The Samuel Goldwyn Company/Feature Productions, 1931).

Struktura krysztalu (*The Structure of Crystals*). K. Zanussi (dir.) (Polish corporation for Film Production Zespoly Filmowe, 1969).

Sud pralad (Tropical Malady). A. Weerasethakul (dir.) (Backup Films/ Anna Sanders Films/Downtown Pictures/[...], 2004).

Sud Sanaeha (*Blissfully yours*). A. Weerasethakul (dir.) Anna Sanders Films/Kick the Machine/La-ong Dao/ [...], 2002).

Sunrise: A Song of Two Humans. F.W. Murnau (dir.) (Fox Films, 1927).

Sunset Boulevard. B. Wilder (dir.) (Paramount Pictures, 1950).

Susana (also known as *The Devil and the Flesh*). L. Buñuel (dir.) (International Cinematográfica, 1951).

Superstar: The Karen Carpenter Story. T. Haynes (dir.) (Iced Tea Productions, 1987).

Sweet Movie. D. Makavejev (dir.) (Maran Film/Mojack Film Ltée/V.M. Productions, 1974).

Symphonie diagonale (*Diagonal symphony*). V. Eggeling (dir.) (Eggeling, 1924).

Ta'm e guilass (*A Taste of Cherry*). A. Kiarostami (dir.) (Abbas Kiarostami Productions/CiBy 2000/Kanoon, 1997).

Tampopo. J. Itami (dir.) (Itami Productions/New Century Productions, 1986).

Taxi Driver. M. Scorsese (dir.) (Columbia Pictures/Bill/hillips/Italo/Judeo Productions, 1976),

Ten. A. Kiarostami (dir.) (Abbas Kiarostami Productions/Key Lime Productions/MK2 Productions, 2002).

Ten Canoes. R. De Heer and P. Djigirr (dirs) (Adelaide Film Festival/Fandango Australia/SBS/Vertigo Productions Pty. Ltd, 2006).

Terminator, The. J. Cameron (dir.) (Hemdale Film/Cinema 84/Euro Film Funding/Pacific Western, 1984).

Terra em transe (*Land in Anguish* also known as *Entranced Earth*). G. Rocha (dir.) (Mapa Filmes, 1967).

Terra Trema: Episodio del mare, La (*The earth trembles*). L. Visconti (dir.) (Universalia Film, 1948).

Tetsuo. S. Tsukamoto (dir.) (Japan Home Video/K2 Spirit/Kaijyu Thatre/SEN, 1989).

There Will be Blood. P.T. Anderson (dir.) (Paramount Vantage/Miramax Films/Ghoulardi Film Company, 2007).

Thin Red Line, The. T. Malik (dir.) (Fox 2000 Pictures/Geisler Roberdeau/Phoenix Pictures, 1998).

This is England. S. Meadows (dir.) (Big Arty Productions/EM Media/Film4/Optimum Releasing/Screen Yorkshire/UK Film Council/Warp Films, 2006).

Tokyo-Ga. W. Wenders (dir.) Chris Sievernich Filmproduktion, Gray City, Westdeutscher Rundfunk (WDR), 1985).

Topkapi. J. Dassin (dir.) (Filmways Pictures, 1964).

Trafic. J. Tati (dir.) (Les Films Corona/Les Films Gibé/Selenia Cinematografica, 1971).

Trois couronnes du matelot, Les (*Three crowns of the sailor*). R. Ruiz (dir.) (Films A2/Institut National de l'Audiovisuel (INA), 1982).

Trois couleurs: Bleu (*Three Colours: Blue*). K. Kieslowski (dir.) (MK2 Productions/CED Productions/France 3 Cinéma/CAB Productions/Zespol

Filmowy 'Tor'/Canal+/Centre National de la Cinématographie/Fonds Eurimages du Conseil de l'Europe, 1993).

Twister. J. De Bont (dir.) (Warner Bros. Pictures/Universal Pictures/Amblin Entertainment/Constant c Productions, 1996).

Umberto D. V. De Sica (dir.) (Amato Film, Astoria Films, De Sica, Rizzoli Film, 1952).

Underground. E. Kustirica (dir.) (Barandov Studios/CiBy 2000/Komuna/Pandora, 1995).

Vacances de Monsieur Hulot, Les (*Monsieur Hulot's Holiday*) J. Tati (dir.) (Discina Film/Cady Film/Specta Film, 1953).

Van Gogh. A. Resnais (dir.) (Canton-Weiner, 1948).

Vayna on 42ⁿᵈ Street. L. Malle (dir.) (Channel Four Films/Mayfair Entertainment/The Vanya Company, 1992).

Velvet Goldmine. T. Haynes (dir.) (Channel Four Films/Goldwyn Films/Killer Films/Miramax Films/Newmarket Capital Group/Single Cell Pictures/Zenith Entertainment, 1998).

Vertigo. A. Hitchcock (dir.) (Alfred J. Hitchcock Productions/Paramount Pictures, 1958).

Virgin Suicides, The. S. Coppola (dir.) (American Zoetrope/Eternity Pictures/Muse Productions/Virgin Suicides LLC, 1999).

Wandâfuru raifu (After Life). H. Koreeda (dir.) (Engine Film/Sputnik Productions/TV Man Union, 1998).

Wavelength. M. Snow (dir.) (Michael Snow, 1967.)

Week End. J.-L. Godard (dir.) (Comacico/Films Copernic/Lira Films/Cinecidi, 1967).

Wicker Man, The. R. Hardy (dir.) (British Lion Film Corporation, 1973).

Wind, The. V. Sjöström (dir.) (MGM, 1928)

Window Water Baby Moving. S. Brakhage (dir.) (Stan Brakhage, 1962).

Wizard of Oz, The. V. Fleming (dir.) (MGM/Loews, 1939).

Workshop Experiment in Animated Sound. N. McLaren (dir.) (Ottawa: National Film Board of Canada, 1948).

Yeogo goedam (Whispering corridors). K.-H. Park (dir.) (Lee Choon-yeon, 1998).

Zangiku Monogatari (The Story of the Late Chrysanthemums). K. Mizoguchi (dir.) (Shôchiku Eiga, 1939).

Zemlya (Earth). A. Dovzhenko (dir.) (VUFKU, 1930).

Zentropa (also known as *Europa*). L. von Trier (dir.) (Alicéléo [...], 1991).

Zvenigora. A. Dovzhenko (dir.) (VUFKU, 1928).

Index